D1563409

The Meanings of Work

Historical Materialism Book Series

The Historical Materialism Book Series is a major publishing initiative of the radical left. The capitalist crisis of the twenty-first century has been met by a resurgence of interest in critical Marxist theory. At the same time, the publishing institutions committed to Marxism have contracted markedly since the high point of the 1970s. The Historical Materialism Book Series is dedicated to addressing this situation by making available important works of Marxist theory. The aim of the series is to publish important theoretical contributions as the basis for vigorous intellectual debate and exchange on the left.

The peer-reviewed series publishes original monographs, translated texts, and reprints of classics across the bounds of academic disciplinary agendas and across the divisions of the left. The series is particularly concerned to encourage the internationalization of Marxist debate and aims to translate significant studies from beyond the English-speaking world.

For a full list of titles in the Historical Materialism Book Series
available in paperback from Haymarket Books, visit:
www.haymarketbooks.org/category/hm-series

The Meanings of Work

Essay on the Affirmation and Negation of Work

by
Ricardo Antunes

Translated by
Elizabeth Molinari

Haymarket Books
Chicago, IL

The English translation has been made possible with the kind support of the Fundação de Amparo à Pesquisa do Estado de São Paulo (FAPESP).

First published in 1999 as Sentidos do Trabalho by Boitempo Editorial, Brazil.
© 2013 Koninklijke Brill NV, Leiden, The Netherlands

Published in paperback in 2013 by
Haymarket Books
P.O. Box 180165
Chicago, IL 60618
773-583-7884
www.haymarketbooks.org

ISBN: 978-1-60846-338-1

Trade distribution:
In the US, Consortium Book Sales, www.cbsd.com
In Canada, Publishers Group Canada, www.pgcbooks.ca
In the UK, Turnaround Publisher Services, www.turnaround-psl.com
In Australia, Palgrave Macmillan, www.palgravemacmillan.com.au
In all other countries, Publishers Group Worldwide, www.pgw.com

Cover design by Ragina Johnson.

This book was published with the generous support of
Lannan Foundation and the Wallace Global Fund.

Printed in Canada by union labor.

10 9 8 7 6 5 4 3 2 1

Library of Congress Cataloging-in-Publication data is available.

To Diva and José,
my parents

'O strange demands of civil society, which first perplexes and misleads us, then asks
of us more than Nature herself.'
Goethe, *Wilhelm Meister's Apprenticeship*

'What times are these, when to speak about trees is almost a crime, because it implies
silence about so many horrors?'
Brecht, 'To Those Born After'

'It is only when man in society seeks a meaning for his life that the failure of this
attempt brings in its wake the antithesis of meaninglessness.'
Lukács, *The Ontology of Social Being*

'The time is out of joint.'
Shakespeare, *Hamlet*

Contents

Foreword

István Mészáros

The capital-apologetic denial of the centrality of labour – a major theme in *The Meanings of Work* – has become most pronounced in the last three decades, coinciding with the onset of capital's structural crisis. The origins of this trend go back a long way. Already in 1925 Karl Mannheim, in his celebrated book *Ideology and Utopia*, had asserted that 'the classes are merging into one another' because, according to a much older idea which he borrowed from Max Scheler, we live in an 'age of equalisation'. The point of such projections was, from the beginning, to do away with the inconvenient reality of labour being the antagonist of capital, denying the very existence of a social force capable of instituting a hegemonic alternative to the established order.

To be sure, we have seen – and continue to be confronted by – *mergers* of monumental proportions. Not between classes, but among giant quasi-monopolistic corporations. Similarly, a real trend of *equalisation* is inexorably advancing. But it is not the trend of creating conditions of equality among social classes – the evidence highlights the exact opposite. The real trend is the *downward equalisation of the differential rate of exploitation*, whereby the labour-force of humanity is being brought under an ever more intense form of exploitation and marginalisation by capital all over the world. Thus, despite all kinds of theoretical mystification which try to dismiss these problems as 'anachronistic nineteenth-century concerns', the need to challenge the hierarchical, structural subordination of labour to capital remains the great issue of our time. And facing up to it, in theory as well as in social practice, is unthinkable without forcefully reasserting the centrality of labour.

The author of *The Meanings of Work* addresses in this regard a whole range of vital issues with rigour and lucidity, faithfully reflecting their complex ramifications. He builds on his earlier books – notably *Adeus ao Trabalho?* (*Farewell to Work?*) – and greatly enlarges the scope of his previous research, providing the reader with a comprehensive framework in which the particular problems come to life and enhance the meaning of one another through their reciprocal connections. He shows convincingly that the 'crisis of Fordism' and the way the 'personifications of capital' attempted to overcome it by restructuring the economy – and fell far short of the expected success – are intelligible only as part of a much deeper crisis of the whole system. He shows that they are manifestations of the capital-system's contradictions, which no amount of 'Toyotism' could possibly remedy.

The theories that postulated the replacement of labour by 'science as the principal productive force' concentrated, with characteristic 'Eurocentrism', on a handful of capitalistically-advanced countries, disregarding the fact that two-thirds of the actually existing labour-force of humanity live in the so-called 'Third World'. Moreover, as Ricardo Antunes demonstrates in an important part of his book dedicated to the analysis of British developments in the last three decades, the conclusions of such theories about the supersession of labour, and the consignment of its combative strategies to the nineteenth century, are devoid of any foundation even in the most advanced-capitalist countries such as England. *The Meanings of Work* explains the reasons behind the two-decade-long Thatcherite-neoliberal project, showing also the attempt by 'New Labour' to revive, under the vacuous ideology of the 'Third Way', the discredited and failed neoliberal enterprise in a new guise.

The Meanings of Work is meticulously researched, and the author's theoretical insights are backed by rich documentation. Antunes is successful in retaining the dialectical complexity of the problems discussed where others might be tempted to offer one-sided interpretations. Thus, to take one example, he underlines that the significant enlargement of female work – in England now constituting 51 per cent of the labour-force – unquestionably represents a partial emancipation of women. At the same time, he puts into relief also the negative side of these developments, showing that capital incorporates women's work in a most unequal way into its social and sexual division of labour by imposing on the female labour-force a greater intensity of exploitative precarisation.

The burning social and political issues discussed in the book are situated within their broad theoretical horizon, highlighting their true significance and undiminished validity. The author's way of focusing on the ontological foundation of labour, putting to imaginative use Lukács's magisterial last work, enables him to connect the much-debated problems of the present with the historical perspective of emancipation. Viable solutions, he argues, are feasible only through labour's hegemonic alternative to the established mode of social-metabolic control, combining the 'sense of life' – i.e. the individual's quest for a meaningful life – with the 'sense of labour'.

Thus, in sharp contrast to those who project a utopian accommodation with capital – by retaining its supremacy in the world of production, and envisaging emancipatory fulfilment *outside* productive activity, in the domain of 'leisure' – Antunes rightly insists that 'a meaningful life *outside* of work pre-supposes a meaningful life *inside* work. It is not possible to make *fetishished, estranged* wage-labour compatible with *(genuinely) free time*. A life deprived of meaning inside work is *incompatible* with a meaningful life outside of work.... A meaningful life in all aspects of social being can only arise with the demolition of the barriers that exist between *working* time and *non-working* time in such a way that, from a meaningful, self-determined, *vital activity – which is beyond the hierarchical division that subordinates labour to capital in force today* and which rests, therefore, upon entirely new foundations – a new sociability can develop.... *In entirely new forms of sociability where freedom and necessity realise one another.'* It could not be put better.

Preface to the English Edition

The English publication of *The Meanings of Work* takes place at a significant moment. Over the last few years, we have entered a new era of social struggle, important examples of which have been seen in Greece, Italy, France, Britain, Spain, Portugal and the US, to mention but a few Western countries. These struggles, while heterogeneous in character, clearly express the connections between the themes of work, casualisation and unemployment and display the rich transversalities that exist between class, gender, ethnicity and generation.

As the structural crisis of capital has significantly increased diverse forms of labour casualisation and unemployment, the rich and complex social scene which is emerging is the globalisation of social struggles. We can recall the riots in France, at the end of 2005, with a vast contingent of immigrants (poor labourers, *sans-papiers*) and the destruction of thousands of cars (symbol of twentieth-century society), or even the demonstrations of early 2006, of students and workers against the so-called 'first job-contract' (*contrat première embauche*, CPE).

As the crisis has deepened at the dawn of the new decade, the social temperature has increased: in Greece, several demonstrations took place against the prescriptions of the European Central Bank and the International Monetary Fund that benefit large financial corporations.

Later came the revolts in the Arab world. Tired of the alternative between dictatorship and pauperism, Tunisia began a period of rebellion that has continued until today. The winds of revolt spread from there to Egypt where demonstrations in Tahrir Square brought together protesters connected through social networks, calling for dignity, freedom, better working conditions, the end of Mubarak's dictatorship and, more recently, the end of military control of the country.

In March 2011, the 'lost generation' of Portugal found its voice. In Lisbon, more than two hundred thousand protesters took to the streets – young people, immigrants, casual workers and the unemployed. A new movement, Precários Inflexíveis ('inflexible precarious workers'), launched a manifesto that captures the character of social struggle in Portugal (and many other countries) today:

> We are precarious in work and in life. We work without contracts or with short-term contracts.... We are call-centre workers, interns, unemployed,... immigrants, casual workers, student-workers.... We are not represented in statistics.... We can't take leave, we can't have children or be unwell. Not to mention the right to strike. Flexicurity? The 'flexi' is for us. The 'security' is for the bosses.... We are in the shadows but we are not silent.... And using the same force with which the bosses attack us, we respond and reinvent the struggle. In the end, there are many more of us than them. Precarious, yes, but inflexible.[1]

Demonstrations in Portugal were followed by the *indignados* movement in Spain against unemployment in the country that, according to Eurostat, has reached nearly 47 per cent for people between the ages of 18 and 24. The message is clear: in education or not, young people are serious candidates for unemployment or casual labour.

Later in the year, revolt moved to British shores after a black taxi-driver was murdered by police. Hundreds of young people from disadvantaged areas including Tottenham and Brixton rioted across London, and within a few days, protests spread to Manchester, Liverpool and other cities.

In the US, the Occupy Wall Street movement emerged, condemning the social tragedy of the country: the hegemony of financial capital, the polarisation between rich and dispossessed, the scourge of unemployment and precarious work, and the disproportionate impact that worsening living conditions has on women, black people and immigrants. In the US, the Occupy-movement has enabled the return to a debate about class that had been off the agenda until now.

Yet, the casualisation of labour is not just a growing feature of the West. In China, since the beginning of the century, there have been high rates of unemployment as the workings of transnational capitalism stretch to the limit the *superexploitation* of the working class. The reasons are many but the example of Foxconn is illuminating. Foxconn, a computing and information-technology enterprise, is an example of Electronic Contract Manufacturing (ECM), a tertiarised firm that assembles electronic products for Apple, Nokia and other transnationals. At its Longhua plant (Shenzhen) where the iPhone is assembled, there have been several suicides amongst the workforce since 2010, most of which condemned the intense exploitation and isolation of the work.

---

1. Available at: <http://precariosinflexiveis.org/p/manifesto-do-pi.html>.

This pattern of labour-exploitation found in many other plants across China on the one hand displays the aggressive tendency of labour-exploitation of large enterprises and, on the other, suggests that recent social struggles and strikes in China originate in precarious working conditions. According to Sacom (Students and Scholars Against Corporate Misbehaviour), at the beginning of 2010, Foxconn-workers work an average of 12 hours per day with a basic monthly wage of 900 yuan (just under US$150) which can reach 2,000 yuan for extra hours worked or for more strenuous work.[2]

In Japan, whose Toyotist model of capitalism became a role-model for Western countries from the mid-1970s, we find young workers who migrate to the cities in search of employment and who sleep in glass capsules, becoming what I called *encapsulated workers*. More recently, in Tokyo's suburbs, homeless, unemployed or underemployed workers, unable to rent even a room, seek night-time refuge in cybercafes that reduce their prices in order to take them in. The workers, between naps, surf the internet in an attempt to secure employment for the following day. They represent one of the layers of the so-called *cybertariat*[3] or *info-proletariat*.[4]

These examples, among many more, highlight the many transversalities between class, generation, gender and ethnicity that are characteristic of social struggles. Yet, the fractures that can be traced back to labour are many: between men and women, young and old, national workers and immigrants, black and white, qualified and unqualified, stable and precarious, formal and informal, employed and unemployed, among many other examples.

Rather than arguing that the significance of work in contemporary society has diminished (theses that are critically analysed throughout the book), our challenge is that of understanding the new *polysemy of work*, its new morphology, whose most distinctive feature is its multifacetedness.

This new morphology comprises not just a working class that is the heir of Taylorism and Fordism, in relative decline especially in the countries of the North (despite a movement in the opposite direction in various countries of the South, like China and India), but also incorporates the new proletarians of the world.

These are an integral and growing part of the *class-that-lives-from-labour*: tertiarised, subcontracted, temporary workers of 'flexible enterprises' whose numbers are swelling, especially in the services- and ICT-sectors – telemarketing and call-centre workers, data-entry workers, fast-food workers and young workers in supermarkets and agribusiness are typical.

---

2. Available at: <http://noticias.bol.uol.com.br/internacional/2010/05/28/suicidios-da-foxconn-revelam-as-duras-condicoes-de-trabalho-na-china.jhtm>.

3. Huws 2003.

4. Antunes and Braga 2009.

xx • Preface to the English Edition

New workers that frequently alternate between heterogeneity in their form of being (gender, ethnicity, age, qualifications, nationality, etc.) and the homogeneity that results from the increasingly precarious condition of work and the erosion of workers' rights that were won through many decades of workers' struggles.

The Meanings of Work starts with a wider conception of work; it seeks to understand its *new morphology* and its transversalities; it suggests connections between these forms of work and the creation of surplus-value and explores the hypothesis that a new morphology of work also signifies a new morphology of struggles, of the organisation and the representation of these social forces.

These theses and ideas could not find, in the current situation, a better laboratory to help understand the role of work in this exceptional moment of global social struggles.

* * *

I would like to conclude this preface to the English edition by thanking in particular Sebastian Budgen and Peter Thomas who are responsible for Brill's *Historical Materialism* Book Series and also Alfredo Saad-Filho and Charles-André Udry for their support.

In Brazil, thanks are due to Fundação de Amparo à Pesquisa do Estado de São Paulo (FAPESP) for making the English translation possible and to Fundo de Apoio ao Ensino, à Pesquisa e Extensão (FAEPEX) from UNICAMP (Universidade de Campinas) for their support.

Ricardo Antunes
Campinas, April 2012

Preface to the Second Edition

This is the 10th reprint of *The Meanings of Work*, ten years after the first edition, published in 1999. In this revised and updated second edition, its central argument acquires even greater strength: we can observe a *new morphology of labour* revealing the essential meanings and significance of the concept of labour and show how, at the start of the twenty-first century, labour still remains a vital question.

More than ever before, billions of men and women depend exclusively on their labour to survive and encounter increasingly unstable, precarious or non-existent conditions of work. As the contingent of workers has grown, there has been a vast reduction in jobs, rights have been corroded and the gains of the past have been eroded.

Perverse machinery and satanic engineering have created an enormous contingent of unemployed workers who have this status because of the destructive logic of capital itself – as it expels hundreds of thousands of men and women from the value-generating, productive world with its stable, formal jobs, it re-creates, in the most remote and distant spaces, new informal and precarious modalities in order to create surplus-value. With an ever growing surplus labour-force, those who survive by working find that their levels of remuneration fall and their impoverishment increases.

Yet, contrary to the simplistic thesis of the *finiteness of work*, work is revealed, in its contradictory essence, as a space of *sociability*, even when it is marked by dominant features of estrangement and alienation – which we can see in the dehumanisation of the unemployed who, especially but not only in the South, have never once experienced the welfare-state.

Rather, therefore, than unilaterally accepting theses that *deconstruct* labour or award it with an uncritical *cult-status*, we know that, throughout the history of human activity, in the never-ending struggle for survival and *social happiness* (which was already present in the Chartist claims of nineteeth-century England), labour is, in itself and for itself, a *vital activity*. Yet, when human life is exclusively reduced to *labour* – which is common in the capitalist world and its *society of abstract labour* – it is also the expression of a painful, alienated, captive and unilateral world.

The conclusion of *The Meanings of Work* is clear: if, on the one hand, we need human labour and its emancipatory potential, we also need to reject conditions of labour that exploit, alienate and deprive social being of happiness. This is because, as we will see throughout this book, *work* that structures capital is destabilising for humanity; on the other hand, *work* that has meaning for humanity is potentially destabilising for capital.

This contradictory labour-process, which emancipates and alienates, humanises and subjects, liberates and enslaves, turns the study of human labour into a critical question for the understanding of our world and our lives in this troubled twenty-first century. The greatest challenge we face is to find a *self-constituting meaning for human labour* and endow our *lives outside of work*, as well as those within, *with meaning*.

*   *   *

This new edition of *The Meanings of Work* includes two new appendices that bring the original arguments up to date, synthesise some of the central theses on the *present* of labour, and also outline a sketch of its *future*.

Readers will be able to see the clear continuity between the appendices and the original version of the book, which, alongside *Adeus ao Trabalho?* (Cortez) and *O Caracol e sua Concha* (Boitempo), completes our trilogy on the centrality of labour in contemporary society.

Finally, I mention that besides the ten reprints in Brazil, *The Meanings of Work* has had a positive reception abroad. Spanish (*Los Sentidos del Trabajo*, Herramienta Ediciones e TEL/Taller de Estúdios Laborales, Argentina, 2005) and Italian (*Il Lavoro in Trappola: La Classe Che Vive di Lavoro*, Jaca Book, 2006) editions already exist and a Franco-Swiss publication is being prepared with Editions Page 2 that we hope to see in the near future.

Ricardo Antunes
Campinas, October 2009

Preface to the First Edition

The Meanings of Work: Essay on the Affirmation and Negation of Work is the result of research undertaken at Sussex University, where I worked as a visiting researcher at the invitation of István Mészáros, Emeritus Professor at Sussex.

I was thus able to further explore questions that I had begun to investigate in *Adeus ao Trabalho?* (*Farewell to Work?*), published in 1995. *The Meanings of Work* returns to the same themes, exploring them more profoundly and developing other dimensions that I believe to be essential when we think of the world of work today, of contemporary forms of labour, its centrality and multiple meanings.

Through a study of relations between *productive* and *unproductive* labour, *manual* and *intellectual* labour, *material* and *immaterial* labour, forms of *sexual division of labour, the new configuration of the working class* – among many other elements that I shall analyse in the text – I have revisited and given substance to the thesis of the centrality of the category of *labour* in contemporary society, against the *theoretical deconstruction* that has occurred in the last few years. In contrast to the much-touted replacement of labour by science, or the replacement of the production of commodities by the sphere of communication, of production by information, I explore the new forms of *interpenetration* that exist between productive and unproductive activities, between factory- and service-activities, between activities of implementation and conception, production and scientific knowledge, that have been expanding within contemporary capital and its productive process.

* * *

Amidst the atmosphere of intellectual exchange in the company of Professors Istvan Mészáros and William Outhwaite at the School of European Studies, Sussex University, I was able to enjoy the conditions to conduct the research that generated this book.

A first, special thank-you is reserved for Professor Istvan Mészáros, for the conversations, discussions, reflections, and more than this, deepest friendship, sensitivity and solidarity that became even stronger during my stay, and in whom, from the very moment of my arrival in the United Kingdom, I found constant support. Our encounters and debates, throughout the year, moulded the shape of this work. My appreciation and thanks extend of course also to my dear friend Donatella, for the memorable times we were lucky to share.

I would also like to thank Professor William Outhwaite for his support and assistance. I am also grateful to John McIlroy at Manchester University for the work we undertook there and our meetings.

Finally, I am also grateful to Fapesp for the Post-Doctoral Scholarship (March 1997 to February 1998) that made the development of this project possible, to CNPq for the research-grant that allowed me to return to this project from March 1999, and to FAEPEX/UNICAMP.

Introduction

In recent decades, contemporary society has undergone profound transformations, affecting both forms of materiality and the sphere of subjectivity, owing to the complexity of relations between these forms of *being* and *existing* of human sociability. The crisis of capital, as well as the responses to it – of which neoliberalism and the productive restructuring of the era of flexible accumulation are an expression – has precipitated, among its many consequences, profound changes within the world of work. Among these are enormous structural unemployment and a growing contingent of precarious workers, as well as the increasing degradation of the metabolic relation between humanity and nature, driven by a societal logic aimed primarily at the production of commodities and the valorisation of capital.

At the same time, however, many have seen new and positive dimensions of social organisation in these forms of (de-)socialisation, as if *labouring humanity* were on the point of reaching its most advanced stage of sociability. There are many forms of fetishism: from the cult of 'democratic society' finally enjoying the *utopia of fulfilment*, to the belief in the de-commodification of social life, the end of ideologies or the advent of a communication-society capable of facilitating subjective interaction through new forms of intersubjectivity, or even those that envisage the *end of labour* and the concrete realisation of the *reign of free time* within the current global structure of social reproduction.

My investigation sets out a rather different analytical framework. In contrast to the formulations above, I argue that contemporary society is at a critical stage affecting both the countries of the so-called Third World, such as Brazil, and the central capitalist countries. The logic of the system of production of commodities is transforming competition and the search for productivity into a destructive process that has led to widespread labour-precarisation and a monumental increase in the industrial reserve-army – the number of unemployed. By way of an example: even Japan, with its Toyotist model committed to 'lifelong employment' for around 25 per cent of its workforce, has had to relinquish this employment-condition in order to keep up with the competition emerging from the 'Toyotised' Western world. Among measures proposed by Japanese capital to tackle the country's crisis is that of increasing the working week – from 48 to 52 hours.[1] In Indonesia, female workers for transnational firm Nike earned US$38 per month with very long working days. In Bangladesh, Wal-Mart, K-Mart and Sears employ female workers to make clothes, who work on average a 60-hour week and earn less than US$30 per month.[2] What can we say about a form of sociability that, according to ILO-figures in 1999, leaves unemployed or casualises more than 1 billion people, which is around one-third of the global workforce?

If it is a serious mistake to imagine the *end of work* in a commodity-producing society, it is also essential to understand the transformations and metamorphoses that are taking place in our world today, what they signify and what important consequences they will have. What we can see in the world of work is a set of critical trends that are unfolding in different parts of the world that are subject to the logic of capital. A critique of the concrete forms of human (de-)socialisation is the condition needed to undertake a critique and de-fetishisation of the forms of representation and ideology that dominate society today.

In an abstract discussion of the forms of (de-)socialisation that exist and are expanding in our world today, Istvan Mészáros refers to *second-order mediations*. In his words:

> Capital's second order mediations – i.e. alienated means of production and their 'personifications'; money; production for exchange; varieties of capital's state formation in their global context; the world market – superimpose themselves in reality itself on the social individuals' essential productive activity and primary mediation among themselves. Only a radical critical scrutiny of this historically specific system of second order mediations could show a way out of its fetishistic conceptual maze. By contrast, however, the

---

1. *Japan Press Weekly* 1998.
2. Data from Collingsworth, Goold and Harvey 1994.

uncritical appearance of the given, historically contingent but powerfully effective, system of the absolute reproductive horizon of human life in general makes impossible the understanding of the real nature of mediation. For the prevailing second order mediations obliterate the proper awareness of the primary mediatory relationships and present themselves in their 'eternal presentness' (Hegel) as the necessary point of departure which is simultaneously also the unsurpassable end-point. Indeed, they produce a complete inversion of the actual relationship as a result of which the primary order is degraded and the alienated second order mediations usurp its place, with potentially most dangerous consequences for the survival of humanity.[3]

Thus, to be effective, the inversion of social logic consolidated the *second-order mediations* that, in turn, came to constitute the founding element of *capital's social-metabolic order*. Deprived of any humanly meaningful orientation, capital assumes, in its process, a logic by which the *use-value* of things is totally subordinated to their *exchange-value*. The system of *second-order mediations* began to overlap with and drive the *first-order mediations*. Societal logic is thereby inverted and transfigured, forging a new social-metabolic order structured by capital.

3. Mészáros 1995, pp. 17–18.

Chapter One

Capital's Social-Metabolic Order and its System of Mediations

Capital's *social-metabolic order* arose as a result of the social-division that created the *structural subordination of labour to capital*. Rather than being the consequence of any immutable ontological determination, this system of social metabolism is, according to Mészáros, the result of a historically-constituted process, whereby a hierarchical-social division comes to prevail that subsumes labour to capital.[1] Social individuals found their interchange mediated and arranged within a structured social whole, by an established system of production and exchange. A system of *second-order mediations* overdetermined its basic-primary mediations, its *first-order mediations*.

The system of first-order mediations

First-order mediations, the purpose of which is the preservation of the vital functions of individual and social reproduction, have the following defining characteristics:

1) human beings are a part of nature who must satisfy their elementary needs through a constant interchange with nature; and
2) they are constituted in such a way that they cannot survive as individuals of the species to which they belong...on the basis of an

---

1. Mészáros 1995.

unmediated interchange with nature (as animals do), regulated by an instinctual behaviour directly determined by nature, however complex that instinctual behaviour might be.[2]

From these fundamental ontological determinations, individuals must reproduce their existence through *primary functions of mediation*, established amongst themselves and in their interaction with nature. Such mediations are given by the *uniquely human ontology of labour*, through which social self-production and reproduction develops. The vital functions of *primary* mediation or *first-order* mediation include:

1) the necessary, more or less spontaneous regulation of biological-reproductive activity using available resources;
2) the regulation of the labour-process, for which the necessary interchange of the community with nature can produce the required goods, working tools, productive enterprises and knowledge for the satisfaction of human needs;
3) the establishment of a suitable system of exchange that can meet changing human needs, and that is able to make optimal use of existing natural and productive resources;
4) the organisation, co-ordination and control of the multiplicity of activities – both material and cultural – with a view to the attainment of a progressively more complex system of social reproduction;
5) the rational allocation of available material and human resources, fighting against scarcity, through an economic (in the sense of economising) use of the means of production, as far as feasible on the basis of existing levels of productivity and within the confines of socioeconomic structures; and
6) the constitution and organisation of societal regulations applicable to all social beings, alongside the other primary mediatory functions and determinations.[3]

None of these primary-mediatory imperatives requires the establishment of structural hierarchies of domination and subordination that configure the system of social metabolism of capital and its *second-order* mediations.

---

2. Mészáros 1995, p. 138.
3. Mészáros 1995, p. 139.

The emergence of the system of second-order mediations

The advent of the *second order of mediations* corresponds to a specific period in human history which profoundly altered the primary mediatory functions to meet the needs of a fetishistic and alienating system of social-metabolic control.[4] This is because:

> the constitution of the capital system is identical to the emergence of its second order mediations. Indeed, capital, as such, is nothing but a dynamic, all-engulfing and dominating mode and means of reproductive mediation, articulated as a historically specific set of structures and institutionally embedded as well as safeguarded social practices. It is a clearly identifiable system of mediations which in its properly developed form strictly subordinates all social reproductive functions – from gender and family relations to material production and even to the creation of works of art – to the absolute requirement of capital expansion, i.e. of its own continued expansion and expanded reproduction as a system of social metabolic mediation.[5]

The explanation for this lies in its essential goal, which is none other than 'the imperative of ever-expanding exchange value to which everything else – from the most basic as well as the most intimate needs of the individuals, to the various material and cultural productive activities in which they engage – must be strictly subordinated'.[6] In this way 'the complete subordination of human needs to the reproduction of exchange-value – in the interest of capital's expanded self-realisation – has been the salient feature of the capital system from the outset'.[7] In other words, to make capital-production become the purpose of humanity, it was necessary to separate use-value from exchange-value, subordinating the former to the latter. This characteristic constitutes one of the main secrets of capital's dynamic success, in that the limitations of need do not constrain the reproductive expansion of capital.[8] 'Naturally, the organisation and division of labour had to be fundamentally different in societies where use-value and need played the key regulatory function.'[9] With capital, a vertical command-structure is erected establishing a hierarchical division of labour that makes the new system of social metabolism viable, one driven by the need for a constant, systematic and

---

4. Mészáros 1995, pp. 139–40.
5. Mészáros 1995, p. 117.
6. Mészáros 1995, p. 14.
7. Mészáros 1995, p. 522.
8. Mészáros 1995, p. 523.
9. Ibid.

growing expansion of exchange-values,[10] in which labour must genuinely be subsumed to capital, as Marx indicated in Chapter VI (unpublished).[11] In this way, Mészáros goes on, the conditions for second-order mediations to emerge with the advent of the capital system, can be found in:

1) the *separation* and *alienation* between worker and the means of production;
2) the *superimposition* of these objectified and alienating conditions over the workers, like a separate power exercising *command over labour*;
3) the *personification of capital* as an egotistic value – with its usurped subjectivity and pseudo-personality – directed at the service of capital's expansionistic imperatives; and
4) an equivalent personification of labour, i.e. the personification of workers as *labour*, so as to establish a relation of dependence with the historically prevailing type of capital; this personification reduces the identity of the subject of such labour to its fragmentary productive functions.[12]

As such, each of the forms of *first-order mediation* is altered and subordinated to the imperatives of the reproduction of capital. The productive and control functions of the social labour-process are radically separated into those that *produce* and those that *control*.

Having constituted itself as the most powerful and all-encompassing system of social metabolism, its system of *second-order mediation* is constituted by a nucleus formed by *capital, labour* and the *state*. These three fundamental dimensions of the system are materially interrelated, it being impossible to overcome them without eliminating the set of elements that constitutes the system. It is not sufficient to eliminate one or even two of the dimensions. The Soviet experience (and its recent collapse) proved the impossibility of destroying the state (as well as capital) while keeping in place the system of social metabolism of alienated and hetero-determined labour. What emerged from that historical experience was, instead, enormous state-hypertrophy, from the moment that the USSR and other *postcapitalist* countries maintained the basic constitutive elements of the *hierarchical social division of labour*. The 'expropriation of the expropriators', the 'political-juridical elimination' of property accomplished by the Soviet system, 'left the edifice of the capital system still standing'.[13]

---

10. Mészáros 1995, p. 537.
11. Marx 1994.
12. Mészáros 1995, p. 617.
13. Mészáros 1995, pp. 493, 137. For Mészáros, the challenge is to overcome the *capital-, labour- and state*-system in its entirety, including its fundamental pillar, the

In Mészáros's synthesis:

> Given the inseparability of the three dimensions of the fully articulated
> capital system – capital, labour and the state – it is inconceivable to
> emancipate labour without simultaneously also superseding capital and the
> state as well. For, paradoxically, the fundamental material supporting pillar
> of capital is not the state but labour in its continued structural dependency
> from capital.... So long as the vital controlling functions of the social
> metabolism are not effectively taken over and autonomously exercised by the
> associated producers, but left under the authority of a separate controlling
> personnel (i.e. the new type of personification of capital), labour itself self-
> defeatingly continues to reproduce the power of capital over against itself,
> materially maintaining and extending thereby the rule of alienated wealth
> over society.[14]

By being neither a *material entity* nor a *mechanism* that can be rationally
controlled, capital constitutes an extremely powerful *totalising* structure of
organisation and control of the societal metabolism, to which all, including
human beings, must adapt. This system maintains control and power over the
totality of social beings because its deepest determinations are *oriented towards
expansion and driven by accumulation*.[15] Whereas social forms preceding capital
'were characterised by a high degree of self-sufficiency with regard to the
relationship between material production and its control',[16] with the development of the global system of capital, capital became expansionistic and

---

hierarchical system of labour with its alienating social division that subordinates *labour
to capital*, with the political state as a link.
14. Mészáros 1995, p. 494.
15. Mészáros 1995, pp. 41–4. For Mészáros, *capital* and *capitalism* are *distinct* phenomena and the conceptual identification of the two has meant that all revolutionary
experiences that occurred during the twentieth century, from the Russian Revolution
to more recent attempts to create a socialist society, have shown themselves incapable
of overcoming the *social-metabolic order of capital*, i.e. the complex characterised by the
hierarchical division of labour that subordinates its vital functions *to capital*. This,
according to the author, precedes *capitalism* and also follows from it. Capitalism is
one of the possible forms of realisation of capital, one of its *historical variants*, present during the phase characterised by the generalised *real subsumption* of labour to
capital. In the same way that *capital* existed before the generalisation of the *system
of commodity-production* (of which merchant-capital is an example), capital can also
continue to exist *after* capitalism, through the constitution of what Mészáros calls
the 'system of post-capitalist capital' that existed in the USSR and various Eastern-
European countries, during the twentieth century. These countries, despite having
a *postcapitalist* configuration, were unable to break with the social-metabolic system
of capital. See, on the Soviet experience, especially Chapter 17, sections 2, 3 and 4 of
Mészáros's text. On the most important differences between capitalism and the Soviet
system, see the synthesis on pp. 630–1.
16. Mészáros 1995, p. 45.

totalising, profoundly changing the system of societal metabolism. And this new characteristic 'makes the system more dynamic than all the earlier modes of social metabolic control put together'.[17] Being a system that has *no limits for its expansion* (unlike previous systems of social organisation that sought, *at all costs*, the attainment of social necessities), capital's social-metabolic order was configured, in the last instance, as an ontologically *uncontrollable* system.[18]

Despite the appearance that a regulatory system can be superimposed on capital and, ultimately, control it, its uncontrollability is the consequence of its own fractures that have existed from the beginning inside the microcosms that make up the base-cells of its social system. The *structural defects* of the system of social metabolism of capital and its *second-order* mediations manifest themselves in different ways. Again, according to Mészáros:

> First, production and its control are radically severed from, and indeed diametrically opposed to, one another.
>
> Second, in the same spirit, arising from the same determinations, production and consumption acquire an extremely problematical independence and separate existence, so that in the end the most absurdly manipulated and wasteful 'overconsumption' in some quarters can find its gruesome corollary in the most inhuman denial of the elementary needs of countless millions.
>
> And third, the new microcosms of the capital system are combined into some sort of manageable whole in such a way that total social capital should be able to enter – since it must – the global domain of circulation…in an attempt to overcome the contradiction between production and circulation. In this way, the necessity of domination and subordination prevails not only inside the particular microcosms – through the agency of the individual 'personifications of capital' – but also across their boundaries, transcending not only all regional barriers but also national frontiers. This is how the total labour force of humanity becomes subjected…to the alienating imperatives of the global capital system.[19]

In the three instances mentioned above, according to Mészáros, there is a structural defect in the mechanisms of control, expressed in the *absence of unity*. Any attempt to create or superimpose unity upon the internally fractured social-reproductive structures is problematic and certainly temporary.

---

17. Mészáros 1995, p. 41.
18. Many attempts to control it, by numerous social-democratic and Soviet-style alternatives, have failed since both pursue, in Mészáros's words, the 'path of least resistance to capital' (Mészáros 1995, pp. 771–2). See especially Chapters 16.1 and 20.
19. Mészáros 1995, pp. 48–9.

The lost unity owes to the fact that the fracture assumes the form of *social antagonism* manifested through fundamental conflicts and confrontations between hegemonic alternative social forces. Such antagonisms are shaped by the specific historical conditions and are of varying intensity, but predominantly favour capital over labour.

> However, even when capital gains the upper hand in the confrontations, the antagonisms cannot be eliminated…precisely because they are structural. For in all three instances we are concerned with capital's vital and therefore irreplaceable structures, and not with – by capital itself transcendable – limited historical contingencies. Consequently, the antagonisms emanating from these structures are necessarily reproduced under all historical circumstances covering capital's epoch, whatever might be the prevailing relation of forces at any particular point in time.[20]

This system avoids a significant degree of control precisely because:

> it itself emerged in the course of history as a most powerful…'totalizing' framework of control into which everything else, including human beings, must be fitted, and prove thereby their 'productive viability', or perish if they fail to do so. One cannot think of a more inexorably engulfing – and in that important sense 'totalitarian' – system of control than the globally dominant capital system [that imposes] its own criteria of viability on everything, from the smallest units of its 'microcosm' to the most gigantic transnational enterprises, and from the most intimate personal relations to the most complex decision making processes of industry-wide monopolies, favouring always the strong against the weak.[21]

Furthermore, under the control of a system of second-order mediations that is superimposed over the first-order mediations (in which individuals relate to nature and with other social individuals with a degree of self-determination), in this

> process of alienation, capital degrades the real subject of social reproduction, labour, to the condition of reified objectivity – a mere 'material factor of production' – thereby overturning, not just in theory but in palpable social practice, the real subject–object relation. However, the trouble for capital is that the 'material factor of production' cannot cease to be the real subject of production. To perform its productive functions, with the consciousness demanded of it by the production process as such – without which capital

---

20. Mészáros 1995, p. 49.
21. Mészáros 1995, p. 41.

itself would cease to exist – labour must be made to acknowledge another subject above itself, even if in reality the latter is only a pseudo-subject. To this effect capital needs its personifications in order to mediate (and impose) its objective imperatives as consciously executable commands on the potentially most recalcitrant real subject of the production process. Fantasies about the coming of a totally automated and worker-free capitalist production process are generated as an imaginary elimination of this problem.[22]

As a mode of social metabolism that is totalising and, in the last instance, *uncontrollable,* given the *centrifugal* tendency that exists in each microcosm of capital, this system assumes an increasingly *destructive* logic. This logic, which is accentuated under contemporary capitalism, led to one of the most important trends of the capitalist mode of production, which Mészáros refers to as the *decreasing rate of utilisation* of the use-value of things. 'Capital treats use-value (which directly corresponds to need) and exchange-value not merely as separate, but in a way that radically subordinates the former to the latter.'[23] Which means that a commodity can vary from one extreme to the other, i.e. from having its use-value realised at one end of the scale, to never being used at all at the other, 'without losing thereby its usefulness as regards the expansionary requirements of the capitalist mode of production'.[24]

Capital thus deepened the separation between production genuinely geared towards human needs and its own self-reproductive needs. The more competition increases between capitals, the more severe the consequences, among which two are particularly nefarious: the destruction and precarisation, unprecedented in the modern era, of the human force that labours and the increasing degradation of the environment, in the metabolic relation between humans, technology and nature, led by a social logic that is subordinated to the parameters of capital and the system of commodity-production.

> Consequently, no matter how absurdly wasteful a particular productive procedure may be, so long as its product can be profitably imposed on the market, it must be welcomed as the right and proper manifestation of the capitalist 'economy'. Thus, to take an example, even if 90 percent of the material and labour resources required for the production and distribution of a profitably marketed commodity – say a cosmetic product: a face cream – goes straight to the physical or figurative (but nonetheless with regard to the costs of production just a real) electronic/advertising rubbish bin, as

---

22. Mészáros 1995, p. 66.
23. Mészáros 1995, p. 566.
24. Mészáros 1995, p. 567.

packaging of one sort or another, and only 10 percent is dedicated to the chemical concoction which is supposed to deliver the real or imaginary benefits of the cream itself to the purchaser, the obviously wasteful practices here involved are fully justified, since they meet the criteria of capitalist 'efficiency', 'rationality' and 'economy' in virtue of the proven *profitability* of the commodity in question.[25]

This trend towards the decreasing use-value of commodities, as well as the necessary acceleration of their reproductive cycle and exchange-value, has been increasing since the 1970s when the system of global capital had to find alternatives to the crisis that was stalling its growth-rates. This is because, 'under the conditions of capital's structural crisis its destructive constituents came to the fore with a vengeance, activating the spectre of total uncontrollability in a form that foreshadows self-destruction both for this unique social reproductive system itself and for humanity in general'.[26] 'It is enough to think in this respect of the wild discrepancy between the size of the US population – less than 5 percent of the world population – and its 25 percent consumption of the total available energy resources. It takes not great imagination to figure out what would happen if the 95 percent adopted the same consumption pattern, trying to squeeze nineteen times 25 percent out of the remaining 75 percent.'[27]

Expansionary, from its microcosm to its most totalising configuration, *globalised*, given the expansion and breadth of the global market, *destructive* and ultimately *uncontrollable*, the social-metabolic order of capital has been assuming an increasingly critical configuration. Its continuation, power and expansion cannot occur without revealing a growing tendency for structural crisis affecting the system as a whole. Rather than long cycles of expansion interspersed with crises, we are witnessing a *depressed continuum* that, in contrast to sustainable development, displays the characteristics of a *cumulative, endemic crisis*, more or less permanent and chronic, with the prospect of a

---

25. Mészáros 1995, p. 569. The computer-industry is another example of this tendency of the use-value of things to decrease. After a short period of time, equipment becomes obsolete, as the new software and systems become incompatible with 'old' machines, even if they are still working. This applies both to the individual consumer and to companies that need to remain competitive in their sector. As Martin Kenney states, '[A]s a result, product life-cycles are becoming shorter. Businesses have little choice except to rapidly innovate or risk being outflanked.' After referring to the product life-cycle of Hewlett-Packard systems he goes on to say 'the lifetime of a product simply [is getting] shorter and shorter' (Kenney 1997, p. 92). The production of computers is a clear example of the *decreasing rate of utilisation of the use-value of commodities*.

26. Mészáros 1995, p. 44.

27. Mészáros 1995, p. xv.

deep *structural crisis*. For this reason, in the advanced-capitalist countries, a 'crisis-management' mechanism has been developing, as an essential part of the action of capital and the state to displace and transfer its present major contradictions.[28] However, 'the *radical disjunction* of genuine production and capital's self-reproduction is no longer some remote possibility but a cruel reality, with the most devastating implications for the future'.[29]

Thus, rather than great crises separated by reasonably long intervals, followed by expansionary phases – as was the case in the crash of 1929 and, subsequently, the post-war 'golden age', *the current crisis has manifested more frequent and continuous shocks* ever since the very first signs of exhaustion which are often mistakenly confused with a crisis of Fordism or Keynesianism.

---

28. Mészáros 1995, pp. 597–8.
29. Mészáros 1995, p. 599.

Chapter Two

Dimensions of the Structural Crisis of Capital

The crisis of Taylorism and Fordism as the phenomenal expression of the structural crisis

After a long period of capital-accumulation that occurred at the height of Fordism and the Keynesian phase, from the 1970s on, capitalism began to show signs of crisis. The most prominent signs included:

1) a fall in the rate of profit caused, among other elements, by the increase in the cost of labour-power in the period after 1945 and by the intensification of social struggles in the 1960s that aimed at the *social control of production*.[1] The combination of these elements brought about a reduction in the levels of productivity of capital, accentuating the tendency of the rate of profit to fall;

2) the exhaustion of the Taylorist/Fordist accumulation-pattern of production (which was, in fact, the clearest phenomenal expression of the structural crisis of capital), caused by the inability to respond to the falling levels of consumption. This drop in consumption was a response to emerging *structural unemployment*;

3) hypertrophy of the *financial sphere*: finance was obtaining relative autonomy compared to productive capital. This was also already an

---

1. I shall discuss this central issue for the understanding of the crisis of the 1970s, at a later stage.

expression of the structural crisis of capital and its system of production, with financial capital positioning itself as a priority area for speculation in the new phase of internationalisation;

4) a greater concentration of capital through mergers between monopolistic and oligopolistic firms;

5) the crisis of the welfare-state, which triggered the fiscal crisis of the capitalist state and the need to retrieve public expenditure and transfer it to private capital; and

6) rapid increase in privatisations, a generalised tendency towards deregulation and the flexibilisation of the productive process, markets and the labour-force, among many other contingent elements that were the expression of this new critical landscape.[2]

Robert Brenner offers a good synthesis of the crisis. It finds:

> its deep roots in a secular...crisis of profitability that has resulted from ongoing overcapacity and overproduction in international manufacturing.
>
> In the first place, then, the major shift of capital into finance has been the consequence of the inability of the real economy, especially the manufacturing sector, to provide an adequate rate of return. Thus the rise of overcapacity and overproduction, leading to falling profitability in manufacturing from the late 1960s, was the root cause of the accelerating rise of finance capital from the later 1970s....
>
> [T]he roots of long-term stagnation and the current crisis lie in the squeeze on manufacturing profits that resulted from the rise of manufacturing overcapacity and overproduction, which was itself the expression of intensified international competition.[3]

Further:

> [B]eginning in the second half of the 1960s, later-developing, lower-cost producers in Germany and especially Japan rapidly expanded their output...reducing the market shares and profit rates of their rivals.
>
> The outcome was overcapacity and overproduction in manufacturing, expressed in reduced aggregate profitability in manufacturing for the G-7 economies taken together....

---

2. Chesnais 1996a, pp. 69, 84. Both Mészáros 1995, especially Chapters 14, 15 and 16, and Chesnais 1996a examine this structural crisis in detail. See also Brenner 1998a. For the purposes of this study, we are able to present here only a schematic outline of the issue.

3. Brenner 1998a.

It has been the major fall of profitability in the United States, Germany, Japan and in the advanced capitalist world as a whole – and its failure to recover – that has been responsible for the secularly reduced rates of capital accumulation at the root of long-term economic stagnation over the past quarter century.

Low rates of capital accumulation have brought low rates of growth of output and of productivity; low rates of productivity growth have meant low rates of growth of wages. Rising unemployment has followed from the slow growth of output and investment.[4]

Indeed, the so-called crisis of Fordism and Keynesianism was the phenomenal expression of a more complex crisis. Its deepest significance lay in a *structural crisis of capital*, with a clear tendency of the rate of profit to fall, as a result of the factors discussed above. It was also the manifestation of both the *destructive* logic of capitalism – present in the intensification of the *law of the tendency of the use-value* of commodities *to fall* – and the *uncontrollability* of capital's social-metabolic order. As its structural crisis was unleashed, the mechanism of 'regulation' that was in place in various advanced-capitalist countries, especially in Europe, began to collapse along with it.

As a response to its crisis, a process of reorganisation began, of capital and its ideological and political system of domination. The most prominent features of this process included the advent of neoliberalism, with the privatisation of the state, the deregulation of labour-rights and the dismantling of the state-productive sector, of which the Thatcher-Reagan era is the strongest expression. To this was added an intense process of production- and labour-restructuring, with a view to providing capital with the necessary tools with which to try to re-establish earlier patterns of expansion.

As Holloway puts it:

Capitalist crisis is never anything other than that: the breakdown of a relatively stable pattern of domination. It appears as an economic crisis, expressed in a fall in the rate of profit, but its core is the failure of an established pattern of domination....For capital, the crisis can be resolved only through struggle, through the restoration of authority and through a far-from-smooth search for new patterns of domination.[5]

This period was also characterised, decisively, by a generalised offensive of capital and the state against the working class and against the conditions

---

4. Brenner 1998a. For a discussion of Brenner's arguments (presented in Brenner 1998b) see McNally 1999, pp. 38–52, and Foster 1999, pp. 32–7).
5. Holloway 1987, pp. 145–6.

present during Fordism's heyday. Beyond the examples mentioned above, one of the central pillars of this new critical landscape was to be found in the financial sector, whose autonomy (albeit *relative*) was increasing in the midst of the complex interrelations between the liberalisation and globalisation of capital and the productive process. This took place amidst the deregulation and expansion of capital, trade, technology, working conditions and employment. As we saw earlier, recession and the crisis of the productive process permitted and incentivised the expansion of speculative-financial capital.

The close of the post-war expansionary cycle saw the complete deregulation of transnational productive capital, as well as widespread growth and the liberalisation of financial capital. New workforce-management techniques, alongside trade-liberalisation and new forms of techno-scientific domination, accentuated the centralising, discriminatory and destructive character of this process. Its nucleus lay in the advanced-capitalist countries, particularly in the triad of US and NAFTA countries, Germany within the European Union and Japan as leader in Asia, with the first bloc taking the leading role.

With the exception of these central nuclei, this process of reorganisation of capital did not incorporate those outside the centre of the capitalist economy, such as the majority of intermediary industrialised countries, not to mention the weaker links with the Third-World countries. Or, rather, it incorporated them (such as the so-called 'newly industrialised countries', in particular the Asian countries), but in a position of total subordination and dependency. Productive restructuring inside these countries occurred in a condition of subalternity.

The crisis was so intense that, after the dismantling a large part of the Third World and eliminating the postcapitalist countries of Eastern Europe, it also affected the centre of the global system of capital-production. In the 1980s, for example, it particularly affected the US as the battle for technological competitiveness was lost to Japan.[6]

From the 1990s, however, as levels of productivity and growth were recovered in the US, the crisis, due to capital's globalised nature, went on to have a profound effect on Japan and elsewhere in Asia, which were engulfed by their own crises in the second half of the decade. And the more capitalist competition advances – the more competitive technology is developed in a particular region or set of countries – the more the financial capital of imperialist countries expands, and the greater the dismantling and de-structuring of those that are subordinate or even excluded from this process, or that are not able to keep pace with it. This may be due to the absence of a solid internal base, as

---

6. Kurz 1992, p. 208.

in the case of the majority of the Asian countries, or because of an inability to keep pace with technological innovation, which is also dictated by the nations that make up this triad. A growing number of countries are excluded from this repositioning of productive and financial capital and the necessary technological expertise, generating profound internal repercussions in the form of unemployment and the precarisation of the human labour-force.

This destructive logic, by reconfiguring and recomposing the international division of the system of capital, has led to the dismantling of entire regions that are gradually being eliminated from the industrial and productive scene, defeated by unequal global competition. The crisis experienced by the Asian countries of Hong Kong, Taiwan, Singapore, Indonesia, the Philippines and Malaysia, among many others, nearly always stemmed from their condition as small countries, with small internal markets, totally dependent on the West for their development. More complicated still are the cases of Japan and South Korea which after a great industrial and technological leap are also entering a period of crisis that is encompassing those countries formerly known as the Asian Tigers.[7]

Moreover, amidst the destruction of productive forces, of nature and the environment, there is also, on a global scale, the destruction of the human force of labour evident in the huge contingent of precarious workers or workers on the fringes of the productive process, intensifying the levels of structural unemployment. Despite significant technological advances (which could encourage, at a global level, a real reduction in the working day or working time), we are seeing policies to lengthen the working day in countries such as England and Japan, among others. England has the longest working day in the whole of the EU, and Japan's government and business-community are trying – as if the country's historically lengthy working day were not enough – to increase it even further, as a means to overcome the crisis.

The very logic that drives these tendencies (which are, in fact, responses of capital to its *structural crisis*) accentuates its most destructive features. The greater the competition between capitals is, the more brutal are the consequences. Amongst these, two are especially severe: the destruction and/or the precarisation of the human labour-force and the growing degradation of the environment, the metabolic relation between humanity, technology and nature, driven by a societal logic that aims primarily at the production of

---

7. These predominantly small Asian countries cannot therefore constitute alternative models of development to be copied or transplanted into *continental* countries such as India, Russia, Brazil and Mexico, among others. The recent Asian financial crisis is the expression of their deep structural fragility, which results from the absence of any internal support within the majority of these Asian countries (see Kurz 1992).

commodities and the process of capital-valorisation. As many authors have stressed before, in the growing use of technology to increase productivity, capital also 'necessarily implies crises, exploitation, poverty, unemployment, the destruction of the natural environment' among many other forms of destruction.[8] Structural unemployment, widespread precarisation of labour and the destruction of the natural environment on a global scale have become constitutive features of the productive restructuring of capital.

---

8. Carchedi 1997, p. 73. See also Davis, Hirschl and Stack (eds.) 1997, pp. 4–10, and Vega Cantor 1999, pp. 167–200.

Chapter Three

The Responses of Capital to Its Structural Crisis: Productive Restructuring and Its Repercussions in the Labour-Process

As discussed above, in recent decades and particularly during the early 1970s, capitalism underwent an acute crisis. Understanding the essential constitutive layers of this crisis is a complex task. The period saw intense transformations at the *economic, social, political* and *ideological* levels, changes that, *taken together*, had powerful repercussions on the *ideals*, the *subjectivity* and the values that constitute the *class-that-lives-from-labour*.[1] Among its many consequences, this structural crisis led to the implementation of a broad process of restructuring of capital in order to recover its productive cycle, which, as we will see further on, strongly affected the world of work. Although the *structural crisis* had deeper causes, the *capitalist response* sought to confront it at a purely superficial, phenomenological level, i.e. without transforming the fundamental pillars of

---

1. A full treatment of the crisis of the world of work cannot be undertaken here, given the complexity of the issue. Apart from the structural crisis of capital and the response of neoliberalism and capital's productive restructuring mentioned above, we can highlight the collapse of Eastern Europe after 1989, the impacts this had on political parties and trade-unions, and also the crisis of social democracy and its repercussions for the working class. It is also important to remember that the crisis of the labour-movement is *particular* and *unique* in accordance with the specific conditions in each country and depending on different political, economic and social contexts. On the more general conditioning factors of the crisis in the world of work, see Appendix 1 to the first edition, entitled 'The Crisis of the Labour-Movement and Centrality of Labour Today'. In the chapter on the UK, I present an outline of the constitutive elements of the crisis in the world of work in that country.

the mode of capitalist production. For the forces of order, it was a case of restructuring the pattern of production of Taylorism and Fordism, in an attempt to re-establish previous levels of accumulation, especially those achieved post-1945, with the use of *new* and *old* mechanisms of accumulation.

Since previous struggles between capital and labour, which reached their climax in the 1960s, had not resulted in the establishment of a *hegemonic project of labour against capital*, it fell upon the latter – once the boldest alternatives proffered by the world of work had been derailed – to offer a response to the crisis. With its attention on the phenomenal sphere, capital's response was to reorganise the reproductive cycle while preserving the essential foundations. It was in precisely this context that an alteration to the pattern of accumulation (and not to the *mode of production*) began that sought to confer greater dynamism on a productive process displaying clear signs of exhaustion. From Taylorist and Fordist production standards, a transition was made towards new flexibilised forms of accumulation.

The limits of Taylorism/Fordism and of the social-democratic compromise

Taylorism/Fordism can be roughly described as the dominant expression of a productive system and its respective labour-process present in large industry for most of the twentieth century, particularly from the 1920s. It was based on the *mass-production* of commodities and was structured upon a *homogenised* and profoundly *verticalised* production-system. In the Taylorist and Fordist automobile-industry, a great deal of the production necessary for making the vehicles was performed internally, with only occasional recourse to external providers of car-parts. It was also necessary for the workers' operations to be streamlined as much as possible, avoiding 'waste' in production, reducing the *time* and increasing the *rhythm* of work, in such a way as to intensify the forms of exploitation.

This productive pattern was based on piecemeal and fragmented labour, on the fragmentation of tasks to reduce the activities to a repetitive series of actions the sum of which resulted in the collective labour that produced the vehicles. Along with the *de-skilling* of the worker, this process of *disanthropomorphisation of labour* and its transformation into an *appendage* of machine-tools intensified capital's ability to extract surplus-labour. In addition to the surplus-value extracted *extensively*, by lengthening the working day and obtaining an *absolute* increase, it was *increasingly* extracted *intensively*, given the relative dimension of surplus-value. The *real subsumption of labour to capital* belonging to the age of machinery was consolidated.

A rigid line of production linked the different tasks, weaving between and interlinking individual actions, setting the pace and marking the time necessary for the completion of the tasks. This productive process was characterised therefore by a combination of Fordist mass-production with Taylorist timekeeping, as well as a clear separation between *elaboration* and *execution*. For capital, it was a case of appropriating the *savoir-faire* of labour and suppressing the *intellectual dimension of industrial labour* which was transferred to the areas of scientific management. The activity of labour was reduced to mechanical and repetitive action.

This productive process transformed capitalist-industrial production, spreading it first across the whole of the automotive industry in the US and then across most of the industrial process of the main capitalist countries.[2] It also grew across much of the service-sector. A system based on intensive accumulation was installed, with mass-production executed by predominantly semi-skilled workers, leading to the emergence of the *mass-worker*, the collective worker of large verticalised and rigidly hierarchical companies.[3]

The introduction of Taylorist-scientific organisation of labour in the automotive industry and its fusion with Fordism came to represent the most advanced form of capitalist rationalisation of the labour-process for many decades of the twentieth century, and only towards the end of the 1960s and early 1970s did this productive model – now *structurally compromised* – begin to show signs of exhaustion.

It could be said that along with the Taylorist/Fordist labour-process, a system of 'compromise' and 'regulation' was erected – within a small portion of advanced-capitalist countries – in the post-war period particularly, that offered the illusion that the system of social metabolism of capital could be *effective*, *lasting* and *definitively* controlled, regulated and founded on a compromise between capital and labour and mediated by the state.

In reality, this 'compromise' was the result of various elements that immediately followed the crisis of 1930 and the management of Keynesian policies thereafter. On the one hand, it was the result of 'the "logic" itself of the earlier development of capitalism' and, on the other, of the 'relative equilibrium in the power-relations between the bourgeoisie and the proletariat that was established after decades of struggle'. Yet this compromise was also *illusory* since, if, on the one hand, it sanctioned a stage in the power-relations between capital and labour, on the other, it was not the result of any discussion

---

2. And it was also manifest in the postcapitalist countries that, by and large, as was the case of the USSR, structured their production by borrowing elements from Taylorism and Fordism.

3. Amin 1996, p. 9; Gounet 1991, pp. 37–9; and Bihr 1991, pp. 43–5.

around clearly established guidelines. This debate occurred later, 'to occupy the "space" opened up by the compromise, to manage its consequences and establish the detail'.[4] Among its binding or intermediary elements were the trade-unions and political parties, as organisational and institutional mediators that positioned themselves as official representatives of the workers and of patronage, with the state appearing to be 'arbitrary' while backing the general interests of capital, taking care to be recognised and accepted by both representatives of capital and labour.

Alternating between social-democratic and outright bourgeois parties, this 'compromise' sought to delineate the arena of class-struggle and to achieve the constitutive elements of the welfare-state in exchange for the abandonment, by the workers, of their socio-historical project,[5] a form of sociability founded on a 'compromise' that would implement social gains and social security for the workers of the central countries, as long as the question of socialism was relegated to a distant future. Moreover, this 'compromise' was sustained by the enormous exploitation of labour in the so-called Third-World countries, that were themselves totally excluded from it.

These mechanisms of 'compromise' led to a process of *integration* of the *social-democratic* wing of the labour-movement – its institutional and representative bodies – eventually transforming the movement into a kind of *cog in the machine* of capitalist power. The 'Fordist compromise' gradually subordinated these institutionalised bodies, trade-unions and political parties, converting them into the 'real joint managers of the global process of capital reproduction'.[6]

Bihr goes on to observe that with the strategy of *integration*, at the heart of the European proletariat's policy-objectives *through the organs that represented it*, was the drive for better wages, better working conditions and social security, demanding of the state that it guarantee and preserve these conquests gained through the 'compromise'.

> But, on the other hand, through *integration*, the labour-movement was gradually transformed into a *mediatory command-structure of capital over the proletariat*. It was in this way that, throughout the Fordist era, trade-union and political organisations tried to channel proletarian conflict proposing and/or imposing upon it objectives and options compatible with the terms

---

4. Bihr 1991, pp. 39–40.
5. Bihr 1991, pp. 40–1.
6. Bihr 1991, pp. 48–9.

of the said compromise, violently attacking any attempt to step outside its boundaries.[7]

The *social-democratic* wing of the labour-movement, tied to its pact with capital and mediated by the state, was also responsible for the growth of a *statist* conception within the labour-movement: 'The idea that conquering the state can lead, if not to liberation from capital's power, at least to lessening its load, received much support in the socio-institutional context of Fordism.' In this way, the belief in 'the legitimacy of statism that was present in the project and strategy of the social-democratic model of the labour-movement' grew stronger.[8] A 'state-fetishism' developed that attributed to state-political power a 'collective' and arbitrary significance, as a power external to capital and labour.[9]

Workers were integrated into social-democratic union and political organisations that purported to represent them.

[B]y transforming negotiation into its sole aim and 'instrumentalising it' as a mechanism of capitalist control over the proletariat, the Fordist compromise accentuated the most detestable aspects of these organisations: because it presupposes a centralisation of trade-union activity at all levels; because by definition only trade-union leaders negotiate; finally, by implying a growing technicality and professionalism among negotiators (in legal, accountancy and financial matters) the systematic practice of negotiation could not but encourage the trend towards the separation between base and top inherent in these organisations, the increasing autonomy of leaders and the gradual reduction of initiatives from the base, in a word, the bureaucratisation of trade-union organisations. By necessarily favouring corporatism, negotiations tended to take place enterprise by enterprise or branch by branch.[10]

For important segments of the European proletariat, this process entailed:

an increased dependence, both practical and ideological on the state, in the form of a welfare-state. Indeed, under Fordism, the state represents, for the proletariat, the guarantee of 'social security' in providing general management of the wage-relation; it is the state that sets the minimum-wage policy...; it is the state that intervenes to conclude and ensure compliance

---

7. Bihr 1991, p. 50.
8. Bihr 1991, pp. 50–1.
9. Bihr 1991, pp. 52–9.
10. Bihr 1991, pp. 52–3.

with collective agreements; it is the state that directly or indirectly generates 'indirect salaries'.[11]

This led to the development of a 'fetishism of the state and of those democratic ideals (and illusions) that the welfare-state gave concrete form to (in more or less guaranteeing the right to work, housing, health, education, career-development, free time, etc.)'.[12]

The expansion and power of the welfare-state, however, showed signs of crisis. Besides the various displays of the exhaustion of its Keynesian 'regulation' phase mentioned above, another decisive element for the crisis of Fordism also took place: *the resurgence of acts of resistance in the world of work and the resulting spread of class-struggle.*

The emergence of mass-worker revolts and the crisis of the welfare-state

From the late 1960s and early 1970s it is possible to talk of the rise of the *mass-worker*, a hegemonic segment of the Taylorist/Fordist proletariat working in the sphere of production. Having lost the cultural identity associated with craftsmanship, this worker was re-socialised in a relatively 'homogeneous' way,[13] as a result of the piecemeal work of the Taylorist/Fordist industry, the loss of dexterity or de-skilling due to repetitive activities, as well as the forms of socialisation that occurred outside of the factory-floor. This enabled the large-scale emergence of a new proletariat, whose form of industrial sociability, marked by *commodification*, offered the grounds for the construction of a new identity and new forms of class-consciousness. If the *mass-worker* represented the social basis for the spread of the earlier social-democratic 'compromise', he or she was also the *main agent of rupture and confrontation, of which the movements for the social control of production at the end of the 1960s were a strong expression.*[14]

The process of proletarisation and commodification that took place during Taylorism/Fordism was, however, deeply contradictory:

> By concentrating the proletariat in the social space, it also tended to atomise it; by homogenising its living conditions, it gave rise, at the same time,

---

11. Bihr 1991, p. 59.
12. Bihr 1991, pp. 59–60.
13. We can say, *relatively* 'homogenised' compared with earlier periods, because clearly (as we will see further on), the *heterogenisation* of workers in terms of their qualifications, social status, gender, race/ethnicity, age-range, nationality, etc. *is a feature that has been present in the world of work since its origins.*
14. Bihr 1991, pp. 60–2.

to the conditions for a process of personalisation; by reducing the part of individual autonomy, it conversely excited the desire for such autonomy, developing the conditions for it; by requiring its geographical, professional, social and psychological mobility, its status was made more rigid, etc. A similar accumulation of contradictions could not but be explosive.[15]

At the end of the 1960s, the actions of workers reached boiling point, shedding doubt on the constitutive pillars of the sociability of capital, particularly the issue of the *social control of production*. With actions across the developed-capitalist world that announced the historical limits of the Fordist 'compromise', they assumed the 'shape of a *genuine mass-worker revolt* against Taylorist and Fordist methods of production, the epicentre of the main contradictions of the process of commodification'.[16]

Taylorism/Fordism carried out an *intense expropriation of the mass-worker*, depriving her of any role in the organisation of a labour-process that was reduced to repetitive and meaningless activity. At the same time, the mass-worker was often called upon to correct the damage and mistakes committed by 'scientific management' and the administration.

This contradiction between autonomy and heteronomy characteristic of the Fordist labour-process, along with the contradiction between production (given the presence of industrial despotism and disciplinary techniques of intensive exploitation of the labour-force) and consumption (which exalted 'individualism' and 'self-realisation'), accentuated the points of saturation of the Fordist 'compromise'. Furthermore, the increase of the essential contradiction that exists in the process of value-creation that structurally subordinates labour to capital can be:

> bearable by the first generation of mass-worker, for whom the advantages of Fordism outweighed the 'price' to pay to access it. But this was certainly no longer the case for the second generation. Raised in the Fordist mould, this generation was not prepared to 'lose its life in order to obtain it': to exchange a job and a meaningless life for the simple increase of its purchasing power, to lose its *being* for a surplus of *having*. In a word, be satisfied with the terms of the Fordist compromise agreed by the previous generation.[17]

The boycott and resistance to despotic, Taylorised, Fordist work took on different forms. It ranged through individual forms of absenteeism, resignation, high turnover, the search for non-factory work, collective forms of action

---

15. Bihr 1991, p. 63.
16. Bihr 1991, pp. 63–4.
17. Bihr 1991, p. 64.

that sought to win power over the labour-process through partial strikes, stealth-operations (marked by special 'care' of the machinery that slowed down production-time), opposition to the hierarchical division of labour and the despotism of factory-bosses, the creation of councils, proposals for self-management, up to the rejection of the control of capital and the call for the social control of production and workers' power.[18]

Thus, a form of interaction between the constitutive elements of the capitalist crisis was under way, elements that made the continuation of the expansionary cycle of capital (that had existed since the end of the war) impossible: as well as the economic exhaustion of the accumulation-cycle (a contingent manifestation of the structural crisis of capital) the class-struggles that took place at the end of the 1960s and early 1970s undermined capital's base, and gave rise to the possibility of a hegemony (or counter-hegemony) from the world of labour. The convergence and numerous reciprocal determinations between these two central elements (economic exhaustion and the intensification of class-struggle) played, therefore, a central role in the crisis at the end of the 1960s and in the early 1970s.

Workers' struggles also expressed discontent towards the *social-democratic path* being followed by the workers' movement that was predominant in labour's representative organisations. On the one hand, this path had adapted to the Taylorist/Fordist proletariat, in particularly its atomisation, and for this reason, the organisations represented moments of re-socialisation. On the other hand, by choosing the path of negotiation and institutionalisation – the contractual path – *these organisations showed themselves to be incapable of effectively incorporating the movement of the social bases of workers*. These organisations were, broadly speaking, defenders of capital, often positioning themselves against the social movements of the worker-base.

As Bihr puts it, 'It was therefore essentially *without* and even *against* trade-union and political organisations constitutive of the social-democratic model of the labour-movement that the proletarian struggles of the era developed. Moreover, these struggles were against this model as a whole. By placing the collective self-organisation of workers permanently at the very heart of the enterprise' these actions in the world of work reclaimed 'the emancipatory virtues of workers' direct action'.[19] They thus strongly opposed the institutionalised path at the heart of the social-democratic project.

It was, therefore, an offensive stage in the workers' struggles, the result of actions that frequently took place:

---

18. Bihr 1991, p. 65.
19. Bihr 1991, p. 67.

outside of trade-union institutions and legally established negotiation-mechanisms [and therefore] named as 'wildcat'-strikes and became known as autonomous movements.... Under these conditions, having direct control over the struggles, during the 1960s and 70s, workers showed that the fundamental question did not simply concern the formal ownership of capital..., but concerned the form in which social labour-relations are organised. During that period there were many cases of workers occupying companies, keeping them in operation without the bosses and administration. But since the control of the movement was directly determined by the bases, when it came to making decisions about production, workers naturally violated the established discipline and began to redesign the internal hierarchies of the company. During the period in which they were occupied, the companies changed their patterns of operation and were reorganised. The workers did not limit themselves to claiming the end to private property. They showed in practice that they were able to take the revolutionary process to a much more fundamental stage, which is that of the transformation of the social relations of labour and production themselves.[20]

At the core of the actions of the workers, therefore, was the effective possibility of the *social control of the material means of production by the workers*. Since such control, over the course of society's development, was alienated and subtracted from its productive social body – social labour – and transferred to capital, these actions of labour, unleashed across various parts of the capitalist world (in the centre as well as in the subordinated periphery), reclaimed and gave vitality and concrete form to the idea of the *social control of labour without capital*.

These actions, however, were constrained by limitations they were unable to transcend. Firstly, it was hard to dismantle a social-democratic organisational structure consolidated over decades that had left its mark on the proletariat. Workers' struggles, despite taking place in the productive space of the factory, attacking Taylorist and Fordist organisation of labour as well as the hierarchical social division that subordinates labour to capital, were not able to make the transition into a hegemonic-societal project against capital. As Bihr argues,[21] 'the struggle against the power of capital over labour did not reach as far as its power outside of work', not managing to articulate itself with the so-called 'new social movements', such as the environmental, urban, anti-nuclear, feminist and gay movements, among many others. Similarly, growing conflict within the proletariat made it unable to consolidate

---

20. Bernardo 1996, pp. 19–20.
21. Bihr 1991, pp. 69–70.

alternative forms of organisation that could oppose the unions and traditional parties. The practices of self-management became limited to the microcosm of the company or the workplace and were not able to erect mechanisms that would ensure their longevity.

Being unable to overcome these limitations, the actions of workers – despite their radicalism – became weaker and receded, unable as they were to hegemonically oppose the sociability of capital. The workers' ability to self-organise, however, 'seriously perturbed the operation of capital' and constituted one of the main reasons for the emergence of the crisis of the 1970s.[22] A huge technological advance was establishing itself as the first response of capital to the open confrontation from the world of work. On the other hand, it also served the needs of the monopoly-phase of inter-capitalist competition.

It was in this context that the forces of capital were able to reorganise themselves, presenting new problems and challenges to the world of work that, from this moment on, would find itself operating in very unfavourable conditions. The reorganisation of capital that followed, with new labour-processes, was influenced by the fact that:

> workers [had shown] they were able to directly control not just the protest-movement but the functioning of the factory itself. They showed, in short, that they did not just possess brute force, but also intelligence, initiative and organisational capacity. The capitalists realised therefore that rather than limiting themselves to the exploitation of the physical strength of workers, depriving them of any initiative and keeping them cloistered in the strict compartments of Taylorism and Fordism, they could multiply their profits by exploiting their imagination, their organisational skills, their capacity to co-operate, the full potential of their intelligence. It was with this goal that they developed electronic technology and computers and redesigned the administrative systems of companies, implanting Toyotism, total quality and other management-techniques. . . . Taylorism was an appropriate management-technique for a context in which each agent knew only what was needed for his immediate work. . . . Indeed, being unable to exploit human economies of scale – since each worker was limited to completing a single task – these companies had to concentrate on material economies of scale. Yet, material economies of scale generate decreasing earnings and at a certain threshold their gains begin to turn into losses. The recovery of workers' ability to self-organise allowed capitalists to overcome this impasse. A worker who reasons during her work and knows more about the technological and economic processes than just the narrow aspects

---

22. Bernardo 1996, p. 19.

pertaining to the immediate scope of her work, is a versatile worker. This is at the heart of human economies of scale. Each worker performs a greater number of operations, assists and replaces others. Co-operation becomes reinforced in the labour-process, increasing, in this way, economies of scale, for the benefit of capital.[23]

Thus, with the defeat of the workers' struggle for the social control of production, the social, ideological and political bases on which to resume the process of capital-restructuring were secured. This process would take a very distinct form from the one established during the Taylorist/Fordist era.

---

23. Bernardo 1996, pp. 19–20.

Chapter Four
Toyotism and the New Forms of Capital-Accumulation

It is in the context outlined above that Toyotism and the age of flexible accumulation emerged in the West. From the 1970s on, what was contingently expressed as a crisis of the Taylorist/Fordist accumulation-pattern was already an expression of a structural crisis of capital that continues to the present day. It resulted in the implementation of a vast process of restructuring aimed at re-establishing capital's reproductive cycle and a project of social domination that had been shaken by the confrontation with labour.

Capital launched a number of transformations to its productive process through the establishment of flexible forms of accumulation, downsizing, forms of organisational management, technological advance, and alternative models to Taylorism/Fordism, particularly Toyotism, or the Japanese model. These transformations, deriving from inter-capitalist competition, on the one hand (at a time of intense crises and disputes between the large transnational and monopolistic groups), and, on the other, from the necessity to control social struggles emanating from labour, began to invoke capital's response to its structural crisis.

Against the resistance emerging from social struggles, capital initiated a process of reorganisation of its forms of social domination, not only reorganising production but also attempting to recover its hegemony in the most diverse spheres of sociability.

It did this, for example, on an ideological level, through a cult of *subjectivism* and extreme individualism above forms of solidarity and collective and social action. Ellen Wood argues that it is a phase in which economic transformations, changes in production and markets, and cultural shifts – generally associated with 'post modernism' – were in fact the expression of a moment of *maturation* and *universalisation* of capital, much more than any transition from 'modernity' to 'post modernity'.[1]

However, these changes, which began in the 1970s and are, to a large extent, still under way, generated more *dissent* than *consent*. According to some scholars, they were responsible for the establishment a new form of industrial organisation and capital-labour relations that offered an improvement over Taylorism/Fordism because it enabled the entry of a more qualified, participatory, multifunctional, versatile worker, able to attain a 'greater degree of achievement in the workplace'. This interpretation, which originated in Sabel and Piore's work (1984), was popular with many other observers who, more or less closely aligned to the thesis of *flexible specialisation*, defended the so-called 'innovatory characteristics' of a 'new phase' of improved interaction between capital and labour able to overcome the basic, constitutive contradictions of capitalist society.

According to others, the transformations were not leading towards a 'Japanisation' or 'Toyotisation' of industry but were instead simply intensifying existing trends and did not indicate a new form of organisation of labour. On the contrary, in the context of advanced-capitalist economies, what could be perceived was a reconfiguration of 'balance of power in the workplace and in the labour market in favour of employers rather than workers'.[2]

For Tomaney, who offers a critical examination of the tendencies described above, new research, particularly in England, reveals that the thesis of a 'new organisation of labour', bestowed with a 'new optimism', is being disproved. The changes that are affecting the world of labour, especially on the 'shop floor', are the result of historical and geographical factors and not simply the result of new technologies and the process of organisational development.[3] In his critique of the theory of flexible specialisation, he shows that 'it is possible to identify three greater sets of problems': 'firstly, the utility of the dichotomy between mass production and flexible accumulation; secondly, the inability to account for the results of the process of restructuring and deal with its political implications; lastly, the fact that, even where it is possible to identify

---

1. Wood 1997a, pp. 539–40.
2. Tomaney 1996, pp. 157–8. See also Pollert 1996; Stephenson 1996; Ackers, Smith and Smith 1996; and Wood 1989, among others that I shall discuss below.
3. Tomaney 1996, p. 158.

examples of flexible specialisation, this has not necessarily brought benefits to labour, as they assume.'[4]

On the contrary, it has been possible to identify a growing number of examples of *labour-intensification* where the *just-in-time* system is used.[5] He concludes that the 'new orthodoxy', based on the idea that 'technical changes are forcing employers to establish a more co-operative relationship with labour', is being re-evaluated by new studies that show different tendencies:

1) where computerised technology has been introduced, this has not resulted in the emergence of qualified labour. Furthermore, large-scale production and forms of intensive accumulation have been consolidated;

2) theses that defend 'post-Fordism' overestimate the breadth of the changes, in particular those that concern qualified and skilled labour, which leads the author to conclude that the changes in the capitalist process of labour are not so profound, but are instead the expression of a continual transformation within the labour-process itself, affecting above all forms of management and the control-flux, but often leading to the intensification of work.[6]

Other authors have accentuated both the elements of continuity and discontinuity with the previous productive pattern, with the *essentially capitalist character of the mode of production and its fundamental pillars* maintained intact. According to this thesis, it is necessary to note the specificity of the transformations and their impact on the system of capitalist production. Here, it is argued, a 'flexible accumulation regime that began in 1973' has emerged, which is characterised by 'shrinking markets, unemployment, rapid shifts in spatial constraints and the global division of labour, capital flight, plant closings, technological and financial reorganisation', among many other changes that mark this new phase of capitalist production.[7] Juan J. Castillo evocatively called it the expression of a process of *organisational lyophilisation* (freeze-drying),[8] with the elimination, offshoring, tertiarisation and streamlining of productive units.[9]

---

4. Tomaney 1996, p. 164.
5. Tomaney 1996, p. 170.
6. Tomaney 1996, pp. 175–6. I shall return to these arguments in more detail when considering the case of Britain.
7. Harvey 1996, pp. 363–4.
8. Lyophilisation, or 'freeze-drying', is a dehydration-process that works by freezing perishable material. The lyophilisation-metaphor is used with regard to organisations to characterise the elimination of living labour that occurs during process of productive restructuring.
9. Castillo 1996a, p. 68, and 1996a.

My reflections have more affinity with this interpretation: the changes taking place are the expression of a reorganisation of capital with the aim of reclaiming its pattern of accumulation and its global project of domination. And it is in this sense that the process of flexible accumulation – examples of which can be found in California, northern Italy, Switzerland and Germany, among many others that followed – as well as the different forms of Toyotism, or the Japanese model, should be the object of critical reflection. We will start with the issue of 'total quality', and later return to reflect upon the *organisational lyophilisation* of the 'lean enterprise'.

The fallacy of 'total quality' under the diminishing utility-rate of the use-value of commodities

A first element concerns the issue of *quality* in the productive processes. During the phase of intensification of the diminishing utility-rate of the use-value of commodities[10] – required for the re-establishment of the process of capital-valorisation – the fallacy of total quality disseminated in the 'modern business-world', inside the lean enterprise of the era of productive restructuring, becomes evident: the greater the 'total quality' of a product, *the shorter should be its longevity*. The imperative to reduce the lifetime-utility of products, to increase the speed of the productive circuit and the speed of production of exchange-values, transforms 'total quality', for the most part, into a *shell*, concerned with *the appearance* or refinement of the *superfluous*, since the products need to last for a short time and be easily inserted into the market. 'Total quality', for this reason, cannot counteract the diminishing utility-rate of the use-value of commodities but has to adapt to capital's socio-economic metabolic order, impacting therefore on both the production of goods and services, as on the equipment and machinery and the human force of labour itself.[11]

As capital's productive system has an intrinsically *expansionary* tendency, 'total quality' needs to become entirely compatible with the logic of *destructive production*. For this reason, in the broadest sense, the capitalist mode of production becomes the enemy of product-*durability:* it even has to make production geared to the longevity of products unviable, which leads to the *deliberate subversion of their quality*.[12] 'Total quality' also becomes the negation of the durability of products. The better the 'quality' commodities *appear* to have (and here *appearance* makes the difference), the more obsolete they

---

10. Mészáros 1995, Chapters 15 and 16.
11. Mészáros 1995, p. 575.
12. Mészáros 1995, pp. 548–9.

should effectively be. Waste and destructiveness end up being their defining features.

In this way, the much acclaimed development of 'total-quality' processes becomes the *phenomenal, apparent* and *superfluous* expression of a mechanism of production that is based on the *diminishing rate of utility of the use-value* of commodities, the condition for the continued reproduction of capital and its expansionary imperatives.

We are not referring here simply to fast-food restaurants (of which McDonald's is an example) that waste tons of packaging to create snacks of barely endurable quality produced to the rhythms of a Fordist factory. Another clear example is the average lifespan of modern automobiles, which gets shorter all the time.

The IT-industry, given its importance in today's productive world, is an example of the depreciative and diminishing tendency of the use-value of commodities. A software-system becomes obsolete and out of date relatively quickly, leading the consumer to replace it as the systems cease to be compatible with one another. Firms faced with the need to reduce the time between production and consumption – because of the intense competition that exists between them – stretch this destructive tendency of the use-value of commodities to the limit. With the need to keep pace with competition, this logic is intensified, making 'total quality' its prisoner. Moreover, it becomes an intrinsic mechanism of its functionality. In order to survive, capital no longer has any choice but to innovate by reducing the useful life-cycle of products or run the risk of being overtaken by competing firms. An example of such a firm is Hewlett-Packard, a firm that by constantly 'innovating' its computing systems has greatly reduced the useful lifetime of its products.[13] The production of computers is therefore an example of the power of the *law of the diminishing tendency of the use-value of commodities,* among many others we could mention.

By this, we are obviously not questioning genuine techno-scientific advance led by real socio-human imperatives, but rather the logic of capital's social-metabolic order that transforms into refuse and waste what should be preserved, in order to meet social use-values as much as to avoid the uncontrolled destruction of nature and the metabolic relation between human beings and nature. Not to mention, moreover, the profound process of destruction of the human force of labour brought about by the process of *organisational lyophilisation* of the 'lean enterprise'.

---

13. See Kenney 1997, p. 92.

The 'lyophilisation' of organisation and labour in the Toyotist factory: new forms of labour-intensification

Flexible accumulation articulates a set of elements of *continuity* and *discontinuity* that result in a *relatively* distinct pattern of accumulation to Taylorism/ Fordism. It is based on an organisationally and technologically advanced productive pattern, the result of the introduction of labour-force management-techniques associated with the information-age, as well as the widespread introduction of computers into the productive process and into services. It developed into a more flexible productive structure, frequently resorting to the devolution of production through subcontracting. It makes use of new labour-management techniques, of teamwork, of 'production-cells', of 'work-teams', of 'semi-autonomous' groups, as well as demanding – at least at the level of discourse – the 'participation' of workers, or rather a manipulated participation that essentially preserves alienated and estranged[14] working conditions. Versatile, 'multifunctional' and 'qualified'[15] labour, as well as a more horizontal structure that is more integrated with other firms, including subcontracted firms, aims at the reduction of labour-time.

The real, essential objective of this process of labour-organisation is the *intensification of the conditions of exploitation of the labour-force*, greatly reducing or eliminating both *unproductive labour*, which creates no value, as well as other equivalent forms, especially activities such as maintenance, supervision and quality-assurance, functions that have become directly assigned to the *productive* worker. Re-engineering, lean production, teamwork, cutting jobs, increasing productivity and total quality are all part of the daily ideals (and of the practice) of the 'modern factory'. If, at the apex of Taylorism/Fordism, the power of a firm was measured by the number of employees, in the era of flexible accumulation and of the 'lean enterprise', the firms that stand out (and that will be considered below) are those with the *smallest* labour-forces but the highest levels of productivity.

Some of the repercussions of these changes in the productive process have an immediate impact in the world of work: extensive deregulation of labour-rights, eliminated on a daily basis in nearly all corners of the world that have industrial production and services; increase in the fragmentation of the working class, precarisation and subcontracting of the human force that labours;

---

14. See Antunes 1995a, pp. 34–5, 91–3, 121–34.
15. This highlights the fallacy of 'work-qualifications', which is often a sign of *ideology* rather than a real requirement of the production-process. The qualifications and expertise that capital requires are more often than not aimed at guaranteeing the *reliability* of the worker, who must place her subjectivity at the disposal of capital.

and destruction of class-unionism and its transformation into docile union-ism, based on *partnership* or even 'enterprise unionism'.[16]

Among the experiences of capital that differ from Fordism/Taylorism, 'Toyotism', or the 'Japanese model', has had greater impact compared with the Swedish example, or the experience of northern Italy (Third Italy), the US (Silicon Valley) or Germany, among others.

From the 1970s on, the Japanese industrial system had a profound impact on the Western world and began to be seen as potential solution to capital's crisis. Naturally, in order to be transplanted into the West, Toyotism had to be adapted to the particularities of each individual country. Its organisa-tional design, its technological advances, its capacity for intensified labour-extraction, as well as teamwork, its participation methods, the control over unions, etc. were all seen by Western capital as a possible route towards over-coming the crisis of accumulation.

And it was in this context that the expansion into the West of the *Japanese model of industrial-capital consolidation* took place. In Sayer's words, the impact of the Japanese model:

> increased in the late 1970s, when after a decade of falling productivity growth in the west the export performance and extraordinarily rapid growth of Japanese manufacturers, particularly in cars and consumer electronics, began to arouse interest in the west.... In addition to well-publicised features of Japanese manufacturing, such as quality circles and lifetime employment, some startling features emerged, such as the practice of assembling completely different models on the same line. Gradually, it became clear that what was involved was not simply a few 'cultural peculiarities' but an innovative and highly integrated system of production organisation.[17]

Toyotism (or Ohnism, after Ohno Taiichi, Toyota's production-control engi-neer), the *Japanese model for the expansion and consolidation of monopolistic indus-trial capitalism*, is a form of labour-organisation that emerged in Toyota in Japan after 1945, and that rapidly expanded amongst other large Japanese companies. It differs from Fordism in the following basic ways:[18]

1) *it is a form of production closely tied to demand* that seeks to respond to the most *individualised* needs of the consumer-market, distinguishing it from Taylorist/Fordist *series-* and *mass*-production. For this reason, its produc-tion is varied and heterogeneous, unlike homogeneous Fordist production;

---

16. See Kelly 1996, pp. 95–8.
17. Sayer 1986, pp. 50–1.
18. On Toyotism, see Gounet 1997, 1992 and 1991; Teague 1997; Ichiyo 1995; Takaichi 1992; Coriat 1992; Sayer 1986; and Kamata 1982.

2) it is based on *team*-work, with *cross-functional teams*, which distinguishes it from the piecemeal work of Fordism;

3) production is structured within a flexible productive process which allows a worker to simultaneously operate various machines (at Toyota, on average five machines), modifying the man-machine relation upon which Taylorism/Fordism was based;

4) it is based on the *just-in-time* principle, the best possible use of production time;

5) it works according to the *kanban*-system, command-tags or -boards for the replacement of parts and stock. Under Toyotism, stocks are minimal when compared with Fordism;

6) firms operating in the Toyotist productive complex, including subcontracted ones, have a horizontal structure, as opposed to the vertical Fordist one. Whereas, under Fordism, around 75 per cent of production was realised inside one factory, the Toyotist factory is responsible for only 25 per cent of production, a tendency that continues to grow. The latter focuses the production-process on what is essential to their expertise (the so-called 'theory of fire') and transfers to third parties much of what used to be produced within its productive space. This horizontalisation extends to subcontracted firms, leading to the expansion of these methods and procedures across the whole network of suppliers. In this way, flexibilisation, tertiarisation, subcontracting, quality-control circles (QCCs), total-quality control, *kanban*, just-in-time production, *kaizen*, teamwork, the elimination of waste, 'participative management' and enterprise-unionism, among many other features, become part of the wider arena of the productive process;

7) it establishes QCCs: groups of workers who are encouraged by capital to discuss their work and performance with a view to improving the productivity of companies. This becomes an important tool for capital to appropriate the intellectual and cognitive *know-how* of the worker that Fordism scorned;[19] and

8) Toyotism set up 'lifetime-employment' for a portion of workers in large companies (about 25 to 30 per cent of the working population, *excluding* women), and increased wages in line with productivity-gains. With 'lifetime-employment', a Japanese worker is guaranteed employment-security, with a transfer, at age 55, to a less important job within the same company.

---

19. In the West, QCCs have differed depending on the specificities of the countries in which they have been implemented.

Taking its inspiration initially from the textile-sector, where workers operated a number of machines at the same time, and later, by importing supermarket management-techniques used in the US (which led to *kanban*), Toyotism also provided a response to the Japanese financial crisis of the end of World-War II, by increasing production without increasing the number of workers. Once this recipe had been adopted across Japanese companies, the result was a return to a scale of production that led Japan, over a very short period of time, to attain very high levels of productivity and capitalist accumulation.

The streamlining of the productive process, which was marked by strong *disciplining* of the workforce and propelled by the need to implant *intensive forms of capital and labour*, characterised the *Japanese model of development of monopoly-capitalism* and its process of *organisational and labour-lyophilisation*. Teamwork, the transferral of responsibilities for the elaboration and control over the quality of production *from* scientific management *to* the workers, gave rise to so-called *management by stress*.[20] As can be seen in the classic statement by Satochi Kamata, the rationalisation of the Toyota Motor Company, undertaken while it was being set up:

> is not so much to eliminate work, as, more directly, to eliminate workers. For example, if 33 per cent of 'wasted motion' is eliminated from three workers, one worker becomes unnecessary. The history of Toyota rationalisation is a history of the reduction of workers, and that's the secret of how Toyota shows no increase in employees while achieving its startling increases in production. All free time during working hours has been taken away from assembly line workers as wasteful. All their time, to the last second, is devoted to production.[21]

The Toyotist production-process, through *teamwork*, thus presupposes the *intensification of labour-exploitation* in the sense of workers simultaneously operating a number of different machines, as well as the rhythm and speed of the production-chain being driven by a system of electric lights. In other words, we see *an intensification of the rhythm of production within the same working time, or even when this is reduced*. In the Toyota factory, when the light is *green*, it signifies normal functioning; when the light is *amber*, it signifies maximum-intensity; and when a *red* light appears, it is because there have been some problems, and the productive rhythm has had to be reduced. The appropriation of the *intellectual* activities of the work that arise from the introduction of automated and computerised machinery present an extremely

20. Gounet 1997, p. 77.
21. Kamata 1982, p. 199.

positive scenario for capital whereby it is able to regain its accumulation-cycles and recuperate its profits.[22]

In this way, like Fordism during the earlier-twentieth century but following a different set of rules, Toyotism inaugurates a new level of labour-intensification, powerfully combining relative and absolute forms of surplus-value extraction. If we recall that a recent proposal of the Japanese government, as mentioned above, 'is to increase…the working week (from 48 to 52 hours)', then we have a clear example of what this entails.[23]

The growth of *part-time* work, as well as labour-forms where capital is able to make use of the *sexual* division of labour and the swelling numbers of immigrant-workers, such as the *dekasseguis* who perform unskilled and often illegal jobs, are clear examples of the vast tendency towards the intensification and exploitation of the labour-force under Toyotism. Its structure *retains* a reduced number of more *qualified* workers within the most important companies, workers who are also *cross-functional* and involved in the company-ethos, while *extending* the fluctuating and flexible mass of workers with an increase in overtime, subcontracting within and outside of the companies, hiring temporary workers, etc., options that vary according to the market-conditions they are faced with. The further the work is from the main companies, the greater is its precariousness. For this reason Toyota workers work an average of '2,300 hours per year, whilst the workers in the subcontracted firms work up to 2,800 hours'.[24]

The transferability of Toyotism, *or of part of its prescriptions*, was of great interest to Western capital as it had been experiencing its own crisis since the early 1970s. Naturally, its adaptability, to a greater or lesser extent, was conditioned by the particularities of each country, in terms of their economic, social, political and ideological conditions, the position of each country in the international division of labour and the characteristics of national labour-movements and labour-markets at the moment Toyotism was adopted.

As Costa and Garanto show, whilst the Japanese model implemented 'lifetime-employment' for a segment of its working class (30 per cent, according to the authors), something very different occurred in the West, where employment-security occurs in a much more limited way, *even in the companies with Japanese capital established in Europe*. 'In fact, employment security is not offered by more than about 11% of companies. It is relatively more accepted

---

22. Ichiyo 1995, pp. 45–6; Gounet 1991, p. 41; Coriat 1992, p. 60; Antunes, pp. 27–8.
23. *Japan Press Weekly* 1998.
24. Gounet 1997, p. 78. In comparison, in Belgium (Ford-Genk, General Motors-Anvers, Volkswagen-Forest, Renault-Vilvorde and Volvo-Gand), employees work on average 1,600–1,700 hours per year (p. 99).

in the UK (in 13% of firms set up there), compared to France (5%) or Spain (6%).'[25] The authors' data leads them *relativise* the 'myth of Japanisation' in Europe.[26] The process of westernisation of Toyotism thus combines elements that are present in Japan with existing practices in the receiving countries, resulting in a *differentiated, particularised and unique process of adaptation.*

Neoliberalism, or the policies it influenced, established conditions that permitted a *differentiated* adaptation of elements of Toyotism in the West. Since *the process of productive restructuring of capital was the material basis of the neoliberal ideologico-political project,*[27] the structure upon which the neoliberal *ethos* and *pragmatic* are built, it was not hard to perceive how from the end of the 1970s and early 1980s, the Western-capitalist world began to develop similar techniques to Toyotism. Toyotism appeared to be the most advanced experience of productive restructuring. It had originated from Japanese Fordism itself and subsequently become *a unique path of capitalist accumulation* that was responsible for a great leap in Japanese capitalism, re-establishing the relevance of the country in the capitalist world at the end of the 1970s.

Against this background, in the mid-1970s, General Motors (GM) began its experience of Toyotism by introducing QCCs. Leaving to one side the full *set* of Toyotism's constitutive elements and making use of only one of its features, GM saw its first attempt at assimilation fall through. This occurred during the worsening the crisis at its Detroit plant, when GM decided to invest a large number of resources in order to challenge Japanese expansion into the North-American market. The company invested in robotics for its assembly-line, starting with 302 robots in 1980 and aiming at having 14,000 by 1990.[28]

Seeking to compete with small Japanese cars, GM also designed a new model that was not, however, able to compete with the prices of similar products produced in Japan by Mazda and Mitsubishi. The result of this phase was the Saturn project that began in 1983 and brought about the construction of a new factory in Spring Hill, Tennessee. The project used just-in-time production, teamwork, advanced automation and computerisation, modular production, tertiarisation and subcontracting, worked with companies in close proximity to GM and reproduced the same production system as Toyota. Like the project that inspired it, closer ties with the consumer led to the production

---

25. Costa and Garanto 1993, p. 98.
26. Costa and Garanto 1993, p. 110.
27. Netto 1998.
28. See Gounet 1991, p. 44. On GM's Saturn project, see also Bernardo 1996. On the Japanese experience in the US, see Berggren 1993.

of vehicles with the requested specifications and, in addition, involved the United Automobile Workers (UAW) union.

During the same period, GM became associated with companies such as Isuzu and Suzuki and, in 1983, established a joint venture with Toyota itself to produce a small car in GM's factory in California, a factory with very dated technology. Toyota oversaw the entire management of this project. While GM recorded disappointing results in the period up to 1986, Toyota, based at NUMMI (New United Motor Manufacturing Inc.) on the other side of the US, was highly profitable even without needing to resort to the introduction of additional robots.

The first conclusion we can draw from the example of GM concerns the use of advanced technology: its implementation was much more complex than it appeared, with numerous faults and frequent problems, in addition to the disparity between the advanced technology and the labour-force. The latter, despite being qualified, did not manage to adapt to the new model. The project of establishing a technologically-advanced factory was therefore abandoned by GM/Saturn, which instead shifted its investment towards improving the qualifications and preparation of its workforce. *It was thus recognised that it would be counterproductive to introduce robots and advanced technology without the equivalent qualification and preparation of the workforce.* Human and organisational transformations would have to occur hand in hand with technological changes. In 1987, a 'Quality Network System' was created with the purpose of transferring to the workers the control of quality, customer-service and increases in productivity. This system was later extended to Europe in 1989.

The result of GM's policy was to keep hold of a slice of around 36 to 37 per cent of the American market, which did not return great profits. In the European market, however, its presence was more aggressive: it was ahead of Ford-Europe and Renault, and just behind Volkswagen, Fiat and Peugeot. Following this path, which wavered during its initial stages and took different turns along the way, GM introduced new labour-processes into its units drawing on elements of the Japanese model.

This assimilation of Toyotism took place in nearly all the large enterprises, starting in the automotive sector and later spreading into the industrial sector and into the various branches of the service-sector, both in the central countries as well as in the intermediary industrialised countries. In the UK, the Toyotist experiment was associated with neoliberalism, in place since the Labour Party lost power in 1979. The following section will be concerned with this experience.

Chapter Five

From Thatcher's Neoliberalism to Blair's 'Third Way': the Recent British Experience

Neoliberalism, the world of work and the crisis of unionism in England

The recent British experience, particularly after Margaret Thatcher and the establishment of the neo-liberal project, has had far-reaching consequences for the world of work in the UK, particularly in England.[1] British society has been profoundly transformed. Changes were made to its productive base through the sale of state-enterprises, the shrinking of the industrial sector, the expansion of a private service-sector and, finally, the reconfiguration of the UK in the new international division of labour. There were also vast repercussions to the *form of being* of the working class, its union-movement, its parties, its social movements, ideals and values.

British trade-unionism experienced periods of growth, through the 1890s and 1970s for example, as well as periods of decline, particularly the 1930s and especially after the 1980s. Periods of rise and decline also occurred in other countries of western Europe, in different ways and with different implications according to the characteristics and specificities of each country. Different national realities created a heterogeneous union-movement with varying political, ideological, religious and occupational configurations.[2]

---

1. Whilst these views often apply to the whole of the UK, they refer mainly to England.

2. Ackers, Smith and Smith 1996, pp. 1–2; Pelling 1987, p. 264.

Whereas unionism in France, Italy and Spain developed with strong competition between Catholics, Socialists and Communists, in northern Europe, especially England, Germany, the Netherlands and the Scandinavian countries, disputes over hegemony were mainly influenced by social democracy (and Labourism, in the case of England). In Sweden, for example, union-membership levels are high (the highest in the world, followed by the Netherlands), whereas the opposite is the case in France and Spain. At the same time, a greater politicisation of union-activities is evident in southern Europe when compared with the deeper institutionalisation and organisation in workplaces of northern Europe.[3]

This varied outline is enough to show the risks involved in trying to describe the trade-union movement in western-European countries in general terms. While it may be possible to capture some general tendencies in the European trade-union context, it is important also to present an analysis that takes into account the different historical realities of each individual country.

In its relationship with labour and the trade-union movement, British capitalism has, in this sense, some very particular traits: compared with Germany, which preserved its contractual system, its welfare-state and stable employment-conditions during the 1970s, in Britain Margaret Thatcher created a 'free-market' system that led the country on a course that differentiated it even further from countries of northern Europe. 'For all these reasons the British trade-union movement calls for special treatment' in order to understand its more general trends as well as the challenges it has faced in light of the current debate 'between the "collectivism" of the European Social Charter and the free market, American "individualist" alternative' that 'may be crucial to the future of trade unionism in Britain and Europe'.[4]

Since the end of the Labour government and especially during 1978, a historic crisis has affected the British labour-movement. '[T]he visible symptom of this malaise (dramatically confirmed the following year) was the declining vote for the British Labour Party.'[5] Important social changes had begun in Britain in the decades that followed World-War II, including a fall in the number of manual labourers, the feminisation of the labour-force and greater ethnic diversity. Throughout this period, strikes began to be met with increasing public opposition. In fact, a significant change in the constitutive

---

3. Ackers, Smith and Smith 1996, pp. 2–3; McIlroy 1995; and Taylor 1989, pp. xiv–v.
4. Ackers, Smith and Smith 1996, p. 4.
5. Ackers, Smith and Smith 1996, pp. 4–5.

features of the labour- and trade-union movement had been under way in Britain since the end of the nineteenth century.[6]

Throughout its history, British unionism was always associated with the ideas of strength and stability. Union-membership levels were high and widespread. In 1920, 8,348,000 workers, representing 45.2 per cent of the workforce, were members of trade unions. 'Whilst these figures were halved during the inter-war depression, growth from the mid-1930s saw membership expand to nine million in the 1940s and to 13.5 million, more than 55 per cent of the labour force, in 1979.'[7] Whilst, in 1910, the unionisation-rate was 14.6 per cent, with 2,565,000 members, in 1933 it reached 22.6 per cent with a total of 4,392,000. In 1955, unionisation-levels reached 44.5 per cent, or 9,741,000 unionised workers.[8]

Institutionally organised, relatively unified politically and in terms of its party-allegiance, the British labour- and union-movement is structured in the following way: its union-arm is based around the national union-federation, the Trades Union Congress (TUC). Its political arm, which emerged from the TUC itself, is formed by the Labour Party. The movement therefore followed a unique path that moved in an opposite direction to the labour-movements in most other advanced-capitalist countries: in Britain, the TUC created the Labour Party and became the pillar that sustained it (although this has changed substantially in the last few years).

The TUC was created in 1868 and throughout a whole century had practically no rivals. It was structured according to:

> complex patterns of organisation and multi-unionism with variants of craft, industrial, occupational and general unionism competing for membership. In the 1960s, more than twenty unions represented workers of one Ford plant. There were 651 unions in England, with 183 unions organising 80 percent of total membership affiliated to the TUC. By the 1970s, a growing number of mergers produced a tendency towards general multi-occupational unionism.[9]

Strongly rooted in factories and workplaces and based on a complex mix of *co-operation* and *opposition*, British trade-unionism had over 90,000 *shop-stewards* at the end of the 1950s, a figure that reached around 350,000 by the 1970s. With its workplace-structure, British unionism had a support-base for its institutionalised and hierarchical policy of negotiation and bargaining. Its

---

6. Ackers, Smith and Smith 1996, p. 5; Pelling 1987, pp. 282–4.
7. McIlroy 1996, pp. 2–3; and McIlroy 1995, p. 11.
8. McIlroy 1995, p. 11.
9. McIlroy 1996, p. 3.

power-base lay in national and private industry. The iron- and coal-industries, among other productive activities of the state, had a strong labour- and union-presence as a result of the nationalisation-policies of previous Labour governments.

Capital, labour and the state rested on:

> the voluntarist regulation of employment relations. There was an absence of detailed legislation – stark in comparison with almost any other national legislation – and priority was accorded to autonomous collective bargaining. Until the 1970s, on some issues beyond that, there was no legal right to affiliate to a union membership or union recognition, no duty on employers to bargain, no enforcement of collective agreements by the Courts and no right to strike.... The already engrained reformism of British trade unionism took on independent organisational form with the creation of the Labour Party.... The unions marked this creation by constitutional domination of the party's decision-making.[10]

The Labour Party's relationship with the unions and the labour-movement was constituted by an industrial wing (the unions) and a political wing (the party itself).

> Socialist rhetoric on the constitution of the Labour Party was divorced from its practice, which only obtained any reformist coherence with the adoption of Keynesianism and state ownership in the 1940s. However, this monopolised the loyalty of working class voters. The Communist Party and other left-wing organisations grew slowly during this period: they had influence in industry but their political importance was marginal. The horizons of the majority of workers were limited by labourism, sustained as they were by the reforms of a complacent state and the success obtained in collective bargaining. Until 1979, Labour had in government for 11 out of the previous 15 years, securing it an important, albeit exaggerated, trade union influence in negotiations with the state, supported by a post-war consensus on full-employment and the Welfare State.[11]

Defending the economic interests of the labour-force and fighting threats to past labour-victories, British unionism:

> made inroads into recruiting a growing number of white collar workers, with union density increasing in this group from 32 percent in 1968 to 44 percent in 1979. As the female labour force grew, density increased from

---

10. Ibid.
11. Ibid. See also Taylor 1989, pp. 121–3.

26 percent in 1965 to almost 40 percent in 1979. More than 70 percent of the workforce was covered by collective agreements. In manufacturing industry and the public sector, 90 percent of workplaces had shop stewards.[12]

The expansion of public-sector unionism was also a defining feature of those years of progress for British labourism. During this period:

> the National Union of Public Employees (NUPE) grew from 200,000 members in 1960 to 700,000 in 1979. NALGO [National and Local Government Officers' Association] had 274,000 members in 1960 and 753,000 in 1979. There were around 370,000 union members in the NHS in 1967 and 1.3 million in 1979. These developments did much to change the face of British trade unionism which had previously possessed the stamp of the private sector.[13]

The growth of the TUC and the Labour Party – the former the expression of the union-arm of the workers and the latter the expression of their political-parliamentary engagement (given the close relationship between the two, their activities often intermingled) – was also marked by an increase in strike-action in England. The 1960s saw a great increase in work-stoppages, reaching an annual average of 3,000 strikes between 1969 and 1974 with up to 12.5 million strikers. Local strikes and national strikes combined on a vast scale, involving public-sector workers in particular. There were also political strikes, such as for example the stoppages against the arrest of dock-workers who defied Conservative government-legislation in 1972, the actions against the restriction of union-activity in 1969, and especially the miners' strike of 1974, which led to the fall of Conservative prime minister Edward Heath.

In addition to the increase in political strikes, the years that preceded the advent of Thatcherism were characterised by an increase in the numbers of shop-stewards, in workplace-organisation and pickets, as well as factory- and workplace-occupations – known as 'work-ins' – in which workers, on many occasions, even assumed responsibility for the management of the enterprise. Broad support for the Labour Party owed mainly to the close ties between the TUC and the Labour Party. Given the extent of unionisation, a significant portion of the British working class was guaranteed to support Labour, conferring a union-base to the political activity of the Labour Party.[14] Notwithstanding its growth and politicisation during the 1960–70s, the British union-movement, through the institutional and political activity of the Labour Party, gradually began to show signs of exhaustion. It began to reveal its limitations in con-

---

12. McIlroy 1996, p. 7.
13. McIlroy 1995, p. 10.
14. See, for example, the electoral data in Callinicos and Harman 1987, especially pp. 83–7.

structing a more solidly *social-democratic* project – like the ones to be found in the northern-European countries – as well as in forging a more clearly *socialist* identity, in the manner of southern-European nations like France or Italy, where left-wing currents were strong, in particular those that were tied to the Communist parties. These limitations were evident in 1979, when Margaret Thatcher and the Conservative Party successfully diverted the earlier trend that was marked by the strong presence of British Labourism. This new phase of recent British history profoundly altered the country's economic, social, political and ideological reality – along with its values – and marked the beginning of the end of British unionism. The arrival of an audacious and virulent strand of neoliberalism in Britain kept the Conservatives in power until May 1997.

With the ascent of Thatcher's conservatism, a *new agenda* radically transformed Labour's previous participatory development path. Gradually, Britain's socio-economic conditions and juridical-institutional structure were altered to make them compatible with the implementation of the neoliberal model. Its primary aim was to strengthen the free market and establish Britain's position in the new capitalist configuration. The *new agenda* sought:

1) the *privatisation* of nearly all that had been under state-control during the labour-era;[15]
2) the reduction and even elimination of state-productive capital;
3) the development of legislation that was *fiercely deregulatory* in terms of labour-conditions and made social rights flexible; and
4) the approval, by the Conservative-led parliament, of a set of strongly anti-union acts that sought to eliminate a range of union-structures from the factory-bases and their shop-stewards, to the more established forms of negotiation between capital, labour and the state such as collective bargaining.

A 'new business-culture' emerged, marked by the proliferation of concepts and practices such as Business School, Human Resource Management, Total-Quality Management, and Employee Involvement and Empowerment. The 'collectivism' that previously existed in Britain's world of work was replaced by individualism, new management and new administration-methods. This *new agenda*, which expanded rapidly in the 1980s, sought an increase of

---

15. With the exception of the underground and postal service, virtually all public services were given over to private capital, after privatisation, and the privatisation of the underground and mail is frequently the subject of debate in the UK.

non-manual jobs, the advance and growth of the service-sector (particularly
the private service-sector), greater self-employment (which doubled between
1979 and 1990) and the huge increase in *part-time* work. The same occurred
with the introduction of streamlining and lean production, the growth of
small productive units and the reduction of bureaucratic management-struc-
tures that resulted in the rapid increase in levels of unemployment (cyclical
and structural), as well as causing significant changes in class-structure and
relations throughout the 1980s and 1990s.[16]

Amid extremely favourable political and ideological conditions, given by
the hegemony of Thatcher's neoliberalism as much as by the subsequent electoral victories (the Conservatives beating the Labour Party in four consecu-
tive elections), along with an impetus to privatise and the ideological defence
of the free market, the soil was fertile for a new phase of capitalism to emerge.
This form of capitalism was less *industrial* and more oriented towards *services*;
less *production*-oriented and more *financial*, less *collectivist* and more *individu-
alistic*, more *deregulated* and less *contractual*, more *flexibilised* and less 'rigid'
in its relations between capital and labour, more rooted in laissez-faire and
in *monetarism* and totally opposed to the *nationalist statism* of the Labour
period – in summary, more attuned to the post-crisis capitalism of the 1970s.[17]

The transformation of unionism into the *core-enemy* of neoliberalism had
direct consequences for the relationship between the state and the working
class. Trade-union leaders were excluded from discussions of state-policy
(in particular unemployment-policies, the economy and the state's role) and
were removed from economic bodies both nationally and locally. The closure
of various tripartite organs also took place, such as the National Enterprise
Board, which established the boundaries of state-intervention, the Manpower
Services Commission, which was responsible for human-resources training
and market-policy, and the National Economic Development Committee,
which since the 1960s had overseen nationalisation and corporate policies.

These exclusionary practices were intensified during the 1980s and 1990s.
In the Training and Enterprise Councils the presence of trade-unionists was
reduced to just 5 per cent or was completely eliminated. There was a boycott on industrial action by the Government Communications Headquarters
(GCHQ) prohibiting its staff from engaging in trade-union activity.[18]

Thatcherism reduced trade-union action at the same time as it introduced
new production-techniques that were based on the individualisation of the
relations between capital and labour and the systematic boycott of trade-

16. Ackers, Smith and Smith 1996, pp. 4–7.
17. Ackers, Smith and Smith 1996, pp. 3–9; and Kelly 1996, pp. 77–82.
18. McIlroy 1995, p. 207; McIlroy 1996, p. 10; and Taylor 1989, pp. 121–3.

union action. This anti-union policy included the systematic outlawing of shop-stewards and limits to closed-shop workplaces where the right to trade-union membership was guaranteed. There was a shift from a legal system that minimally regulated labour-relations, *to a system of tight regulation that sought to deregulate labour-conditions, on the one hand, and heavily repress and restrict trade-union activity, on the other.* In other words, from a system of minimal regulation that permitted widespread trade-union activity to a system of heavy regulation that was restrictive to trade-unions and deregulatory with respect to labour-market conditions.

Strike-action is a clear example. For a strike to be decreed legal, a ritual of complex, bureaucratic voting practices has to be performed, preceded by the announcement of the strike and subsequent navigation through a web of restrictions. Solidarity-strikes were outlawed; repressed also were awareness-raising activities such as pickets or union-pressure – pressure traditionally exerted on workers who ignored collective decisions, made in secret ballots, to go on strike. Only those stoppages that successfully navigated this restrictive legal-bureaucratic ritual were accepted. When unions did not systematically adhere to all the bureaucracy, they suffered heavy fines and penalties, making their activity and efforts redundant.

> Union autonomy has been significantly compromised: compulsory ballots, with complex, detailed requirements cover industrial action, internal elections and decisions over unions' political activities. Almost all aspects of union activity, from finance and arrangements for collecting members' subscriptions, to the TUC's Bridlington Agreement regulating inter-union disputes, have been the object of legal intervention. Despite opposition to state intervention, the Conservatives have established two new state commissions to finance individuals exercising rights against their unions. Simultaneously, rights against employers, from protection against dismissal or redundancy to rights to maternity benefits, have been whittled away.[19]

Thatcher's form of Conservatism was so virulent as to stop the UK from adhering to the European Social Charter that established a set of social rights to be followed by the participating countries. British neoliberalism, which continued under Major, sought to restrict and discredit, *as much as possible,* decisions that pertained to the Charter.

With strong restrictions upon unionism in the state's productive sector – such as in the coalmining- and steel-industries – with limits to (or the total absence of) the participation of unionists in the decision-making processes

---

19. McIlroy 1996, pp. 12–13.

of public enterprises, and with individual negotiations between capital and labour replacing obligatory collective bargaining, social relations between capital, labour and the state changed radically in the UK.

British neoliberalism, however, faced widespread opposition from miners' strikes, particularly the historic strike of 1984–5 against the closure of the mines, which lasted almost a year. More than 220,000 mining jobs were lost under Thatcher from 1979, resulting in the near-extinction of one of the most important segments of the British labour-movement, which had been responsible for a historic tradition of struggle and resistance and a militant unionism opposed to neoliberalism under the leadership of Arthur Scargill.[20] Despite the wave of solidarity for the miners that spread across the country, the strong bonds between the miners and their families, especially the women, international solidarity and the miners' fierce resistance, after nearly a year the strike ended without achieving its goal, which was *to stop the closure of the mines*.[21]

Between 1989 and 1990, another wave of social unrest hit Thatcher's conservatism, with the riots against the poll-tax.[22] These were due to a general increase in taxes that disproportionately affected the poor. Indeed, they constituted the largest public protest against the erosion of neoliberalism – the miners' strike of 1984–5, despite its enormous social, political, ideological and symbolic significance, had not had a good outcome for the workers. In the protests against the poll-tax, there was a rejection of the government, motivated by a fierce social and political discontent with neoliberalism and Margaret Thatcher.

Among the deep repercussions for the structure of the British working class throughout nearly twenty years of neoliberalism, it is also important to emphasise the vast process of deindustrialisation that profoundly shook the world of work. As Huw Beynon argues, 'the dramatic change that has taken place in the composition and organisation of work and employment in the UK can be seen most dramatically in the changes in the coal and steel industries. Once the centre of a state managed "smoke stack" economy, today they are privately owned and with a combined labour force of less than 40,000 reduced to just three percent of their post-war strength'.[23]

---

20. Arthur Scargill was the then general secretary of the National Union of Mineworkers (NUM).
21. McIlroy 1995, p. 213; McIlroy 1996, pp. 11–12; and Pelling 1987, pp. 288–90.
22. Strange 1997, p. 14.
23. Beynon 1997, p. 21.

Industrial production in the UK in 1979 employed around 7 million workers, falling to around 3.75 million in 1995. The figures below highlight the intensity of job-losses:

Changes to employment-patterns in the UK (in millions)

	Manufacture	Services	Total *
1979	7.013	13.68	22.97
1985	5.307	13.86	21.073
1995	3.789	15.912	21.103

Source: *Employment Gazette*, various years[24]
*Includes 'other activities.'

While unemployment greatly affected the textile- and leather-manufacturing industries, where employment fell from 723,000 workers in 1979 to 366,200 in 1995, there was also the introduction of capital from North America, Germany, Japan, Korea, etc., that benefited from incentives and concessions from the neoliberal government. The companies involved specialised mainly in microelectronics, but also in automotive manufacturing, such as for example Nissan Motor Manufacturing, set up in the north of England. But these were not able to stop levels of unemployment increasing substantially in the 1980s and early 1990s. By the end of the first two years of Thatcher's government, there were 2 million unemployed people in the UK, reaching 3 million in 1986. Unemployment stood at 5 per cent in 1979, reaching 12 per cent in 1983, spreading to areas where union-presence was particularly strong.

In recent years, unemployment-figures have been distorted by statistics that hide certain forms of unemployment. One consequence of the vast process of labour-deregulation, of the lack of mechanisms to regulate working conditions and of the vast flexibilisation of the market has been an unprecedented expansion of *part-time* work; however, by classifying these workers as part of the contingent of employed workers, unemployment-figures appear sharply reduced.[25]

At the same time as industrial labour declined, especially in areas with the greatest union-density, the number of service-sector workers grew, whose

---

24. Quoted in Beynon 1995, p. 2.
25. While official figures in June 1997 calculated unemployment in the UK at 5.7 per cent, estimates based on ILO-established criteria place it at 7.2 per cent (*Financial Times*, 17 July 1997, p. 9). From February 1998, the government began to adopt internationally approved standards for the measurement of official rates (*Financial Times*, 4 February 1998, p. 18).

levels of unionisation were much lower. Female workers approached around 50 per cent of the labour-force and there was a rapid increase of part-time and temporary workers.[26] The same process was occurring with the growth of administrative jobs, freelance-workers and especially self-employed workers. Even within the service-sector trade stands out, with the spread of large supermarket-chains (Tesco, Safeway, etc.), as well as insurance, financial-services companies and tourism. As Huw Beynon shows, in 1995 more than half of Britain reaped greater rewards from the financial and services-sectors than the industrial one. In the same year, there were nearly 1.25 million people employed in the hotel- and leisure-sector, which corresponded to a larger labour-force than the one that existed in different traditional industrial branches that were the heirs of Fordism.[27]

From this complex scenario of transformations both in class-structure as well as in social, political and ideological relations, the British working class saw the development of a varied group of workers, who included *part-time, temporary, casual* and *self-employed workers*, among others, constituting what Beynon refers to as *'hyphenated workers.'*[28] In his words, 'These are the *hyphenated* workers of the *hyphenated* economy. The old industrial economy of Britain was highly regulated; it employed large numbers of highly unionised workers employed on full-time contracts.'[29] The largest portion was made up of male workers, responsible for the bulk of family-earnings. As a consequence of these changes in the world of work, the female salary became essential to the domestic budget. Beynon even shows that, as well as the fall in male workers as a proportion of the workforce in the UK, there was also a reduction in the number of workers under the age of 18 and older than 54.[30]

This complex and contradictory set of transformations in the structure of class in Britain led the author to argue, 'Curiously, at a time when "work is becoming scarce" more and more people are working longer hours.'[31] These new tendencies, based on the techniques of lean production, just-in-time, total quality and teamwork, were responsible for a clear process of labour-*intensi-*

---

26. According to researcher Sheila Rowbotham of Manchester University, at the end of 1997, the Office for National Statistics (ONS) announced that the contingent of female workers had overtaken male workers for the first time in England in the last 50 years (*The Guardian,* 3 January 1998).
27. Beynon 1995, p. 4. Beynon discusses at length the heterogeneity of these 'new service-sector workers', comparing them to the manual labourers of traditional industry. He also shows the extent of female labour in this economic sector, as a result particularly, of the increase in part-time work (p. 25).
28. Beynon 1995, p. 30.
29. Beynon 1995, p. 37.
30. Beynon 1995, p. 16.
31. Beynon 1995, p. 12.

fication, with resulting increases in employment-insecurity, stress and work-related illnesses.[32]

These changes to the structure of the working class had important consequences for the union-movement. While industrial sectors that had the greatest levels of unionisation retracted, there was an expansion of those sectors whose workers were self-employed or part-time and who nearly always had a weaker tradition of unionism, given their relatively recent development.[33]

If the union- and strike-movement that unfolded in the 1960s and 1970s in Britain had been significant, from 1979, under Thatcher, the government displayed a strong anti-union policy that profoundly affected the way workers were represented. As McIlroy argues:

> membership of all unions fell from 13.5 million in 1979 to 8.2 million in 1994. Membership of TUC affiliated unions dropped from 12.2 million in 1979 to 6.9 million in 1994. The gains of the 1960s and 1970s have been reversed with a vengeance: there were a million more union members in 1948 than in 1994. Today unions organise just a third of the workforce. TUC unions less than that. For individual unions decline was differential. Worst hit were those recruiting manual workers in the private sector.[34]

UNISON, the public-sector union that represents health-sector workers and civil servants, suffered a less severe decline. UNISON is the result of a merger, in 1983, between three unions that often organised in the same sectors, mostly in the public sector: the Confederation of Health Service Employees (COHSE), the National Union of Public Employees (NUPE), and the National and Local Government Officers' Association (NALGO), which represented white-collar workers in the public sector as well as workers in the health-, gas-, electrical-energy, water-, transport-, and higher-education sectors. After privatisation, UNISON began representing workers in the private sector as well.[35]

According to TUC-data, in 1992 the unions with the highest membership in Britain were UNISON with 1,486,984, the Transport and General Workers' Union (TGWU) with 1,036,000, the Amalgamated Engineering and Electrical Union (AEEU) with 884,000, the General Municipal Boilermakers (GMB) with 799,101, and the Manufacturing, Science and Finance Union (MSFU) with 552,000 members.[36]

---

32. Beynon 1995, pp. 15–22. On work-illness in England, see also London Hazard Centre 1994, pp. 23–5.
33. Beynon 1995; and McIlroy 1996.
34. McIlroy 1996, p. 19.
35. McIlroy 1995, p. 14; and McIlroy 1996, p. 19.
36. McIlroy 1995, p. 15.

As discussed above, this process of reduction of membership has been intensifying even more in the last few years, affecting the TGWU in particular. *The merging of unions became one of the most common responses of British unionism as it faced the dismantling and reduction of its membership-base.* While, in 1979, the TUC had 112 affiliates, in 1994 this number had fallen to 69.[37]

The reduction of unionisation-rates throughout the post-1979 period was the result of a range of features of the Thatcher and Major governments and was the result of both structural changes as well as anti-union policies. The complexity and diversity of elements pertaining to the world of work led to one of the most difficult phases in the union- and labour-movement in the UK. The restrictions on the political activity of trade-unions, along with the restrictions on workplace-organising, within an adverse and deeply anti-social political environment, led the union-movement in Britain to take on an intensely defensive stance.

The shrinking of the movement is also apparent when we compare the number of strikes: whilst in the second half of the 1970s the average number of strikes was 2,412, in the first half of the 1980s that figure fell to 1,276. This tendency was even more pronounced between 1986 and 1989, when the average was around 893 strikes per year. During the 1990s, the trend continued: in 1990 there were 630 strikes; in 1993, 211 and in 1994, only 205. While, in 1980, the first year in which neoliberalism was in force in the UK, the number of strikes reached 1,330, involving 834,000 workers and totalling 11,964,000 working days lost, in 1993 the 211 stoppages involved 385,000 workers and amounted to 649,000 working days lost. 'Statistics demonstrate substantial decline in industrial conflict since 1979 and reflect the changed environment – and the erosion of coal, cars and the docks. The number of strikes declined sharply in the early 1980s and underlying decline continued to 1988.'[38]

The number of workplaces that recognised trade-unions also fell. In 1984, 66 per cent of companies recognised trade-unions and in 1990 this figure fell to 53 per cent. Only 30 per cent of new companies recognised trade-unions, 23 per cent amongst the private sector. Similarly, collective bargaining also became much less widespread, having had significant reach in the pre-1979 period: in 1984 it encompassed 71 per cent of the working class, while in 1990, it had fallen to around 54 per cent and continued to shrink with intensity.

---

37. McIlroy 1996, p. 27.
38. McIlroy 1995, pp. 120–1; and McIlroy 1996, p. 22.

Again, in workplaces, the number of shop-stewards fell from 54 per cent in 1984 to 38 per cent in 1990.[39]

This critical landscape profoundly affected trade-unionism in the UK. The TUC in particular, having distanced itself from its working-class roots, throughout the 1980s and especially during the 1990s came to view its ties with the Labour Party (which later became 'New Labour') as increasingly tenuous. It also saw itself representing a smaller percentage of the working class as a whole. *It increasingly became the institutionalised expression of an interest-group and less a class-representative union-movement.* During the 1997 Congress, the greatest challenges of the TUC were defined as being:

1) to increase the qualifications of the workforce;
2) to increase employability;
3) to maintain a partnership with the Confederation of British Industries (COB) and with local enterprises; and
4) to work with the 'new' employer-ethos that emphasised new management-techniques, the acceptance of privatisation and the recognition of the necessity to flexibilise the labour-market, among many other aspects. In this way, a similar process to the metamorphosis that occurred within New Labour has been undertaken by the TUC within the trade-union movement. During the Congress in 1997, Tony Blair stated that *there was a need for a New TUC, along the same lines as the 'modernisation' undertaken by New Labour.*[40]

Proximity to New Labour's recent project, however, entailed a *greater distancing of the unions from the party-structure. The influence of the unions on the political command of New Labour has become weaker and an enormous transformation has taken place compared to the original project.*

These political transformations had a clear relationship with both neoliberal transformations taking place in the UK's productive structure, as well as with the changes occurring in the global arena. All these elements had a profound effect on relations between the TUC and the Labour Party.

---

39. McIlroy 1996, p. 21.
40. *Financial Times*, 10 September 1997. Tony Blair incited the TUC to abandon its image of opposition to employers and join New Labour in the 'crusade to make Britain more competitive' (*Financial Times*, 10 September 1998). John Monks, Secretary-General of the TUC and Adair Turner, Director-General of the Confederation of British Industry (CBI), discussed possible forms of partnership and co-operation between the two entities (*Financial Times*, 4, 10 and 11 September 1998).

Elements of productive restructuring in Britain: ideas and practice

In order to be compatible with techniques present in the main advanced-capitalist economies, productive units in the UK adapted to downsizing (or lean-production) processes, to the introduction of machinery, to 'Japanisation' and Toyotism, to flexible accumulation, etc., in other words, to the whole array of mechanisms required by capital in this phase of competition and transnationalisation. The most stable forms of employment, heirs of Fordism, were dismantled and substituted by flexibilised, tertiarised forms from which emerged a completely deregulated world of work, widespread unemployment, as well as legislative reforms to capital-labour relations. This process, as Elger suggests, affected trade-union organisation in the workplace in unequal ways as well as substantially and increasingly weakening it.[41]

The arrival of foreign capital – with the practices and experiences of trade-union relations in the originating countries (Japan, for example) and new technologies, especially computers and IT – was part of the process of Britain's integration with the transnationalised economic world.

Research into the different experiences of the UK in recent years clearly shows some of the most important trends in this process. Much of the literature on production in the UK in the last few decades has, however, emphasised the need for more empirical studies, in order to understand the significance of these transformations and demystify the dominant thinking that defends the 'values' that pertain to the 'new enterprise', to the 'new forms of relations' between capital and labour, to the 'new productive universe' and to the 'new forms of collaboration', etc.[42]

New research shows some of the main trends in the recent experience of 'industrial relations' in the UK. It has shown how the implementation of new productive techniques has led to the deterioration of working conditions, the intensification of the rhythm of production and an increase in labour-exploitation, often resulting in the exclusion of trade-union activity itself. In other cases, something altogether different has occurred: after the initial attempt by management to exclude the unions, and in the absence of mechanisms to represent the workers, the unions have returned to the factory-environment from which they had been excluded. This illustrates the complexity and diversity present in the so-called 'new management techniques' in the UK.

---

41. Elger 1996, p. 2; and Beynon 1996, pp. 10–13.
42. Ackers, Smith and Smith 1996; Pollert 1996; Stephenson 1996; Amin 1996; and Tomaney 1996.

The key question therefore is to understand how workers experienced these new conditions, and the ways in which these transformations affected their *form of being*. I shall show this by presenting the results of some recent research into the experience of the implementation of the new techniques.[43]

I shall start by outlining the key elements of two Japanese enterprises in the UK that are tied to automotive manufacturing: the case of Nissan Motor Manufacturing, in the North, and Ikeda Hoover, in the North East, the latter being the result of a partnership between Nissan and Hoover and a supplier to Nissan. Both Nissan and Ikeda Hoover implemented the *just-in-time* system, but whereas at the Nissan plant the process took place without any resistance to the logic of labour-flexibilisation, at Ikeda Hoover flexibilisation and lean production met with opposition.[44]

Nissan, the fourth-largest automotive-manufacturing company in the world behind General Motors, Ford and Toyota, is spread across the world (24 units) and its production has already surpassed 2,600,000 units.[45]

To understand the process experienced by Nissan in the UK we need to return to the end of the 1970s and early 1980s, when economic recession – the result of the first phase of neoliberalism – had led to high levels of unemployment, particularly in the northern region that had been the heartland of industrialisation in England. In 1981, there were 40,000 unemployed workers in the North, mainly ex-industrial workers, and this trend could be seen in many other parts of the country. In this same year, Nissan began to take an interest in establishing plants in the US and Europe in order to increase production and establish productive units before the development of new disadvantageous tariffs.

It is also interesting in relation to Nissan that 'after the Second World War, various western methods were being implemented by Japan, emanating from its Productivity Centre. One example – ironic in retrospect – was the licence that Nissan obtained from British Austin to learn the advanced production methods in 1950s England'.[46] Once the new skills had been learned, in the 1980s the company began competing on British soil.

From the 1970s and 1980s, the British market welcomed Nissan and it was increasingly able to export cars to the European market. Imports of vehicles to Britain from Japan were limited to 12 per cent, with Nissan responsible for 6 per cent, which amounted to more than Toyota, Honda and Mazda put together. Moreover, both local and national governments offered various

---

43. Ackers, Smith and Smith 1996; Stephenson 1996; and Pollert 1996.
44. Stephenson 1996, pp. 210–11.
45. Stephenson 1996, p. 237.
46. Sayer 1986, p. 59.

incentives, worth in excess of £100 million, to encourage plants (assembly and supply) to be set up in the region. Nissan established a relationship with 177 suppliers, 18 of which were in the region. Directly employing around 4,000 workers (of whom 400 were made redundant in 1993), Nissan claimed to be responsible for the creation of around 8,000 jobs in the region.[47]

According to view expressed by its administration, the success of the enterprise lay in the implementation of three basic principles: flexibility, quality control and teamwork. These, in turn, depended on three other principles:

1) the transferral of responsibility to individual workers themselves;
2) since workers have knowledge, they should be incorporated into the productive process and the 'environment of the firm'; and
3) workers are much more productive when they are involved in teamwork.

As far as trade-union activity was concerned, apart from the adverse conditions on the labour-market as a result of high unemployment, Nissan determined the terms for the acceptance of a union-presence. The AEEU was recognised by the two production-plants.[48] Although the company recognised the existence of shop-stewards inside the factory, they were not recognised as representatives of the union during negotiations.

Under Nissan's model, the relation between the workers and the company's board is given by the participation of a maximum of 10 shopfloor- and office-workers in the board. In this way, the union experienced the shrinking and weakening of the shop-steward's role. Even though around one-third of Nissan's workforce was a member of the union, its role was relatively discredited.

The *kaizen*-system 'incentivises' workers to 'make their own changes'. In Carol Stephenson's research:

> 'Kaizen' (meaning continual improvement) is achieved by workers meeting in teams to develop projects to improve any part of the work process or experience of work. Managers evaluate the projects, and those judges to be the best are put into operation. Kaizen projects have related to such diverse matters as bus routes, sports facilities, the standard of canteen food and improvements in the production process itself.

---

47. Stephenson 1996, pp. 214–15.
48. This union was the result of the merger between the Amalgamated Engineering Union (AEU) and the Electrical Electronic Telecommunication and Plumbing Union (EETPU) in 1992. It thus became another important union with regard to the number of its members (Stephenson 1996, pp. 217–18; McIlroy 1995, pp. 14–15).

The Kaizen meeting performed a number of both practical and ideological functions with Nissan. It allowed communication to occur between shop floor workers and senior managers, without the interference of a third party (i.e. a trade union) or the threat of stoppages. It therefore allowed workers to identify areas of potential unrest and dissatisfaction in a safe environment. Kaizen allowed managers to access workers' knowledge of the production process. Garraghan and Stewart noted that workers have suggested changes which have led to the speeding up of work. Garraghan and Stewart also acknowledged that through Kaizen workers learn how to participate in the Nissan way of working in a way which is acceptable to their employers. In addition to this, it is important to note that the legitimacy of Kaizen has been maintained as projects are not narrowly defined or directed towards improvements in the labour process or other areas which directly affect the accumulation of profit. Workers interviewed were able to point to changes which had occurred as a result of Kaizen and which have improved their experience of work, even if those are as simple as changes to the local bus service.[49]

The author also argues that changes of this kind resulting in a new communication system led to the workers legitimising it and adopting this new means of communication within the factory. It led to the revitalisation of communication between the shop-floor and management, clearly resulting in the firm's 'improvement'. The system brought with it benefits in the use of transport, in nutrition, in sports, but also changes to the labour-process, increasing its intensity and speed by eliminating time 'wasted'.[50]

Since its establishment in the UK, Nissan, a company clearly allied to the 'spirit' of Toyotism, defined itself as a 'factory of the new age'.[51] With this new communication-system, the company firmly reduced trade-union activity, making it almost 'superfluous', as well as managing to avoid – by pre-empting complaints – the threat of strikes or worker-resistance. *Kaizen*, however, performs the clearly *ideological* function of encouraging worker-involvement in the company-project. The ethos of Toyota, whose motto was 'Protect the company to protect your life', present since the 1950s in Japan, now found its counterpart at the Nissan factory in the UK.

Nissan became the closest experience of the *British* version of the *Japanese* model of Toyotism, a very different experience when compared with other sectors or branches of production, as we will see below. Nissan is possibly

---

49. Stephenson 1996, p. 220.
50. Ibid.
51. Holloway 1987.

the most celebrated of Japanese companies in the UK. It was the first large Japanese manufacturing plant to receive an incentive from the Conservative government to introduce new industrial relations inspired by the Japanese model in the UK.[52]

Ikeda Hoover, a Nissan supplier, is the result of a partnership between Ikeda Bussan Co. of Japan and Hoover Universal Ltd., of Britain. The former holds 51 per cent of the shares and the latter, 49 per cent. Ikeda Hoover is responsible for the supply of some of the interior finishings of Nissan's cars, and uses the *just-in-time* system. A computer-system makes the connection between the two in such a way that Ikeda Hoover responds to demands from Nissan on aspects such as the colour and type of car being assembled at Nissan. Every 15 minutes, Ikeda Hoover provides materials to the manufacturing plant. The term 'synchronised production' is used to describe the sophisticated precision of its *just-in-time* system. It has to have the same administration-system, the same practices and the same operations-systems as Nissan, because, if the equipment is not supplied *on time*, the manufacturer faces the possibility of stoppage. Yet, given that they are different companies, it would be misleading to imagine that Nissan's operations-systems were entirely *transplanted* onto Ikeda Hoover. There are differences, even when the project implemented is relatively similar. To be viable, there needs to be room for adaptation to the particularities of each case.[53]

The experiences of Nissan and Ikeda Hoover, as examples of the transplanting of the Japanese model and its technical prescriptions to the UK – both in the sense of wholly Japanese capital (in the first case), or of a joint venture (in the second case) – led to, in Stephenson's view, a 'combination of Taylorist and post-Fordist practices' in the labour-process.[54] Both depended on standardised operations and timescales. The workers in both companies were involved in the process of intensification of their own jobs, self-control over their own quality-standards and quality-control over their colleagues.

Yet there was a clear separation between the two projects: 'Nissan workers were involved in additional self-subordinating activities such as Kaizen and the monitoring of a variety of actions of their peers in accordance with the philosophy of active participation in corporate goals. At Ikeda, workers had the introduction of new technologies and practices (e.g. the standing sewing machine) and some workers interviewed offered a critique of flexible work practices which indicated an understanding of the possible dangers associated with participation in continual improvements strategies.' The relative

---

52. Ackers, Smith and Smith 1996, p. 30.
53. Stephenson 1996, p. 216.
54. Stephenson 1996, p. 233.

prevention of tension that took place at Nissan could not also occur in the supply-firm because the system of meetings (*kaizen*) was not implemented at Ikeda.[55]

Whereas at Nissan the 'involvement' of the workers was greater, at Ikeda tensions and conflicts between the workers and the administration were more common. At Nissan, *kaizen* and the communication that developed from it ended up 'substituting' for the union as a means of dialogue between the workers and the company-management. The gains this brought about, by saving time, introducing new benefits, etc., occurred in the labour-process through the appropriation of the know-how of the workers and not through the performance of managers and administrators, which reduced any vertical conflict inside the factory. 'The style of management within the two companies was qualitatively different, the Ikeda management style was described by workers as confrontational, and workers claimed managers had adopted an interventionist approach.'[56] Whilst, at Ikeda Hoover, the conflicts had a vertical structure (between workers and administration) since the behaviour of management was often interventionist, at Nissan the conflict took on the more horizontal shape of competition between the workers themselves.

Carol Stephenson's research confirms the weight that unemployment and the depressed economic context had on the workers' reconciliation to their 'involvement' in the factory's objectives and the company's dismissive attitude towards the union. The very choice of location for the Nissan factory was determined by the fact that it was an area with greater possibilities of worker-*consent* and receding union-control.

The research also shows that, as well as the need to investigate activities at the central plants, it is also important to examine the working conditions in the supply-chains. These provide supplies using the *just-in-time* system and semi-skilled or even unskilled labour, in addition to female and migrant-workers who experience greater levels of exploitation and more precarious living conditions.[57]

A wider study of the different working conditions, which covers the company and its suppliers, shows that arguments that make a *cult of the new ideals* and their capacity to instill new, positive conditions of integration in the relation between capital and labour, need to be questioned. There is a clear need for further study on the changes that took place in different branches in order to avoid generalisations and the common misrepresentation of the workers' acceptance of the new conditions. The reservations shown by many workers

---

55. Ibid.
56. Stephenson 1996, p. 234.
57. Stephenson 1996, pp. 235–6.

towards the union, highlighted in Stephenson's research, was often the result of the unquestioning acceptance, by the union, of the new factory-conditions. Further, the context of recession and unemployment and the need to stay in employment did not create the conditions for a more outright critical stance by the workers, steering them instead in the direction of *involvement* in order to preserve their jobs. What became pressing for workers, over and above the need for involvement and adherence to the company-values, was the need to remain employed despite the most adverse conditions, where even the most insignificant act of questioning could be construed as a sign of indisposition and entail the risk of dismissal.

Unlike the Toyotist model implemented in the most important Japanese companies, *in the West*, it was *implemented and made feasible without the counterpart of 'lifetime-employment'*. Furthermore, it was accomplished within a labour-market, in the UK, that was strongly deregulated, flexibilised and had high levels of unemployment that had and still has a fiercely intimidating impact on workers.

Under these conditions, *my argument is that, while workers are expected to display a 'spirit of co-operation' with the companies – the general condition for the 'successful implementation' of the Toyotist model – their performance is achieved on a platform that is unstable. The possibility of redundancy, while pushing a worker to accept new conditions, creates an unfavourable basis for capital in this process of 'integration' because workers perceive themselves under the constant threat of unemployment. This contradiction inside the factory-walls has proved to be one of the most difficult elements in capital's attempts at 'involvement' of the worker.*

Another key example of the tendencies under way in the process of productive restructuring in the UK can be found in the food-industry, which has grown recently as a result of the increasingly important service-sector and especially the large supermarket-chains. Anna Pollert's study of Choc-Co, a large company in the food-sector, seeks to investigate the operation of teamwork, with a view to understanding the different perceptions that exist from the upper echelons of the company down to the factory-floor.

Within the ideology of teamwork, its origin, the discourse of employers and what actually occurs in the workplace, the ethos of a *new company* and its practice, there is a chasm that constitutes the focus of the research. It explores not just the role of the shop-stewards, their relationships with the work-teams and with the union. It also examines the labour-process by focusing on the issue of how qualifications and de-skilling are articulated in the productive space of an industry that has a long tradition, as well as the ways in which the changes taking place relate to questions of gender. The choice of a branch of the food-industry came from the desire to investigate other experiences that could highlight female labour and its interface with male labour.

Whereas the food-, drink- and tobacco-industries employ 59 per cent male workers and 41 per cent female, the gender-division in the industrial sector in general is 70.3 per cent male and 29.7 per cent female, with male employment in the automotive industry reaching 88.5 per cent.[58]

The food-, drink- and tobacco-industries have the second-largest number of workers in British industry, with 500,800 workers, mostly concentrated in the food-processing sector. As the author shows, this sector is largely responsible for Britain's economic growth, despite the recession of the 1980s. From the long period between 1974 and 1992, the number of jobs provided by this sector increased from 9.9 per cent to 11.4 per cent. It is a fiercely competitive, highly-concentrated sector that receives a great deal of foreign capital.[59]

In the food-processing branch, Choc-Co had a Quaker-influenced administration-policy inherited from its origins in the Victorian era, with strong paternalistic features and close, personal relationships with the workforce. From 1918 the company used Taylorist methods and the participation of workers on the company-board can be seen from 1919.

This past history meant that the 'new' management-techniques introduced in the 1980s and 1990s met with a company that was steeped in tradition. In 1992, when the research began, Choc-Co had 3,400 workers in production, predominantly in its chocolate-manufacturing line. Earlier, in 1988, the company had been bought out by Food-Co, an important transnational company in the field. However, Choc-Co had already initiated a process of restructuring and large-scale streamlining that had led to the closure of some of its plants. Between 1984 and 1987 two factories were closed and the company opened a new chocolate-production unit specialising in this activity. By this stage, teamwork had already been introduced.

After the acquisition by Food-Co, the process of introduction of 'new' techniques gathered speed, in a highly competitive market given by the new configuration of production in the UK. The primary objective was 'the reduction of man hours for each ton produced'.[60] The use of teamwork and the process of involving the workers through quality-control circles, from the 1980s on, was thus intensified. In the plants in which workers showed a greater resistance to the introduction of these methods, the response of management was harsher. Instead of a 'consensual involvement', direct interference by management was common, combining 'new' and old forms of industrial relations. Or, in other words, there was an introduction of the 'new' through the use of 'old' means. The introduction of teamwork was conceived as fundamental

---

58. Pollert 1996, p. 180.
59. Ibid.
60. Pollert 1996, p. 182.

for a 'new entrepreneurial culture' to emerge that would reduce the levels of supervision. The team-leaders' duties included:

1) motivating work-teams;
2) planning, organising and overseeing quality;
3) identifying training and development-needs;
4) assessing work-performance and costs and preparing budgets;
5) establishing production-standards and discussing performance; and
6) responsibility for communication, disciplinary procedures and other problems.[61]

Team-leaders had an important role in facilitating communication between the shop-floor and management, which lead to the reduction of trade-union activity and the isolation of shop-stewards.

> With 150 teams and only twenty nine shop stewards across the whole factory it was difficult for the union to maintain vigilance over every aspect of change introduced via these routes. As observed in other studies of team working, the aim was for greater group cohesion, but also the accompanying team competition and pressure (Garraghan and Stewart, 1992). Team performance score boards, some with liquid-display messages, were put up throughout the factory.[62]

The disclosure of the results of production showing the performance of the teams was intended to create a climate of competition in the factory.

Choc-Co's strategy was to begin the implementation of work-teams in sectors composed of both semi-skilled and unskilled workers. The effects of this, however, were few. In Pollert's words, 'Indeed, despite the rhetoric of "involvement", the Fordist production system of specialised machinery, task fragmentation and standardisation of components was not challenged by management's enthusiasm.'[63] The greatest obstacle arose from the diffi-culty of adapting the system of work-teams to the production-line, a problem that commonly occurs in trying to transfer Toyotist patterns to Fordist-based production-units. In the mass-production system, '[w]ork is repetitive, machine-based, with few opportunities for direct participation in terms of influencing production. For the majority of employees, the "flexibility" of team working is limited to job rotation, greater integration of quality con-

---

61. Pollert 1996, p. 183.
62. Ibid.
63. Pollert 1996, p. 185.

trol into production, cleaning up around the production area and work intensification'.[64] The introduction of microprocessing and new technologies did not have a significant impact on the production-line routine as a whole, especially since the new technology met with a workforce that was not apt to operate the machinery, which created an even greater gap between the proposals to introduce 'new work-methods' and the existing productive structure based on Fordism. The much-vaunted 'involvement' of workers in the relationship between capital and labour was very often simply a greater intensification of the rhythm of work.[65]

As far as the *sexual division of labour* is concerned, a distinction can be seen between male and female labour. Whereas the former operates *predominantly* in *capital-intensive* areas, with computerised machinery, female labour is concentrated in *labour-intensive* areas, performing routine-work. For example, the more valued areas of work in the manufacturing of chocolate (often called the *kitchen* by the workers) are dominated by male labour, whereas the more manual areas, such a packaging, are dominated by female labour. There are also differences in terms of working time, with far fewer women working night-shifts, a tendency that continued even after 1986 when the legal restrictions on night-time work for women were lifted.

The areas where advanced technology is used sees women involved in the more routine activities that require fewer qualifications. Although the management states that it is the male workers themselves who do not want female workers in the same work-space, the male workers claim that the management does not install the facilities necessary for female workers to enjoy reasonable working conditions.[66]

In different production-areas, in the packaging section as much as in other areas where female labour is predominant – in *labour-intensive* areas – part-time work is also more common. 'At Choc-Co, the perpetuation of the sexual division of labour, with men concentrated in capital-intensive and women in labour-intensive production, meant that team working, even in its most limited form for all semi-skilled production workers, was an even more artificial construct for most women than for most men.'[67] In other words, in the sexual division of labour in this company, the implementation of new systems led to an even greater intensification of female labour.

---

64. Pollert 1996, p. 186.
65. Ibid.
66. Pollert 1996, p. 188.
67. Ibid.

For this reason, Pollert argues, the existence of notions such as 'flexibility', 'involvement', etc. in an environment marked by the presence of semi- and unskilled work, and *especially, in a system of labour-intensive work realised by a female workforce* where mass-production is the norm, is highly contradictory. It highlights, moreover, the gap between management's quest for a 'culture of business improvement' and the reality of the production-process. Further, at Choc-Co the activity of team-representatives minimised the impact of unions, with team-leaders chosen by the administration, by-passing shop-stewards and the union and acting as intermediaries between management and workers. Yet, when communication and the capacity of the team-leaders to negotiate were lagging, shop-stewards were called upon once again to represent the workers.

Choc-Co is an example that shows how despite the attempt to eliminate trade-union and shop-floor representation, the team-leaders' capacity to act upon issues that normally fell within the remit of the union or shop-stewards was limited. As a result, a system developed in which shop-stewards were often consulted by mid-level managers and team-leaders on employment-related topics, health-issues, working hours and the whole range of matters that arise in a working day. The system, which sought to exclude or greatly restrain trade-union activity, regularly made recourse to it, developing a *parallel* system between the 'new' and the 'old' procedures. The former became, in everyday experience, largely dependent on the latter. Once again, we see here another aspect of the contradictory nature of the ideology present in these 'new techniques' and the reality of their implementation in the UK.[68]

Perception of the operation of the system of work-teams varied according to the degree of engagement of the participants, with nuances between the perspectives of the leaders, workers or the union, as well as the range of positions within each of these categories. Amongst the team-leaders, for example, it is hard to make generalisations since there were variations even from department to department within the factory. However, Pollert's research does show that only a minority-group composed of young workers genuinely welcomed the introduction of 'new techniques', while the majority considered themselves to be overburdened and dissatisfied.

Work became increasingly intensified yet despite this, management always seemed to judge the results to be beneath expectations. This view is common in the statements collected in the study, as one worker and team-leader shows: '[They] don't call us team leaders, [they] call us mushrooms,' with the mushroom metaphor used again in 'Keep 'em in the dark and feed them shit.'

---

68. Pollert 1996, pp. 191–2.

A similar view is expressed in the statement of another team-leader: 'More and more gets pushed down on us and it's going to get worse.'[69]

The author quotes other interviewees who offer a less critical perspective, but reiterate that there is a 'systemic contradiction between the social demands of team building and a productivity strategy for labour intensification. Senior management's exhortation for greater team leader delegation to the team as a resolution to work overload was in vain. There was insufficient labour slack to do this.'[70] The intensification of labour and the requirement to be constantly beating targets that had already been met, or even the idea that 'the company is always in the red', had a demotivating effect, making any real discussion of 'new techniques' in a factory such as Choc-Co redundant. The distance and the disgruntlement of shop-floor workers confirmed the idea the changes were taking place much more at the level of discourse than in the reality of everyday work. Only 206 workers, less than 10 per cent of the workforce, were tied to the 46 quality-control circles.[71]

According to Pollert, the research conducted inside Choc-Co showed that work-teams – conceived of as a system of labour-organisation and of worker-involvement – were not working and were, instead, generating various kinds of tensions. There are 'structural contradictions at the heart of the strategy: between worker alienation in a production system that still depends on unskilled, repetitive jobs and the aim of winning hearts and minds to the objectives of business improvement; between the needs of wider production units in the collective labour process and the narrow needs of the team', in sum, 'between the wider dynamics of capitalist restructuring involving work intensification, employment reduction and insecurity and the aims of building worker commitment to the company'.[72] It is as if the discourse on the *rational involvement* of the workers, celebrated by capital, were facing, on a daily basis, its effective negation in the form of constraints that instead entail *irrationality* in the world of work: the intensification of labour, the imminent risk of unemployment, gender-segregation, qualifications, age, etc. (among many other fractures in the world of production).

The experiences of a company like Choc-Co in the food-processing sector and of Nissan and Ikeda Hoover in the car-manufacturing sector give us an indication of how the expansion of Toyotism (or of elements of this new form of labour-organisation) in the UK assumes specific forms that make generalisations about its application redundant. Toyotism displays significant

---

69. Pollert 1996, pp. 196–7.
70. Pollert 1996, p. 198.
71. Pollert 1996, p. 200.
72. Pollert 1996, p. 205.

differences not just in virtue of the different countries in which it has been implemented, but also between different sectors within the same country.

We can argue therefore, on the basis of the British experience analysed above, that in companies that have implemented techniques based on *just-in-time, kanban, total-quality control, kaizen, etc.,* there has been a reduction in trade-union activity and an attempt to substitute shop-stewards with a new communication-system that capital has sought to implement inside the factories. While trade-unions in Japan were, in many cases, *enterprise-unions,* frequently participating in management's human-resource activities, in other countries, such as the UK, management forced the reduction and even the elimination of trade-union activity. In the Nissan case, recognition of trade-union activity was conditional on the acceptance by the union of the company's plans. The very choice of location for Nissan's and Ikeda Hoover's plants took into consideration this weakness of trade-unions in the North, the severe unemployment and the attractive incentives offered by the neoliberal government.

The neoliberal project, with its implications for juridical-political and ideological restructuring and the *process of productive restructuring of capital,* had enormous consequences for the British working class. In particular, we can highlight the absence of any regulation of the labour-force, large-scale flexibilisation of the labour-market and precarisation of workers *especially in terms of their social rights.* As a result, during the recession in the 1980s, primarily, there was also growing structural and conjunctural unemployment, which transformed Britain into the country with the sharpest deterioration of labour-conditions compared to other countries of the European Union. This can be seen in the following data:

1) between 1987 and 1997, Britain was the only country in the European Union in which the working week increased;
2) the average number of hours worked per week by a full-time worker was around 40 (42 for men and 38 for women). German workers, for example, worked 36 hours per week;
3) manual labourers worked 44.2 hours per week and non-manual labourers 38.2; and
4) in 1996, 3,900,000 people worked more than 48 hours per week compared with 2,700,000 in 1984.[73]

---

73. Data from *The Observer,* 30 November 1997.

In such a flexibilised and deregulated labour-market, we can understand the refusal by the Thatcher and Major neoliberal governments to accept the terms of the European Social Charter. Tony Blair too, as leader of New Labour, did not initiate any labour-market policy-revision. The existence of a highly flexibilised and deregulated labour-market became the distinguishing feature of the productive restructuring of capital under neoliberalism.

The implementation of these policies did meet with resistance, however. I referred earlier to some confrontations during the 1980s. The 1990s also saw the eruption of different movements of workers protesting against the radical transformations affecting the world of work.

British strikes in the 1990s: forms of confrontation with neoliberalism and the casualisation of work

Between mid-1995 and early 1996, Vauxhall Motors, the subsidiary of General Motors in the UK, was the stage for an act of resistance by workers who objected to the introduction of 'new industrial relations' based on *lean production*. For the first time in more than a decade, the company saw itself faced with organised action from the workers in two factories, one at Ellesmere Port (manufacturing plant for the Astra) and one in Luton (manufacturing plant for the Vectra). The entire ideological construct surrounding the 'new production-systems' was questioned and came under fire. As Stewart argues, 'Workers at the two sites which together employ almost 10,000 workers took action in support of their claim for a reduction in the working week and an across the board wage rise. Their campaign included a ban on overtime and a two hour unofficial strike every Friday.'[74] The rhetoric of 'consensus and participation', formulated and defended by the company as it tried to introduce lean production, was not able to achieve the support and acceptance of the shop-stewards or the shop-floor workers. Along with another unofficial strike that took place in 1995 at the Ford factory, the Vauxhall dispute represented a watershed in the process of productive restructuring of the automotive industry in the UK.

After a ballot, more than 70 per cent of Vauxhall workers voted in favour of strike-action in support of their demands, amongst which were the reduction of the working week from 39 to 38 hours and an increase in wages, both of which they obtained.[75] The reduction of working time was a real gain because the strike directly attacked managerial discourse that defended the ideal of

---

74. Stewart 1997, pp. 1–2.
75. Stewart 1997, pp. 3–4.

'new conditions' of work, but in practice introduced an intensification of work. This resistance brought to the surface the real state of dissatisfaction felt by the workers on the shop-floor and their perception of the gap between the participatory rhetoric expounded by management and the reality of intensification and stress and their physical and emotional repercussions on the subjectivity of the employees. The more capital spoke of new working conditions, the more the shop-floor factory-rhythms intensified. The strike constituted a victory of the workers against the fallacy of the new working conditions.[76]

Perhaps the most expressive and symbolic movement of resistance against British neoliberalism and its destructive forms in the 1990s was that of the dock-workers' strike in Liverpool. Beginning in September 1995, it was a reaction against forms of labour-flexibilisation introduced to the ports-system that made working conditions extremely precarious. The action, which was ruled illegal, resulted in the dismissal of 500 workers who, from that moment on, began an important strike-movement that survived until February 1998. At the same time as it directly confronted neoliberal policies that destroyed labour-rights and legislation that repressed worker-action, during its two years of existence, this movement carved the boundaries of traditional British unionism. Indeed, the TUC's support and solidarity were minimal and, on more than one occasion, its actions revealed a political stance that hindered the spread of the dock-workers' struggle to other ports and other categories of workers.[77]

The recent history of this movement goes back to 1988, when Thatcher announced that she intended to repeal the system of permanent contracts that dockers had (previously) won. The Dock Workers' Strike Committee reacted with actions and meetings across the country, to fight against the decision and as a result, a strike was started. It was begun in two ports, Tilbury in London, and Liverpool. The leadership of the Transport and General Workers' Union (TGWU), which also represented the dock-workers, positioned itself against the strike fearing that its 'illegal' status would pit it against the government. Although the shop-stewards had begun an unofficial stoppage, it was unsustainable without the support of the TGWU. Once the legal requirements had been met, a strike against Thatcher's policies began that lasted 22 days.

Expressing a trend that had been growing for a number of years, the movement did not count on the participation of the TGWU, much as the miners had done in the strike of 1984–5. The striking dockers were sacked; the warehouses were closed by the company and then later reopened with

---

76. Stewart 1997, p. 6.
77. Gibson 1997, pp. 1–2.

different names and with a casual workforce. Whilst the strike was derailed in Tilbury, in Liverpool, pickets and solidarity-actions kept the strike going. Opposition to the strike by the TGWU on the grounds that 'it is not possible to defend trade-unionism in Great Britain today' (in the words of the secretary-general, Ron Todd), and the defeat in Tilbury, brought the movement to a close. Whilst at Tilbury, casual labour remained and the shop-stewards were sacked – resorting to the courts for reinstatement – in Liverpool the dockers managed to keep the unofficial strike going for more than a week, returning subsequently to their jobs with structured and intact independent organisation. The dockers had created an independent movement, outside the institutional boundaries of official unionism, named the Unofficial Docks' Shop Steward Committee (UDSSC), which played an important role in the dockers' movement from 1988 onwards.

So began the preparation for the struggle of resistance that erupted in September 1995. The Mersey Docks and Harbour Company (MDHC), after the strike of 1988, set out a series of measures designed to weaken the dock-workers' organisation. It split up the workforce and forced a significant number of workers who had been employed by the company for many years to take on cleaning tasks (such as toilets) and similar jobs, in an act of retaliation designed to humiliate the workers. Bobby Morton, a shop-steward at the dock, said that 'a sense of failure spread among the dockers'.[78] In this context, in 1995 the company increased the pressure and announced its intention to dismiss 20 workers and replace them with temporary workers. The dock-workers' resistance recommenced in the form of a long strike-movement that lasted until the beginning of 1998. As well as receiving a great deal of support from British workers, the movement organised a number of international meetings, such as the International Conference of Dockworkers in February 1996 in Liverpool, in order to establish co-ordinated action with dock-workers around the world.

Once again, the actions of the TGWU and TUC were afflicted with doubt, in refusing to defend a movement in clear opposition to neoliberal policy that had originated with the dock-workers but increasingly affected other sectors of British labour. An intense international campaign sought to put pressure on the company and make it retract its proposal to introduce casual labour to the docks. For a long period, thanks to the pickets and widespread solidarity, the dockers' movement kept up its resistance to the proposed changes to working conditions. It rejected, more than once, management-proposals offering funds of up to £28,000 individual compensation for the striking work-

---

78. Gibson 1997, p. 2.

ers to abandon their demands and end the dispute, since the jobs they used to have had already been taken by other workers who had accepted the new (precarious) conditions.

The dockers' dispute was replete with symbolism: it echoed the miners' strike of 1984–5 and it positioned itself clearly in opposition to neoliberal policy. It represented a real example of resistance to the changes that made working conditions even more precarious. 'The dockers' strike received strong support from the British working class and from various movements throughout the world, which provided resources, including funds, to carry on the struggle. Many ports across the world refused to receive cargo that was initially destined for Liverpool, forcing the transport companies to incur huge losses.'[79]

At the end of January 1998, after a number of months of the New Labour government, without any further sign of its contribution to finding a solution to the confrontation and without *any effective union- and political support from the TGWU*, the Liverpool dockers had no alternative but to accept the employers' offer of £28,000 that they had earlier rejected. The material and political conditions for the strike, which had lasted nearly two and half years, were gone.[80]

The dispute did not end without controversy, as this account shows:

> The dockers did not climb down, they were let down, and forced to end their remarkable two-year struggle not because of any failure on their part. On the contrary, the action they inspired across the world, against the return of exploited, casual labour, galvanised thousands on every continent and was without precedent this century.
>
> Their struggle in this country was lost because the Transport and General Workers' Union virtually guaranteed its failure. Had this rich and powerful organisation launched a national campaign challenging the sinister circumstances and the sheer injustice of the dockers' dismissal along with an assault on anti-trade union laws that most of the democratic world regard as a disgrace in a free country, the battle could have been won there and then. Instead, it was the craven silence of the union leadership that finally ended the imaginative and courageous efforts of men once described by

---

79. Gibson 1997, p. 3.
80. The strike lasted two years, three months and 29 days, according to information from *The Guardian*. The payment of £28,000 accepted at the end of the strike had been rejected earlier by the workers, as mentioned above. By the end of the strike, there were still 250 strikers (*The Times*, 27 January 1998).

Lloyds List as 'the most productive work force in Europe' and who represent Britain at its best.[81]

The dockers' strike was a vivid expression of a scenario common today of increased distance between traditional unions and their social bases, evident in the TUC's stance and by the enormous bureaucratisation and institutional emphasis of the unions. This, coupled with trade-unions' need to 'modernise' and establish 'partnerships' with capital to improve the qualifications of the workforce in the UK and endow it with 'employability', illustrates the current landscape of crisis of traditional unionism.[82]

When the dockers expected that under the New-Labour government their working conditions would return more or less to what they were, something unexpected occurred. The absence of any real support for the workers and New Labour's need to obtain the endorsement of capital for its project of government, led it to gradually distance itself from the working class and gave the dockers no other option but to end the strike. In less than a year from the outset of his new government, in 1998, Tony Blair put a nail in the coffin of one of the most important movements of resistance and opposition to British neoliberalism, for its level of confrontation and its symbolic significance. This was, however, merely the start of what was to come.

New Labour and Tony Blair's 'Third Way'

In addition to the growing cleft between the unions and their social bases, there was also an increasing divide between New Labour and the unions, which had had a central role in the *origin and historical development* of the party. The trade-unions progressively lost their influence in the party-structure, at the same time as New Labour separated itself from its *working-class and reformist* roots. A 'new' political posture began to emerge within the Party, from 1994 on, that sought an *alternative path* that could preserve a social-democratic quality alongside the basic features of *neoliberalism*. When

---

81. Exchange of letters in *The Guardian* between John Pilger and Bill Morris, 2 February 1998 (available at: <http://www.hartford-hwp.com/archives/61/079.html>). Further details on the strike can be found in Gibson 1997; Gibson 1996; Dockers' Charter 1997; *The Guardian*, 27, 29, 30 and 31 January 1998; *Daily Mail*, 27 January 1998; and *The Observer Review*, 1 February 1998.

82. This crisis not only affected British trade-unionism and the TUC, but was widespread, affecting the CGT and CFDT in France, the CGIL in Italy, the DGB in Germany and the AFL-CIO in North America, among others. For details about these countries, see Mouriaux et al. 1991; Armingeon et al. 1981, which discusses France, Germany, Italy, the UK and Spain; Visser 1993; and Rosanvallon 1998, in addition to the references above.

Tony Blair began the process of transforming the Labour Party into New Labour in 1994, the objective was not only a greater separation from the Party's working-class origins, but also to sever ties with the unions as much as possible. Furthermore, the transformation sought to eliminate the legacy of the Party's association with 'socialism' that was, at least formally, still referred to in its statutes.

The debate put forward by Tony Blair around the *removal* of Clause 4 from the party-constitution (which defended *the communal ownership of the means of production*) resulted in its replacement by wording that provides a clear example of the set of changes that were under way in the Labour Party. The clause that referred to *collective ownership* was replaced with one that defended *market-entrepreneurism and the rigour of competition*, marking the victory, within New Labour, of the free market over its previous vision. *Socialist* rhetoric and *working-class* and *reformist* practices that had upheld a belief in a strong statist and mixed economy were replaced by the defence of a market-economy that mixed 'liberalism' with traces of a 'modern' social democracy. This marked the beginning of what Tony Blair, with the intellectual support of Anthony Giddens and David Miliband, would later call the 'Third Way'.

At a deeper level, New Labour's 'Third Way' sought to give *continuity* to the project, launched by Thatcher, of repositioning Britain and creating a *British* alternative to the new configuration of contemporary capitalism. The new stance, as we have seen, consolidated the separation of the Party from the unions and the TUC and instead pressurised them into supporting New Labour's project. Meanwhile, it allied the Party more closely to 'modern British business', whose interests it came to represent, leading *The Economist* to present New Labour as the British version of Clinton's Democratic Party.[83]

In this new era of neoliberalism, which had begun in the mid-1990s, New Labour, despite signing the European Social Charter, systematically upheld its commitment to *maintaining* legislation of labour-market flexibilisation and deregulation that Thatcher had imposed on the working class. 'Flexibilisation, yes, but with fair play,' as Blair proposed during the Labour conference on 30 September 1997. The preservation of flexibility, introduced by Thatcher and defended by Blair, would be counterbalanced by measures to recognise unions inside the workplace, the introduction of a minimum-wage, the adhesion to the European Social Charter, among other initiatives announced by the prime minister.[84]

83. *The Economist*, 8 November 1997, p. 35.
84. *The Guardian*, 1 and 2 October 1997; and *Le Monde*, 4 October 1997.

The 'Third Way' represented a form of *continuity* with what was at the core of the Thatcher era. This was due to the weakening of classical neoliberalism over the previous two decades, which made it necessary to search for an alternative that would preserve, in its essence, the transformations that took place during that period. When New Labour came to power in May 1997, on a wave of deep social and political discontent, its political agenda already included the preservation of the essence of the neoliberal project. There would be no revision of privatisation; labour-flexibilisation and -casualisation would be preserved and in some cases intensified; trade-union activity would be restricted; the ideals of 'modernity', 'employability' and 'competitiveness', among many others, would continue to be pursued with conviction.

New Labour's *discontinuity* with Thatcher's policies can be seen in certain political – indeed, *politicised* – decisions made by Blair's government such as the establishment of the Scottish Parliament, which did not however constitute an obstacle for the continuation of British capital's project. The victorious New Labour of 1997, having cut its ties with its working-class and reformist past, became New Labour post-Thatcher: 'modern', and a staunch defender of the 'market-economy', of labour-flexibilisation, of deregulation, of the 'modern globalised economy', in other words, of all that had been fundamentally restructured during the phase of classical neoliberalism. The defence of the welfare-state, for example, was completely different from classic social democracy. Blair wanted to 'modernise' the welfare-state. However, 'modernising it' entailed the destruction of labour-rights that he once described as an 'archaic inheritance'.[85]

Giddens presents New Labour's project clearly: 'The third way presents a scenario significantly distinct from the two alternatives (social democracy and neo-liberalism). Some of the critiques of the Welfare State formulated by the new right are valid. Its institutions are frequently alienating and bureaucratic: old-age pensions create acquired rights and can have perverse consequences, undermining what they had originally aimed to achieve. The Welfare State needs radical reform, not to reduce its size, but to make it relevant to the world we are living in today.'

Politically, 'the Third Way represents the modernisation of the centre. While it accepts the basic socialist value of social justice, it rejects class politics, searching out a support base that cuts across class lines'.

Economically, 'the Third Way advocates a defence of a new mixed economy' that seeks a 'balance between regulation and de-regulation and between

---

85. See Mészáros 1995 for a pre-emptive critique of the essential meaning of Tony Blair's New Labour. See especially Chapter 18. See also McIlroy 1997.

economic and the non-economic elements of society'. It must 'preserve economic competition when it is threatened by monopoly'. It must also 'control natural monopolies' and 'create and sustain the institutional bases of the market'.[86]

In line with the *essence* of capitalism's values in the 'era of modernity', the *scope* of the discourse and the *ambiguity* of 'Third-Way' ideology (defined as between social democracy and neoliberalism) are conditioning factors that capitalism *assimilated* and *moulded*, as the condition under which it could preserve its project when faced with the exhaustion of its classical neoliberal variant in the UK after nearly 20 years. As Blair asserts:

> The third way is the route to renewing and securing a successful modern social democracy. It is not simply a compromise between left and right. Rather, it consists of recuperating the essential values of the centre and the centre-left and applies them to a world of social change and economic fundamentals, and frees them of old-fashioned ideologies.... In regard to the economy, our approach opts for neither *laissez-faire* nor state intervention. The role of government is to promote macroeconomic stability, expand the tax base and welfare, ...equip people for work by improving education and infrastructure, and promote an entrepreneurial mentality, particularly in the knowledge-based industries of the future. We are proud to enjoy as much support from the employers as from the trade unions.[87]

An anti-union and anti-working-class stance as shown in response to the Liverpool dockers' strike, adherence to the essence of Thatcherism, the preservation of policies to dismantle labour-rights (and at times, their intensification, which was the case with the erosion of the social rights of single mothers and those with disabilities that provoked a wave of protest against Blair), the attempt to continue the privatisations (with a proposal to privatise the London Underground), not to mention the unconditional adherence to the politico-military domination of the US with the resulting military interventions, are all evidence that the 'Third Way' expressed *the preservation of what was fundamental to neoliberalism, dressed in a thin, gradually fading, varnish of social democracy.*

---

86. Giddens 1999, p. 5. See also, from the same author, the book *The Third Way: The Renewal of Social Democracy*, Polity Press, 1998, that *The Economist* described as 'in some ways disturbingly vacuous' (see 'The Third Way Revealed', *The Economist*, 19 September 1998, p. 48).

87. *Clarín*, 21 September 1998, p. 15.

Indeed, Tony Blair is the expression of the subjectivity and political project of 'modern' British capital after the inevitable exhaustion of Thatcher's neoliberalism. It was necessary to find, in the ranks of opposition, a *new*, more far-reaching *variant* of neoliberalism that could maintain the original project and could, therefore, protect the interests of British capital *even with the electoral defeat of the Tories*; that could, moreover, maintain those political and ideological elements that are in tune with British Conservatism.[88]

As one of the most advanced laboratories for the implementation of European neoliberalism, firstly in its *classical form* – dismantling the earlier experience of the working class and vigorous productive restructuring of capital – and most recently, under the auspices of New Labour's 'Third Way', the world of work underwent one of its most profound critical transformations.

---

88. As the journalist Robert Taylor recently stated, 'New Labour is socially authoritarian and represents a threat to civil liberties. It doesn't tolerate political dissent. It adopts a punitive stance towards poor people and destitutes. Immigrants and refugees that could once expect a human response from the party...are treated as enemies of the state.' He adds, 'It is also extremely a-critical towards the whims of global capital. Neoliberalism fell in love with the super-rich, especially those that finance the Labour Party.' (*O Estado de S. Paulo*, 29 November 1998, p. 3.)

Chapter Six

The Class-that-Lives-from-Labour: the Working Class Today

Towards a broader notion of the working class

The expression 'class-that-lives-from-labour' used in this study is concerned in the first instance with giving *contemporary validity* to the Marxist concept of the *working class*. With many theories asserting the analytical *loss of validity* of the notion of class, our designation aims *to emphasise the current meaning of the working class*, its *form of being*. Therefore, in contrast to the authors who defend the idea of the extinction of social classes, of the working class or even of work itself, the expression *class-that-lives-from-labour* seeks to update and broaden the concept of the *social being that labours*, of today's working class, to comprehend its *effective reality*, its *processes* and its *concrete form*.[1] The definition of this class includes a set of analytical elements that I outline below.

The *class-that-lives-from-labour*, the working class, today embraces the totality of those who sell their labour-power, with *productive* workers (in the sense Marx attributed to this, especially in Chapter VI,

---

1. The thesis of labour as *a value on the route to extinction* is explored at length in Méda 1997. A more empirical text, where the growing reduction of employment leads a trend towards the *end of work*, is provided by Rifkin 1995. See also Pakulski and Waters 1996, which defends the notion of the dissolution of social classes and the loss of their conceptual validity in advanced societies. Harvie 1997, pp. 192–3, provides a critique of their thesis. Castells 1998, in a dense and wide-reaching study, offers new elements with which to think of the centrality of labour today starting from a contractualist defence of the wage-society.

unpublished) representing the *central* nucleus. It is not therefore restricted to *direct manual labour*, but incorporates the *totality of social labour*, the totality of *collective wage-labour*. As *productive* labour directly produces surplus-value and *directly participates in the process of capital-valorisation, it plays a central role within the working class, with the industrial proletariat as its primary nucleus.* Therefore, *productive labour*, where the proletariat is to be found, in our reading of Marx, *is not restricted to direct manual labour* (despite it being its central nucleus), *but also incorporates forms of labour that are not productive, that produce surplus-value, but are not directly manual.*

Yet, the *class-that-lives-from-labour* also comprises *unproductive* workers, those whose forms of labour are used as a service, either for public use or for the capitalist, and who are not constituted as a directly productive element, as a live element in the process of capital-valorisation and creation of surplus-value. They are those, according to Marx, whose labour is consumed as a *use-value* and not as labour that creates *exchange-value*. They constitute a growing wage-earning segment of contemporary capitalism, despite some branches within it being in decline, as we will see below. They are constituted as 'non-productive, anti-value generating constituents of the capitalist labour process [but who] share the same premises and are built on the self-same material foundations. They belong to those "false costs and useless expenses of production", which are, nevertheless, absolutely vital to the survival of the system.'[2]

Given, therefore, that *all productive workers are wage-earners* and *not all wage-earners are productive*, an updated notion of the *working class* must, broadly, embrace *the totality of wage-earning workers*. This does not deny, as mentioned above, *the central role of the productive worker, of collective social labour* that creates exchange-value, of the *modern industrial proletariat*, within the *class-that-lives-from-labour*, which is evident as the reference draws on Marx's formulation. But, since there is a *growing overlap* between *productive* and *unproductive* labour in contemporary capitalism and the working class incorporates these two basic dimensions of labour under capitalism, this *broader notion* seems fundamental for an understanding of what the working class is today.[3]

We know that Marx (often in collaboration with Engels) used the notions of *proletariat*, *working class* and *wage-earners* as synonyms, as can been seen in, for example, the *Communist Manifesto*. But he also often emphasised, especially in *Capital*, that the proletariat was essentially made up of producers of

---

2. Mészáros 1995, p. 533.
3. On *productive and unproductive labour*, and on the meaning of *socially-combined labour*, see Marx 1994. Mandel also provides some succinct and insightful considerations on how to think of the working class today.

surplus-value, who experienced the conditions given by the *real subsumption* of labour to capital. In our analytical framework, we will endeavour to broadly maintain this distinction: I shall use *'industrial proletariat'* to indicate those who *directly create surplus-value and directly participate in the process of capital-valorisation*, and I shall use the notion of *working class* or *class-that-lives-from-labour* to include both the industrial working class as well as wage-earners who sell their labour-power (and, naturally, those who are unemployed as a result of the destructive logic of capital).[4]

A broad notion of the working class includes, therefore, all those who *sell their labour-power in exchange for a wage*, incorporating, in addition to the industrial proletariat and wage-earners in the service sector, the rural proletariat that sells its labour-power to capital. This notion includes: the *precarious proletariat; the modern sub-proletariat; part-time* work; the new proletariat of fast-food restaurants; the *hyphenated workers* whom Beynon refers to; the tertiarised and precarious workers of *lyophilised* enterprises referred to by Juan José Castillo; *wage-earning* workers of the so-called 'informal economy'[5] who are very often indirectly subordinated to capital; as well as unemployed workers, expelled from the productive process and from the labour-market as a result of capital restructuring and expanding the industrial reserve-army, during the phase of expansion of *structural unemployment*.

The working class of today obviously *excludes capital-owners, its high-level functionaries* who have control over the labour-process and processes of valorisation and reproduction of capital inside companies and who earn high salaries,[6] and those who have accumulated capital and live by means of speculation and interest. It also *excludes* small-business owners and the urban and rural *propertied* bourgeoisie.[7]

To understand the *class-that-lives-from-labour* in this broad way, as a *synonym* of the *working class*, allows us to recognise that the *world of work* has undergone significant changes. We will therefore provide an assessment of

---

4. I return to this discussion in Appendix 2, 'The New Proletarians at the Turn of the Century'.

5. Here I am mainly referring to wage-workers *without* a work-permit, rapidly increasing in contemporary capitalism, and also in those who are *self-employed*, who provide maintenance, cleaning, etc. services, excluding, however, small-business owners. The analytical key for defining the working class is given on the basis of earning a wage and the sale of one's labour-power. For this reason, we refer to *class-that-lives-from-labour*, an expression that seeks to capture and incorporate the *totality of wage-earners who live by the sale of their labour-power*.

6. Bernardo 2009.

7. These parts of the petty bourgeoisie could, of course, constitute important allies of the working class, although they do not form part of its constitutive nucleus.

these changes: a descriptive account in the first instance followed by some analytic observations.

Dimensions of the diversity, heterogeneity and complexity of the working class

A common trend has been the reduction of the industrial, factory-, traditional, manual, *stable and specialised* proletariat, heir of the era of verticalised industry. This proletariat developed extensively during the Taylorist/Fordist period and has been in decline since the productive restructuring of capital, the development of lean production, the Western expansion of Toyotism and of forms of horizontalisation of productive capital, and the flexibilisation and decentralisation (and often *de-territorialisation*) of the physical productive space. Further still, its decline is also the result of, among others, the introduction of computerised machinery and telematics (that allows for direct relations between far-flung companies by means of computers, in addition to the introduction of new forms of 'domestic labour').[8]

There has been, on the other hand, a huge surge in a *new industrial and services-proletariat*, reflected in the remarkable growth on a global scale of what has been referred to as *precarious labour* (which I refer to in *Adeus ao Trabalho?* (*Farewell to Labour?*) as the *new sub-proletariat*, precisely because of its instability). It is 'outsourced,' subcontracted, part-time labour, among many other similar forms, that is proliferating in numerous parts of the world.

Decades ago, these jobs were mainly taken by immigrants: the *gastarbeiters* in Germany, *lavoro nero* in Italy, the *Chicanos* in the US, the *dekasseguis* in Japan, among many other examples. But, today, they have expanded to include *the remaining workers of the era of Taylorist/Fordist specialisation*, whose activities are gradually disappearing, directly affecting workers in core-countries, who, with the increasing disintegration of the welfare-state, the growth of *structural unemployment* and the crisis of capital, are forced to find alternative work in very adverse conditions compared with those existing previously. This process also affects, albeit differently, the *intermediary industrialised subordinate countries*, such as Brazil, Mexico and Korea, among many others that, after a huge expansion of their industrial proletariat in previous decades, recently started to experience significant processes of deindustrialisation and de-proletarianisation, resulting in the growth of precarious, partial, temporary, outsourced and informal labour.

---

8. See, for example, Beynon 1995; Fumagalli 1996; Castillo 1996b; and Bihr 1991.

However, the metamorphoses under way within the world of work do not end here, as we shall see in the following section.

The sexual division of labour: transversalities between the dimensions of class and gender

There has been a significant increase in the amount of female labour that has been absorbed by capital, reaching over 40 per cent of the workforce in several advanced countries, particularly in the form of part-time, precarious and deregulated work. In the UK, as we have seen, the female contingent recently surpassed the male one in the composition of the workforce. It is known, however, that this expansion of female labour has not translated into equality of earnings despite women's increased participation in the labour-market. Women's earnings remain much lower than those of their male counterparts. The same often occurs with respect to labour-rights and working conditions.

In the *sexual division of labour* established by capital in the *factory-space*, conceptual activities or those based on *intensive capital* are generally performed by male workers, whereas those that require fewer qualifications, that are more elementary and often based on *intensive labour*, are generally allocated to female workers (and very often also immigrant- and black workers).

In research conducted in workplaces in the UK, Anna Pollert, addressing the issue through the prism of the *sexual division of labour*, observes a clear distinction between male and female labour. Whereas the former is mainly found in environments with a predominance of *intensive capital* (with more advanced machinery), female labour is more frequently restricted to routine-work, where there is a greater need for *intensive labour*.

Examining a traditional food-plant in the UK – Choc-Co – Pollert shows that in the most valued areas of the chocolate-factory *male workers* predominate and in the more routine areas that require manual labour the presence of female workers has been increasing. And, in more technologically sophisticated units, her research showed that female labour is reserved for routine-activities that require lower levels of qualification and where temporary and part-time work are more common. Pollert was able to conclude that at Choc-Co, in the *sexual division of labour* under way in the productive restructuring of capital, exploitation in the world of female work had intensified.[9]

---

9. Pollert 1996, pp. 186–8.

In her study on the female labour-force, Helena Hirata also makes important observations similar to those outlined above. She considers that 'theses about the universal reach of flexible specialisation or of the emergence of a new productive paradigm to replace the Fordist model of production are highly questionable in light of empirical studies that take into account North-South and gender differences.... Flexible specialisation or labour organised into small islands or modules is not performed indiscriminately when we consider the gender of the workforce and whether it is performed in highly industrialised or so-called "underdeveloped" countries.'[10]

In a comparative study conducted by the author on Japan, France and Brazil that covered parent-companies and their subsidiaries, Hirata found a great variety in the organisation and management of the workforce, according to the sexual division of labour and the North-South divide. In her words:

> In terms of the organisation of work, the first conclusion is that on the premises of establishments in all three countries, the staff was male or female according to the type of machine, the type of work and the organisation of work. Repetitive, manual work was attributed to women and work that required greater technical knowledge attributed to men.
>
> Another common feature: employers in all three countries easily recognised the qualities of female labour, but they were not recognised as qualifications.... The movements of Taylorisation/de-Taylorisation do not follow the same path in both very industrialised and 'semi-industrialised' countries, like Brazil.[11]

The piecemeal character of labour is much more common in countries such as Brazil.

The author continues: 'In terms of the workforce-management policy, the first conclusion, similar to the organisation of work, is that it differs according to gender.'[12] In Japanese companies, for example, two remuneration-systems, based on gender, are openly adhered to. Another example is that of discrimination against married women. In France, during the selection process, the parent-companies do not discriminate against married women as they do in the Brazilian subsidiaries.

> Finally, with regard to the system of participative management, the study of the quality-control circle showed that there were differences in the degree of participation, according to the country (very high in Japan, relatively

10. Hirata 1995, p. 86.
11. Hirata 1995, p. 87.
12. Ibid.

high in Brazil and intermediary in France) and gender; women were often less involved in group-activities and less encouraged to make suggestions about technical improvements and, especially, more commonly excluded from decision-making processes.[13]

Among the many consequences of this sexual division of labour, we can recall, for instance, that unions often exclude working women as well as *contracted and precarious workers*. The modern working class is increasingly composed of these different segments, women and contracted or precarious workers (and even more often by female contractors), that are a central constituent of the world of work. If the unions are unable to allow the (self-) organisation of women and/or of part-time workers within the union, it is easy to imagine an even deeper worsening of the crisis of representation of workers by the unions.

These elements allow us to move further into the complex interactions between class and gender.

We have seen that female labour has increased even more significantly in the *productive sphere of the factory*. This has shaped a (new) *sexual division of labour* in which, save a few exceptions, female workers occupy areas of *intensive labour*, with even higher levels of labour-exploitation, whereas those areas known for *intensive capital*, endowed with greater technological development, continue to be reserved for male workers.

As a result, female labour has grown to occupy, in particular, *more precarious work*, part-time work, and work characterised by an even greater *informality*, where wage inequality is even more marked and working hours are longer.[14]

Another crucial element in the study of *gender in labour* is that of class. Working women, in general, perform their work *twice, both inside and outside of the home*, or if we prefer, *inside and outside the factory*. And, in doing so, despite the *twofold nature of the act of work*, they are doubly exploited by capital. Firstly, by exercising, in the *public sphere*, their *productive* labour in the factory. Secondly, in the realm of *private life*, by dedicating hours to *domestic work*

---

13. Hirata 1995, p. 88. Helena Hirata concludes by stating that the forms of female labour-force utilisation, taking into account civil status, age and qualifications, vary considerably from country to country. 'Significant differences also exist in the practices of discrimination that appear to be directly related to the evolution of the social relations of the sexes in the society as a whole' (p. 89).

14. A special edition of *Le Monde diplomatique* in 1999 with the title 'Bilan du Monde' ('Balance Sheet of the World'), showed, 'Women work more than men in nearly all societies. The disparity is particularly high in rural parts of the developing world. In the industrialised countries, the disparity is smaller, but exists particularly in Italy (28%), in France (11%) and in the US (11%), when compared to men' (p. 19).

that secures their *reproduction* – a sphere of *not directly commercial work* in which the *indispensable conditions for the reproduction* of the labour-force of her husband, children and herself are created.[15] Without this sphere of not directly commercial *reproduction*, the conditions for the *reproduction* of capital's social-metabolic order would be severely compromised, if not completely unviable.[16]

The necessary interactions between gender and class are clear, particularly when exploring the world of work. As Lilian Segnini states, 'the analytic category "gender" enables a search for the meaning of representations of both the feminine and masculine, placing them in their social and historical contexts. An analysis of gender relations also implies and analysis of power-relations', and it is in this sense, as Segnini remarks quoting Joan Scott, 'that this relation enables the understanding of two dimensions:

> gender as a constitutive element of social relations, based on the perceivable differences between the sexes;
> gender as a basic form of representation of power-relations in which the dominant representations are presented as natural and unquestionable.[17]

Relations between *gender* and *class* show us how, in the sphere of the productive and reproductive world, we experience a *sexualised social construction*, where working men and women – from the home through school – are qualified and equipped *differently* to enter the labour-market. And capitalism was able to appropriate itself, unequally, of this *sexual division of labour*.

It is clear that the increase in female labour in the productive world in the last few decades is part of the process of *partial* emancipation of women, both in relation to the class-society as well as to innumerable forms of male oppression that are based in the traditional social and sexual division of labour. However, crucially, capital incorporates female labour in an *unequal and differentiated way in its social and sexual division of labour*. As we saw in the studies mentioned earlier, *female labour is more intensively precarious.* Salaries, rights,

---

15. Helena Hirata argues that when analysing *non-waged labour* and, particularly, *the sexual division of labour*, unremunerated work should also be included, such as domestic labour carried out by women who, despite working as wage-earners, also engage in non-wage labour inside the home. In her words, 'An account of domestic and wage-work, remunerated and unremunerated work, formal and informal work, as modalities of labour, broadens the concept of labour and the affirmation of its centrality, If waged work diminishes, the real activity of work continues to have a strategic place in contemporary societies' (Hirata 1993, p. 7).
16. See, for instance, *Reventando*, a journal of the Corriente Marxista Feminista Clara Zetkin, Cordoba, Argentina, 1998, p. 8.
17. Segnini 1998, p. 49.

working conditions, in sum, *the precarisation of working conditions has been even greater when studies take into account the gender-dimension as well.*[18]

Yet capital was also able to appropriate the *versatility and multitasking* ability of female labour, derived from the activities they fulfil in the sphere of *reproductive, domestic labour.* Whilst men – given existing socio-historical conditions that are, as we have seen, a *sexualised social construction* – have greater difficulty in adapting to the new polyvalent dimensions (which in fact are associated with greater levels of *exploitation*), capital has been able to make use of this social attribute associated with women.

What was, therefore, a real moment – albeit limited – of *partial* female emancipation from capital's exploitation and male oppression is converted by capital into a source of further inequality.

These issues allow us to draw some conclusions as to the analytic interactions between gender and class.

In the deeper process of emancipation of the *human race*, united action between working *men and women* is essential. This action finds in capital and in its system of social metabolism, the source of *subordination and estrangement.*[19] A meaningful life that can lead to the flourishing of an *authentic subjectivity* is a struggle against this system of social metabolism; it is the act of the *working class against capital.* The very same condition that creates distinct forms of *estrangement,* for a life *without* meaning in work, offers the conditions for the development of an *authentic subjectivity* that can create a life *endowed with meaning.*

However, women's struggle for emancipation is also – and decisively – an act against the sociohistorical forms of male oppression. In this domain, feminist struggle is precapitalist, it comes into force under the power of capital; it will also be postcapitalist, because the demise of the class society *does not mean the direct and immediate end of gender oppression.* It is clear that if the end of forms of class-oppression can create an authentically free, self-determining and emancipated form of society, it will lead to the emergence of egalitarian socio-historical conditions *never before seen, that can engender genuinely different, free and autonomous subjectivities.* Here, gender-differences become completely distinct and authentic and capable of establishing relations between men and women that are completely free from the forms of oppression that exist in different forms of *class society.*

---

18. See Lavinas 1996, pp. 174ff.

19. I use 'estrangement' (*Entfremdung*) in the same sense as is commonly attributed to 'alienation,' for the reasons outlined in Antunes 1995a, pp. 121–34. I use 'alienation' specifically when I am citing or making explicit reference to a particular author. See also Ranieri 1995.

While the emancipation of humanity and the creation of a 'free association of individuals' is the task of men and women who labour, of the working class, the specific emancipation of women in relation to male oppression is decisive and primarily a *female conquest towards the real and all-encompassing emancipation of the human race*, in which free men can and should participate, but *without a leading or controlling role*.[20]

Wage-earners in the service-sector, the 'third sector' and new forms of domestic labour

Let us thus return to other distinctive trends in the world of work. There has been, in the last few decades, a significant increase in moderate wage-earners and service-sector workers, made up of a broad contingent of workers that emerged from the process of productive restructuring and deindustrialisation. In the US, this contingent surpasses 70 per cent of the workforce, a trend similar to that of the UK, France and Spain as well as the other main capitalist economies.[21] Yet, it is important to remember that the service-sector has also been affected by organisational and technological changes and transformations in forms of management, and that this sector has increasingly yielded to the rationality of capital.[22] We see, for example, the sharp reduction of banking jobs or the widespread privatisation of public services over the last decade and the resulting vast numbers of unemployed workers. This scenario led Lojkine to observe that, from 1975 to 1980, there was a reduction in the rate of growth of the service-sector, increasing the levels of structural unemployment.[23]

If we include the *growing* overlap between the productive sphere and the service-sector, as well as the increasing subordination of the latter to the former, service-sector wage-work has become increasingly close to the logic and rationality of the productive world, establishing a *reciprocal interpenetration* between the two, between *productive* and *unproductive* labour.[24] This absorption of labour by the service-sector led to a significant increase in the levels of unionisation of moderate-wage earners, which was not, however, sufficient to

---

20. While I am not able, in the space available, to explore the connections between race and class, or the gay rights and green movements, it is important to state that these movements achieve much greater vitality and emancipatory force when they are articulated with the struggle of labour against capital. See, for instance, Saffioti 1997.

21. Wood 1997b, p. 5.

22. A trend that clearly contradicts Offe's thesis (1989).

23. Lojkine 1995b, p. 261.

24. Lojkine 1995b, p. 257.

compensate for the fall in trade-union density in the industrial sectors. None-theless, it did entail a strong contingent of wage-earners in the new configura-tion of the working class.

In the central countries – with repercussions within intermediary indus-trialised countries – the world of work is witnessing an increasing process of exclusion of young people and of workers considered 'old' by capital: the former have frequently joined the ranks of neo-Nazi movements, having no prospects in a *society of structural unemployment*. And those over 40, once excluded from the labour-market, have great difficult *re-qualifying* in order to re-enter it. They increase the pockets of so-called informal labour and the industrial reserve-army. The growth of religious movements has made ample use of these groups of unemployed people. The modern capitalist world of labour is explicitly hostile to these workers who are generally heirs to a 'Ford-ist culture,' with specialisations that, as a result of their unilateral nature, con-trast with the versatile and multifunctional worker (often in the *ideological* sense of the term) required by Toyotism. Alongside this exclusion, there is the precocious and criminal inclusion of children in the labour-market, not just in Asian or Latin-American countries, but also in various central countries.

There has also been an expansion of work in the so-called 'third sector,' especially in the advanced-capitalist countries, such as the US and the UK, among others. A new form of occupation has emerged in community, not-for-profit enterprises, operating with various forms of predominantly volun-tary labour, performing a wide array of activities centred on support- and assistance-services and that developed somewhat on the fringes of the market. The growth of 'third-sector' work derives from the retraction of the industrial labour-market as well as the decline of the service-sector as a result of struc-tural unemployment.[25] Indeed, it is the consequence of the structural crisis of capital, of its destructive logic and the means employed for its productive restructuring that seek to reduce *living* labour and increase *dead* labour.

While I disagree with those who attribute to this sector an important role in a globalised-capitalist economy[26] it is important to note, however, that this form of social activity, driven predominantly by motives other than trade, has shown some growth, with work performed by NGOs and other similar associations and organisations. An *extremely limited* alternative to replace the loss of jobs caused by the destructive logic of contemporary society, the 'third sector' has, nonetheless, deserved investigation in some countries. In the US and the UK, for instance, it is also an example of exclusion of labour from the productive

---

25. See, for example, Dickens 1997, pp. 1–4.
26. As Rifkin does (Rifkin 1995).

system, due to the growth of *structural unemployment*, since the 'third sector' absorbs a relatively small portion of those workers who are expelled from the capitalist labour-market. Thus, in our view, the 'third sector' is not a real and lasting alternative to the capitalist labour-market, but has a *functional* role in absorbing portions of workers unemployed by capital.

Within the 'third sector,' *solidarity-economy* activities have the advantage of acting outside the logic of commerce, yet to characterise them as a *real transformative alternative to the logic of capital and its market*, capable of undermining the mechanisms of the productive capitalist unit, is a serious misunderstanding. It would be as though, through the growth of the *solidarity-economy*, starting at the fringes of the system, we could invert and *substantially* alter the essence of the logic of the system of commodity-production and valorisation of capital.

It is one thing to understand the different forms of *solidarity-economy* and 'third-sector' activity as a mechanism that incorporates men and women rejected by the labour-market and wage-labour relations into non-profit making and non-commercial activities, reinvesting in the limited (but necessary) forms of sociability that labour brings about in contemporary society. These social individuals see themselves not as *unemployed* or *excluded*, but as people performing real activities, endowed with some social meaning. This, certainly, represents a moment of useful and positive activity, on the relative fringes (directly, at least) of the mechanisms of accumulation. Yet, it is important to remember that these activities fulfil a functional role in relation to a system that nowadays wishes to have no public or social concern with unemployment.

With the dismantling of the welfare-state, in the small number of countries where it existed, these solidarity-associations or -organisations to some extent fill those gaps. Now, to attribute to them the capability of expanding and thus *replacing, changing and ultimately transforming* the global system of capital seems to us an enormous mistake. As a mechanism for minimising the barbarity of structural unemployment, they play an effective (albeit very limited) role. However, when conceived of as a real moment of *deep social transformation*, they turn out to represent a new form of mystification that (in a generous understanding) seeks to 'replace' the radical, deep-rooted and totalising forms of transformation of societal logic with more palatable and partial mechanisms that can somehow be assimilated by capital. In a less generous interpretation, they seek to *avoid* those transformations capable of *eliminating* capital.

To conclude this outline of the trends characterising the world of work, we should also mention the growth of domestic labour, instigated by the devolution of the productive process, by the expansion of small and medium-sized units of production, as exemplified by the 'Third Italy'. With the introduction of *telematics*, the growth of forms of labour-flexibilisation (and precarisation), the increasingly horizontal nature of productive capital and the necessity to meet the needs of an increasingly 'individualised' market, domestic work has begun to display new forms of expansion in different parts of the world. As Chesnais observes:

> Teleinformatics (sometimes called 'telematics') arose from convergence of new satellite- and cable- telecommunications-systems, information-technologies and microelectronics. For enterprises and banks, it presented greater possibilities to control the expansion of their assets on an international scale and strengthen their global operations....
>
> Telematics increases tertiarised relations, especially between enterprises located hundreds of thousands of miles from one another, as well as the relocation of routine-tasks to industries that rely heavily on information-technology. It opens the door to the fragmentation of labour-processes and new forms of 'work from home'.[27]

Its effects concern, according to the author, the economy of labour and of capital, as they allow:

- greater flexibility over production-processes;
- a reduction in the stock of intermediary products through the use of the just-in-time system and the stock of finished products;
- shorter delivery-times;
- a reduction in working capital; and
- the employment of electronic equipment in the sales- and franchise-sector, among other advantages.[28]

It is my view, however, that these last two trends – that of the 'third sector' and of 'working from home' – despite being visible and forming part of a more heterogeneous and fragmented *class-that-lives-from-labour*, are still limited: in the case of the 'third sector,' it is composed of forms of community- and care-work that are growing primarily in the wake of *the collapse of the welfare-state*, in an attempt to perform the activity once performed by the state. In the case of 'work from home,' its use cannot reach many productive sectors, such as the automotive, the steel-, the petrochemical industries, etc. Yet, where it has proliferated, its ties to the capitalist productive system are

---

27. Chesnais 1999, p. 28.
28. Chesnais 1999, pp. 28–9.

much more evident, *its subordination to capital is direct*, being a mechanism for the reintroduction of *bygone* forms of labour, such as the *piecemeal-work* that Marx described, that capitalism in the era of globalisation is renewing on a vast scale. It is sufficient to recall the massive expansion of Benetton and of Nike across the world, among the innumerable examples of labour performed in the domestic space or in small production-units.

It is important to add that the *productive* work at home that these companies make use of is combined with domestic *reproductive* work, which we mentioned above, bringing to light once again the importance of female labour.

Transnationalisation of capital and the world of work

This more complex configuration of the working class, in the context of contemporary capitalism, assumes a decisive dimension with the *transnational* nature of capital and its productive system. Its local, regional and national character extends through linkages and connections in the productive chain that is becoming more and more internationalised. This is because 'the singular and particular forms of labour are subsumed by the social, general and abstract labour that is expressed in the sphere of global capitalism and are realised there. In the same way that the most diverse singular and particular forms of capital are subsumed to capital in general, which finds its expression in the sphere of the global market, something similar occurs with the most diverse forms and meanings of labour.'[29]

In the same way that capital is a global system, the world of labour and its challenges are also increasingly transnationalised, though the internationalisation of the productive chain has not, to date, come up with an *international* response on behalf of the working class. It keeps itself predominantly within its national structures, which poses an enormous limitation on workers' action. With the reconfiguration of the *space* as much as of the *time* of production, in the global system of production, there has been a process of both *re-territorialisation* and *de-territorialisation*. New industrial regions emerge and many disappear, as well as more and more factories becoming *globalised*, such as the automotive industry, where *global* cars have virtually replaced the national car.

This positions the class-struggle at an increasingly international level: the strike of the autoworkers at the General Motors plant in the US, in June 1998, which began in Michigan in a small plant that was strategically important

---

29. Ianni 1996, p. 169.

to the company, had profound repercussions in many countries such as Mexico, Canada and Brazil. The movement spread as other plants ran out of the equipment and parts supplied by the Flint factory, the *space* where the strike had been triggered. Little by little, other plants were affected, bringing virtually the whole of General Motors' productive process to a halt because of the absence of equipment and parts.

This new productive configuration of capital presents, therefore, growing challenges to the world of labour, since the centre of present-day social confrontation is given by the contradiction between *total social capital and the totality of labour*.[30] In the same way that capital makes use of these globalised mechanisms and its *international* organs, workers' struggle must be characterised also, increasingly, by its international formation. And, on this terrain, as we know, capital is well ahead of labour when it comes to solidarity and class-action. Very often, the success or the failure of a strike in one or more countries is dependent upon the support, solidarity and action of workers in productive units of the same company elsewhere.

Existing international labour-union organisations nearly always have a traditional, bureaucratic and institutionalised structure that leaves them completely incapable of offering an alternative social vision opposed to the logic of capital. They tend to assume a defensive stance or one that is subordinate to the logic of internationalisation of capital, opposing merely some of its most dire *consequences*. The conflict between native and immigrant-workers is another clear example of this process of economic transnationalisation, *of the re-territorialisation and de-territorialisation* of the labour-force, to which the labour-movement has been unable to provide a satisfactory response.

In this way, besides the cleavages that exist between secure and precarious workers, men and women, young and old people, native and immigrant, black and white, skilled and unskilled, 'included' and 'excluded,' and many other examples to be found with the national space, *the stratification and fragmentation of labour are also accentuated as a function of a growing process of internationalisation of capital*. This broader, more complex and fragmented world of labour is manifested, therefore:

1) within a particular group of section of work;
2) within different groups of workers belonging to the same national community;
3) between nationally different bodies of labour, pitted against one another in the context of international capitalist competition...;

---

30. Mészáros 1995.

4) [between] the labour-force of advanced capitalist countries – relative ben-
eficiaries of the global capitalist division of labour – and the relatively
more exploited labour-force of the 'Third World';

5) [between] labour in employment, separated from and opposed to objectively differentiated interests – and generally politically and organisationally unarticulated – and the 'unwaged' or unemployed, including those
that are increasingly victims of the 'second industrial revolution'.[31]

This *composite, diverse and heterogeneous* picture of the *class-that-lives-from-labour*
will allows us, in the next part of this book, to make some considerations of
an analytical nature. I shall consider contemporary forms of value-theory, as
well as the distinct modalities of contemporary labour.

31. Mészáros 1995, p. 929.

Chapter Seven

The World of Labour and Value-Theory: Forms of Material and Immaterial Labour

The growing interaction between labour and scientific knowledge: a critique of the thesis of 'science as primary productive force'

I begin with the existing linkages between *labour* and the new demands of the *law of value*. In conceiving of contemporary forms of labour as an expression of *social labour*, which is *more complex, socially combined* and even more *intense* in its rhythms and processes, I cannot defend arguments that minimise or even ignore the process of creation of exchange-values. On the contrary, I argue that the society of capital and its law of value have *increasingly less* need for *secure* labour and an ever *greater* need for diversified forms of partial or part-time, contracted labour, forms that in a growing scale are becoming a constitutive part of the process of capitalist production.

Similarly, the reduction of *living labour* and the expansion of *dead labour* is quite apparent. Yet, precisely because capital cannot eliminate *living labour* from the process of value-creation, it needs to increase the *use and the productivity of labour so as to intensify the forms of extraction of surplus-labour in an ever smaller amount of time*. The reduction of the physical time of labour and of direct manual labour, combined with the expansion of qualified, multi-functional labour endowed with a greater intellectual dimension, shows how the thesis that *capital no longer has an interest in exploiting abstract labour* ends up turning the *tendency* for the *reduction* of living labour and the expansion of dead labour into the *extinction* of the former, something which is entirely different. At the same time that it establishes these trends, capital increasingly resorts to precarious and intensified forms of labour-exploitation, which become even more essential for the realisation of its reproductive cycle in a world in which competitiveness is the guarantee of survival of capitalist firms.

Therefore, it is one thing to *have the pressing necessity to reduce the variable dimension of capital and the concomitant necessity to expand its constant part. It is another, entirely distinct, to imagine that after eliminating living labour capital can continue to reproduce itself.* It would not be possible to *produce capital* nor would it be possible to complete the reproductive cycle through consumption, since it would be abstraction to imagine consumption without *wage-earners.* The articulation between *living labour and dead labour is the condition upon which the capitalist system of production is maintained.* The thesis of the *elimination of abstract labour,* understood as the expenditure of physical and mental energy for the production of commodities, finds neither theoretical nor empirical support in the advanced-capitalist countries, such as the US, Japan or Germany, and even less so in the so-called Third World.[1] Further, its main analytical drawback consists in ignoring the interactions that exist between – as Francisco de Oliveira expresses well – the *constituent power of living labour* and the *constituted power* present in *dead labour.*[2]

The reduction of the 'stable' proletariat, heir of Taylorism/Fordism, the expansion of *abstract-intellectual labour* inside modern factories and the generalised growth of forms of precarious labour (*abstract-manual labour*) in the shape of subcontracted, part-time labour developed intensively in the 'era of the flexible firm' and the de-verticalisation of production, *are clear examples of the validity of the law of value.* The increase in workers who experience conditions of unemployment (the expression 'excluded', often used to indicate such workers, contains a sense of criticism and denunciation, but is analytically weak) is a constitutive part of growing *structural unemployment* that affects the

---

1. An analysis of the relationship between value and machinery, updated for the information- and computer-age, can be found in Caffentzis 1997, pp. 29–56. The author draws on Marx's analysis to demonstrate the impossibility of a machine creating exchange-value.

2. The idea was expressed by Francisco de Oliveira, known for his analytical richness, during a joint project with Nobuco Kameyama, José Paulo Netto, Evaldo Amaro Vieira and myself, at UFRJ (Universidade Federal do Rio de Janeiro) in April 1999. In his book *Os Direitos do Antivalor* (1997), particularly in the first part, can be found a number of elements that help conceptualise the relationship of living labour to dead labour and, in particular, the *automation* of constant capital.

world of work, according to the destructive logic that presides over its system of societal metabolism. As Tosel remarks (drawing on J.-M. Vincent's analysis), since capital has a powerful aspect of waste and exclusion, it is the very 'centrality of abstract labour that produces the non-centrality of labour, found in the mass of those excluded from living labour' who, once (de-)socialised and (de-)individualised by labour's expulsion, 'desperately search for forms of identification and socialisation in the isolated spheres of non-labour (training and charity- or service-activities)'.[3]

For these reasons, I cannot agree with the thesis of the transformation of science into the 'primary productive force', replacing a no-longer-operative labour-value.[4] Habermas argues:

> Since the end of the nineteenth century the other developmental tendency characteristic of advanced capitalism has become increasingly momentous: the scientisation of technology.... With the advent of large-scale industrial research, science, technology and industrial utilisation were fused into a system. Since then, industrial research has been linked up with research under government-contract, which primarily promotes scientific and technical progress in the military sector. From there information flows back into the sectors of civilian production. This technology and science become a leading productive force, rendering inoperative the conditions for Marx's labour theory of value. It is no longer meaningful to calculate the amount of capital investment in research and development on the basis of the value of unskilled (simple) labour-power, when scientific-technical progress has become an independent source of surplus-value, in relation to which the only source of surplus-value considered by Marx, namely the labour-power of the immediate producers, plays an ever smaller role.[5]

This formulation, in 'replacing' the thesis of labour-value with that of science as primary productive force, ignores an essential element given by the complexity of relations between value-theory and scientific knowledge. Or rather, it ignores that 'living labour, in conjunction with science and technology, constitute a complex and contradictory unity under the conditions of capitalist developments' since 'the *tendency* of capital to give production a scientific character is *counteracted* by capital's innermost limitations, i.e. by

---

3. Tosel 1995, p. 210. To which he adds, 'Is it not, in fact, based in this apparent decentralisation (*decentration*) of labour that theories opposing the paradigm of labour for the competing paradims of communicational action or the public sphere, find their roots?' (p. 210). We will return to this further on.

4. Habermas 1975, p. 320.

5. Habermas 1975, pp. 320–1.

the ultimately paralysing, anti-social requirements "to maintain the already created value as value" so as to contain production within capital's *limited foundation'*.[6]

Released by capital to expand, but *ultimately* prisoner of the necessity to subordinate itself to the imperatives of the process of creation of exchange-values, science cannot be transformed into a 'primary productive force', into independent science and technology, *because this would blow apart the material basis* of the system of production of capital, as Marx warned in the *Grundrisse*.[7] His preparatory notes show that, from the mid-nineteenth century, the relation between labour-value and science was extremely important. Yet, even acknowledging the hyper-dimensionality of science in the contemporary world, social knowledge generated by scientific progress is *restricted* in its goals by the logic of capital-reproduction. Unable to establish a social order that *produces useful things in disposable time*, it is up to the *scientisation of technology* to adapt to the *necessary time to produce exchange-values*. The absence of *independence* from capital and its reproductive cycle prevents it from breaking from this logic.

This is not to say that the labour theory of value does not recognise the growing role of science, but that science is hampered in its development by the material base of relations between capital and labour that it cannot overcome. It is as a result of this structural restriction, which *releases* and even *forces* science's expansion to increase the production of exchange-values, *but prevents a qualitative social leap towards a society that produces useful goods according to the logic of disposable time*, that science is not able to become the primary productive force. Prisoner of this material base, rather than a process of *scientisation of technology* there is, as Mészáros suggests, a process of technologification of science.[8] Deeply linked to the social constraints of the system of capital, science and technology do not have an autonomous logic nor an independent path, but have solid ties with its reproductive movement. In Mészáros's synthesis:

> The great dilemma of modern science is that its development was always tied to the *contradictory dynamism* of capital itself.... Modern science could not help being oriented towards the most effective possible implementation of the *objective imperatives* that define the nature.... To bring about the much needed disjunction between science and destructive capitalist determinations is conceivable only if society as a whole successfully escapes from capital's

---

6. Mészáros 1989, pp. 135–6.
7. Marx 1974, pp. 705–9.
8. Mészáros 1989, p. 133.

orbit and provides new ground – with different orienting principles – on which scientific practices can flourish in the service of human ends.[9]

This entails *removing* the relation that prevails today where the production of use-values is subordinated to their exchange-values. Without ignoring the dialectic of reciprocal interactions, the structurally dominant importance of exchange-value ultimately imposes itself on scientific and technological advances.[10] The *second-order mediations* discussed above, imposed by capital's system of social metabolism through private property, exchange, the hierarchical social division of labour, etc., besides impacting on and transforming the primary mediations, also affect other aspects of the activity of social beings. Science has also suffered these negative consequences as it has had to yield to social, institutional and material imperatives, reified by the system of *second-order mediations*.[11]

Ontologically imprisoned in the material soil of capital, science cannot become its *principal productive force*. Science *interacts* with labour, with the powerful necessity to participate in the process of capital-valorisation. *Science does not override value, but is an intrinsic part of its mechanism.* This interpenetration between labour and science associates and articulates the *constituent power of living labour with the constituted power of techno-scientific knowledge in the production of values (material or immaterial).* Scientific knowledge and knowledge deriving from labour are mixed more directly in the contemporary productive world *without the former 'bringing down' the latter.*

Many experiences, of which General Motors' Saturn project is an example, failed with the attempt to automate the productive process *minimising and ignoring* labour. Intelligent machines cannot replace workers. On the contrary, their introduction makes use of the intellectual labour of the worker, who, by interacting with the automated machine, transfers part of his new intellectual and cognitive attributes to the new machine that results from this process. A complex interactive process is therefore established between labour and productive science that does not (and cannot) bring about the extinction of *living labour* and its *constituent power* in capital's social-metabolic order. This feedback process requires capital to find an *even more complex, multifunctional workforce, to be exploited even more intensely and sophisticatedly,* at least in those branches of production with greater technological development.

Japan's superiority in the 1980s was not based *only* on its technological advances, but also upon *a growing interaction between labour and science,*

9. Mészáros 1989, pp. 195–6.
10. Mészáros 1989, pp. 199–200.
11. Mészáros 1989, p. 507, note 525.

between execution and development, between technological advancement and the adequate 'involvement' of the workforce. It contrasted with Fordism, which was based on the rigid separation between *production* and *development*, *execution and conception* and which exhausted its capacity of expropriation of the *intellectual know-how of labour, of abstract intellectual labour*, of the cognitive dimension present in living labour. The main change within the process of capital-production in the Toyotist, flexible factory is not, therefore, the *transformation of science into the primary productive force that replaces and eliminates labour in the process of value-creation, but, instead, the growing interaction between labour and science, material and immaterial labour, essential elements in the contemporary productive (industrial and service-) world*.

Given these observations concerning science and labour, we can explore other developments in the relation between *labour and value*. The first of these is the one that allows the conversion of *living labour* into *dead labour*, from the moment in which, thanks to the development of software, the computerised machine begins to perform activities that are characteristic of human intelligence. There is, thus, a process of *objectification of cerebral activities in the machinery*, of transfer of *intellectual and cognitive knowledge* from the working class to the computerised machinery.

As Lojkine summarises:

> The supreme phase of mechanisation, the automated factory remains part of the industrial revolution, because its principle is still the replacement of the human hand. Yet, at the same time, hyper-mechanisation objectified the 'intelligent hand' (the most refined gestures).... The principle of automation entails the flexibility, that is, the capacity the machine has to not only correct itself, but at the same time adapt to different demands and in so doing, change its programming.[12]

The transfer of intellectual capacities to computerised machinery reinforces the tendency (mentioned by Marx in Volume I of *Capital*) of the reduction and transformation of *living labour* into *dead labour*.

Another trend engineered by capital during the phase of productive restructuring that concerns the relation between labour and value is the one that *reduces the levels of unproductive labour in the factory*. The elimination of various activities such as *supervision, monitoring, inspection, middle-management, etc. –* a measure that constitutes a central element of Toyotism and the modern capitalist enterprise based on lean production – aims to transfer and incorporate into *productive* labour-activities that were previously performed by

---

12. Lojkine 1995a, p. 44.

unproductive workers. By reducing unproductive labour and incorporating it into productive labour, capital dispenses itself of its obligation to groups of workers who do not directly participate in the process of value-creation. *It is important to remember, as we saw in the previous chapter, that capital cannot eliminate unproductive labour entirely, work that generates anti-value (that is indispensable to the process of value-creation), but can reduce or reallocate some parts of these activities to its productive workers.*

The interaction between *material and immaterial* labour

Besides the reduction of unproductive labour, there is another trend deriving from the growing overlap between *material* and *immaterial* labour. In the contemporary world, we are witnessing the expansion of labour carrying a greater intellectual dimension, in the *most computerised industrial activities,* as much as in the *service- and communications-sectors,* among many others.[13] The advancement of work in the areas of research, software-creation, marketing and publicity, is also an example of the *spread of labour in the immaterial sphere.* The growth of labour among the services, in not directly productive spheres that however perform activities that *overlap* with productive labour, is another important characteristic of the *broader notion of labour,* when we seek to understand its meaning in the contemporary world.

Let us consider manual and intellectual activities. In the capitalist social division of labour, *although it is possible to see, particularly amongst tertiarised and precarious labour, a huge expansion of manual labour in numerous sectors* (especially, but not exclusively, in so-called Third-World countries), there is also a trend towards the *intensification of intellectual activities in the sphere of productive labour, especially in those sectors at the cutting edge of the productive process* (which are more common in the central countries, but also not exclusive to them).[14] The *uneven* character of the *global system of capital* means the incidence of these

---

13. It strikes me as essential to stress that these tendencies present in the most advanced centres of production cannot, without the risk of performing a generalised abstraction, be taken as expressing the entire productive process, where labour-precarisation and de-skilling are common and are clearly on the rise, if we consider the totality of the productive process on a global scale. But to falsely generalise the ubiquity of the forms given by immaterial labour appears so misleading as to be worth rejecting.

14. Clearly, in highlighting the quantitative aspects, the trend for the incidence of precarious manual labour to expand is much more common than that of forms of abstract intellectual labour. However, when the analysis highlights the qualitative aspects, the importance of the latter also becomes apparent.

trends varies, but they are present in nearly all the countries with centres of modern industrial production.

J.-M. Vincent characterises these new configurations of the productive world in the following way: 'In the context of very rapid technical progress, relations with technology change rapidly. Automated systems of production are made by increasingly complex dead labour and increasingly control more operations and operational chains. They are not simply a set of machines, but systems in evolution that can perfect the functions of demand and programmed innovations.' Given that, according to the author, in the world of techno-science, the production of knowledge becomes an essential element in the production of goods and services, he goes on to say, 'The capacity of workers to increase their knowledge...becomes a decisive characteristic of working capacity in general. And it is no exaggeration to say that the labour-force is increasingly presented as an intelligent force of reaction to changing situations of production and the resolution to unexpected problems.'[15]

The growth of forms of *immaterial labour* becomes, therefore, another trend of the contemporary system of production, since it is increasingly in need of research, communication and marketing activities to obtain advance information about the market.[16] As firms need more direct ties with the consumer-market, as we saw above, the sphere of consumption begins to impact more directly on the sphere of production. 'A product, before being made, has to be sold (even in heavy industry, like the automotive industry, a car is put into production only after the sales-networks give the go-ahead). This strategy is based on the production and consumption of knowledge. It mobilises important communication- and marketing strategies to gather information (to know the market tendencies) and circulate (create a market).' While, under the Taylorist/Fordist system of production, goods were standardised (recall the black Ford Model T5, the only 'choice' offered by the manufacturer), today the automotive industry produces made-to-measure cars, according to demand.[17]

In productive enterprises and services we are thus witnessing an expansion of so-called immaterial activities:

> Immaterial labour can be found at the interface of this new production-consumption interface. It is immaterial labour that activates and organises the production-consumption relation. The activation of productive co-operation, along with the social relation with the consumer, is materialised in and

15. Vincent 1995, p. 160.
16. Lazzarato 1993, p. 111.
17. Lazzarato 1993, p. 112.

for the process of communication. It is immaterial labour that continually innovates the form and conditions of communication (and, therefore, of labour and consumption). It gives shape to and form to the necessities, the imagination, tastes. The particularity of the commodity produced by immaterial labour (its use-value being essentially its informational and cultural content) consists in the fact that it is not destroyed in the act of consumption, but expands, is transformed and creates the ideological and cultural environment of the consumer.[18]

In this way, immaterial labour 'does not produce only commodities, but above all the relation to capital itself.... Immaterial labour produces both subjectivity and economic value, showing that capitalist production has invaded all of life, breaking down the barriers between economy, power and knowledge.'[19]

Immaterial labour, therefore, again according to Lazzarato, expresses the power of the informational sphere of the commodity-form: it reflects the *informational* content of the commodity, showing the transformations of labour inside large enterprises and the service-sector, where direct manual labour is being replaced by labour endowed with a greater intellectual dimension, or in the words of the author: 'the indices of immediate labour are increasingly subordinated to the capacity of information-handling and horizontal and vertical communication'.[20]

Immaterial labour within *large industry* represents a meeting point between the sphere of labour-subjectivity (its more intellectual and cognitive features) and the productive process, that commonly compels the worker to 'make decisions', 'analyse situations', offer solutions when faced with unexpected events. The worker has to convert herself into an element 'of integration more and more involved in the team/system relation', displaying the 'integration that is more and more involved in the team/system relation', expressing a 'capacity to activate and manage productive co-operation. The worker must become an "active subject" of the co-ordination of different functions of production, instead of simply being commanded. Collective apprenticeship becomes the principal feature of productivity.'[21]

---

18. Lazzarato 1993, p. 114.
19. Lazzarato 1993, p. 115.
20. Lazzarato 1993, p. 54. Lazzarato also includes the cultural content present in the commodity-form, orientated more towards cultural and artistic processes, tied to fashion, to consumption patterns, etc. (Lazzarato 1993, pp. 117–20).
21. Ibid.

In the *reified* world of capital's project and operations, labour acquires an active form of subjectivity and capital makes it its main goal to place this at the service of its drive for accumulation. As I highlighted earlier, the weaker division between *development and execution* brings the active dimension of labour to the fore, since its sphere of subjectivity is urged towards *involvement* with the firm's goals and its process of value-creation.

It is, however, the construction of an *inauthentic* subjectivity, as in Tertulian's clear formulation,[22] because the dimension of subjectivity present in this labour-process is hindered and directed toward the valorisation and self-reproduction of capital, toward 'quality' and toward 'customer-service', among many forms of ideological, valorative or symbolic representations that capital introduces into the productive process. Worker-subjectivity has to transcend the sphere of *execution*, in order to not just produce but think on a daily basis of what is best for the company and its goals. Even within work with a greater intellectual, immaterial significance, the exercise of subjective activity is *constrained* in the last instance by the logic of the *commodity-form and its realisation.*

In the interpretation that I am proposing, the new dimensions and forms of labour entail a greater extension and complexity of working activities, of which the growth of immaterial labour is an example. *Material* and *immaterial* labour, in the increasing overlap that exists between them, are, however, subordinated to the logic of commodity-production and of capital. In the sphere of the extension of intellectual activity within production:

> the value form of labour itself is transformed. It increasingly assumes the value form of abstract/intellectual labour. The intellectual labour-force produced inside and outside of production is absorbed as commodity by capital that incorporates it to give new qualities to dead labour: flexibility, rapid displacement and constant self-transformation. Material production and production of services increasingly require innovations, becoming as a result more and more subordinated to an increasing production of knowledge that is converted into commodities and capital.[23]

In this context, the intellectual labour that participates in the process of value-creation is also trapped inside the realm of commodity-fetishism. It is illusory to believe that it is intellectual work that possesses meaning and self-determination: it is firstly *intellectual/abstract labour.* As Vincent goes on

---

22. Tertulian 1993, p. 442. This is a concept I shall return to in the chapter dedicated to Lukács and Habermas.
23. Vincent 1993, p. 121.

to explain, a reflexive dimension, aimed at authentic knowledge and understanding, 'i.e. all that is far from generalised commodification, the repetitive
reproduction of social relations, the obstinate operation of social automatisms,
is implicitly outlawed. It is not important to know where we are going, or to
question whether we are heading for self-destruction: for capital, producing
is enough.'[24] And perhaps one could say that the expenditure of physical
energy of the workforce is being transformed, *at least in those sectors with
more technologically advanced production-processes*, into expenditure of intellectual capacities.[25]

In order to discuss the centrality of labour today, I offer a reworking of the
meaning of *immaterial* forms of labour. It should be understood as an expression of the *constituent* force of *living labour*, both in its manifestation as *material* labour – in my view, still *strongly prevalent* when we consider the *global*
production-system – as well as in its manifestation as *immaterial* labour, which
is *not dominant today but which is becoming an increasingly present trend at the
cutting edge of production*.

Contrary to Habermas's formulation – which I shall outline in the next
chapter – the power of immaterial labour neither confers centrality to the
sphere of communication nor releases it from the instrumental sphere of the
system. *Immaterial* labour, even when it is closer to the sphere of circulation,
interacts with the productive world of *material* labour and is imprisoned by
the system of social metabolism of capital. My analysis not only rejects the *disjunction* between *material* and *immaterial*, it also strongly refutes, as discussed
below, the *binary and dualist disjunction* between 'system' and 'lifeworld', as it
appears in Habermas's analysis.

Thus, the reflection on living labour and its importance today should revisit
the discussion on immaterial labour *as a trend in the productive world of the
modern capitalist firm* that interacts with forms of material labour. This interpretation is decisive for an accurate understanding of the productive world.
We agree therefore with Toni Negri and Michael Hardt when they observe
that 'attempts to replace the law of value as the constitutive element of the
social fabric, for monetary, symbolic and political horizons, occasionally

24. Vincent 1993, p. 123.
25. Vincent 1993, p. 124. The attempt to reclaim the Marxian idea of the 'general
intellect' (*Grundrisse*) is worth mentioning to think about the increasing importance
of intellectual labour within capitalist production, of a general intelligence present in
the productive process, or even, of interrelations between immediate and mediated
forms of labour (given by science) in the contemporary world. See Vincent 1993, pp.
122ff. and Tosel 1995, pp. 212ff.

manage to exclude labour from the sphere of theory, but cannot, exclude it from the reality'.[26]

Contemporary forms of estrangement

Whether as a result of *manual* or *immaterial* labour, because both are controlled by the system of social metabolism of capital, *labour-estrangement* [*Entfremdung*] is in its essence preserved. Although phenomenally minimised by the reduction in the separation between development and execution, by the reduction of hierarchy within firms, the subjectivity that arises within the factory or in contemporary productive spheres is the expression of an *inauthentic* and estranged *existence*. With greater 'participation' in quality-control circle projects, with greater 'involvement' of workers, the subjectivity that thus emerges is *estranged* from *what is produced and for whom it is produced.*

The benefits that workers apparently receive during the labour-process are greatly outweighed by capital, since the workers *always have to prioritise the intrinsic objectives of the company, which are often masked by the need to meet the requirements of the consumer-market. But since consumption is a structural part of the productive system of capital, it is obvious that to defend the customer and his or her satisfaction is the necessary condition of preserving the company itself.* More complex still is the appearance of more freedom in the productive space but, as a counterpart, the fact that the *personifications of labour* must become even more *personifications of capital.* If not, if they fail to show these aptitudes ('willingness', 'proactivity' and 'desire'), the workers can be replaced by others who demonstrate the 'profile' and 'attributes' to accept these 'new challenges'.

In this phase of capital, characterised by *structural unemployment* and the erosion and precarisation of working conditions, we witness a materiality that is adverse to workers, a social terrain that places even greater *constraint* on the development of an authentic subjectivity. Multiple fetishisms and reifications pollute and permeate the world of labour with enormous repercussions in life *outside of work*, in the sphere of social reproduction, where the consumption of commodities, material or immaterial, is also to a large extent structured by capital. From increasingly *privatised public* services, to tourism where 'free time' equates with consumption in shopping malls, the evidence of the *domination of capital outside of work* is everywhere apparent. An even stronger example is that of the increasing need to be *better qualified and prepared* in order to find work. An increasingly large part of workers' 'free time' is

---

26. Negri and Hardt 1998–9, pp. 6–7.

spent improving their 'employability', a word that capital has used to transfer onto the worker the requirement for qualifications, something that used to be largely provided by capital.[27]

Besides worker-*knowledge*, which Fordism expropriated and transferred to the sphere of scientific management and development, the new phase of capital, of which Toyotism is the best example, transfers *know-how* back to labour, but with a view to appropriating its *intellectual* dimension, its cognitive capacities and *attempting* to involve the workers' subjectivity more intensely. Teamwork, quality-control circles, the suggestions from the shop-floor, are collected and appropriated by capital in this phase of productive restructuring. Workers' ideas are absorbed by the company after they have been analysed and proved to be viable and to the benefit (profit) of capital. The process goes further, however, since a part of the *intellectual knowledge* is transferred to the computerised machinery, which becomes *more intelligent, reproducing part of the activities transferred to it by the intellectual know-how of labour.*

Since a machine cannot replace human labour, it requires a greater *interaction* between the subjectivity that labours and the new intelligent machinery. *And, in this process,* the interactive involvement *increases* the *estrangement of labour*, the modern forms of *reification*, to an even greater degree, further distancing the subjectivity of the exercise of an authentic, self-determined everyday life. Despite the appearance of a milder form of despotism, the commodity-producing society makes the condition of *estrangement* of worker-subjectivity even deeper and more internalised.

In his discussion of the different ways to understand estrangement (or alienation), John Holloway argues:

> If humanity is defined by activity – a basic presupposition for Marx – then alienation means that humanity exists in the form of inhumanity, that human subjects exist as objects. Alienation is the objectification of the subject. The subject alienates her or his subjectivity, and the subjectivity is appropriated by an other.... At the same time as the subject is transformed into an object, the object which the subject produces, capital, is transformed into the subject of society. The objectification of the subject implies the subjectification of the object.[28]

But alienation, understood as a contradictory expression under capitalism, as a process, is also the expression of struggle and resistance.[29]

---

27. See Bernardo 1996.
28. Holloway 1997, p. 146.
29. Holloway 1997, p. 147.

As alienation is 'the production of capital by the worker' it should be understood 'as activity, always in dispute.... In other words, alienation is the struggle of capital to survive, the struggle of capital to subordinate labour, ...capital's unceasing struggle for power. Alienation is not an aspect of class struggle: it is the struggle of capital to exist.'[30] The process of alienation is therefore experienced daily by labour; the struggle against alienation is inseparable from this process, the 'unceasing rebellion of activity against passivity, of doing against suffering'.[31] It is the expression of the revolt of activity against its *estranged* condition.

If *estrangement* persists and becomes even more complex at the cutting edge of the production-cycle, in the apparently more 'stable' and integrated part of the workforce that performs *abstract intellectual labour*, the reality is even more extreme amongst the precarious workforce, those most deprived of rights and who, on a daily basis, experience the instability of part-time and temporary work.

Ramtin describes the *estrangement* (alienation) among this segment of the working class:

> For the permanently unemployed and unemployable the reality of alienation means not only the extension of powerlessness to its upmost limits, but the greater intensification of spiritual and physical *dehumanization*.... A vital aspect of alienation is that the fact of powerlessness is based on, and a condition of, social integration through work. If that form of social integration is being increasingly impaired by the advance of technology, then the social order begins to show clear signs of instability and crisis, leading gradually towards general social disintegration.[32]

Under the condition of absolute separation of labour, alienation *loses its unity*: *labour- and leisure-time, means and ends, public and private life*, among other forms of disjunction of the elements of unity present in the *society of labour*.

In this way, the forms of alienation of those at the fringes of the labour-process grow. In the words of the author once again, 'In opposition to interpretations of technological transformation as a movement towards a golden age of prosperous, harmonious, sanitized capitalism' we 'have in fact a historical process of disintegration, a movement towards the disunity of opposites...towards increasing antagonism, deepening contradictions and incoherence. The more

---

30. Holloway 1997, p. 148.
31. Ibid.
32. Ramtin 1997, p. 248.

the technological system of automation advances, the more alienation tends towards its absolute limits.'[33]

When we think of the vast numbers of *unemployed*, there are multiple forms of *absolutisation* of alienation. They vary, according to the author, from the rejection of social life, isolation, apathy and silence (of the majority) to violence and direct aggression. The points of contradiction between the unemployed and society as a whole increase, between the 'rationality' of the productive sphere and 'irrationality' in the societal sphere. Conflicts become a social problem, rather than an issue of business, transcending the factory-space and entering the public and social sphere. From the riots in Los Angeles, in 1992, to the unrest amongst France's unemployed that has been growing since the beginning of 1997, many expressions of revolt against *estrangement* were led by those expelled from work and who as a result were deprived of a meaningful life. This segregative dehumanisation leads, again according to the author, to individual isolation, to crime, to the formation of ghettos of excluded groups, to more ostentatious social explosions that, however, 'cannot be looked at merely in terms of social cohesion, of society as such, in isolation from the contradictions of the capitalist form of production (that is, value and surplus-value production and so on)'.[34]

At the more intellectual pole of the working class – those who exercise *abstract intellectual labour* – forms of reification are more complex (more *'humanised' in their dehumanising essence*) owing to the new forms of 'engagement' and interaction between living labour and computerised machinery. In the strata most affected by precariousness/exclusion from labour, reification is *directly* more dehumanised and brutalised. This makes up the contemporary picture of *estrangement* in the world of capital, differentiated in its impacts, but affecting the entire class-that-lives-from-labour.

I have sought to show above how the relations between *productive and unproductive* labour, *manual and intellectual* labour, *material and immaterial* labour, as well as the *sexual division of labour*, amongst other elements discussed, allow us to reposition and give concrete form to the thesis of the centrality (and transversality) of the category *labour* in modern society.

I can therefore state that, instead of the replacement of labour by science, or the replacement of the production of exchange-values for communication, or the substitution of production by information, what is taking place in the contemporary world is the greater *interrelation*, the greater *interpenetration*,

---

33. Ramtin 1997, pp. 248–9.
34. Ramtin 1997, p. 250.

between productive and unproductive activities, between manufacturing and services, between performative acts of labour and conception, between production and scientific knowledge, that is rapidly growing in the world of capital and its productive system.

I can now discuss the analytical connections between *labour and interaction*, between *working practice and interactive or intersubjective practice*, which have decisive analytic ramifications when we consider the centrality of labour to contemporary sociability. This brings us to the debate between Habermas and Lukács.

Chapter Eight

Excursus on the Centrality of Labour: the Debate between Lukács and Habermas

In these final chapters, I discuss the more *theoretical* aspects that constitute the core of the category *labour*. I begin with a discussion of the points of analytical divergence between Lukács's and Habermas's respective theses, and consider the connections between *labouring* and *interactive or intersubjective practice*, between *labour* and *interaction*. My aim is to discover the connections that exist between these levels of social practice and their founding ontological elements.

The centrality of labour in Lukács's *Ontology of Social Being*

I begin with the following question: why does the category *labour* have a position of centrality in Lukács's *Ontology*?[1]

When we begin with an ontological perspective, 'the answer is more simple than it might appear at first sight. It is because all other categories of this

---

1. For our purposes, I shall focus on Lukács's theorisation on the founding ontological character of labour, in order to offer elements for a critique of Habermas's thesis. Lukács's last publication was posthumous and incomplete at the time of his death and this is apparent in many of the passages. I prefer, in the passages that follow, to maintain this characteristic of Lukács's last work. For the purposes of this text, I use the English *edition The Ontology of Social Being: Labour* (1980), translated by David Fernbach. On occasion, I make use of the Italian edition (Lukács 1981), translated by Alberto Scarponi. General introductions to *The Ontology of Social Being* as a whole can be found in Tertulian 1990 and Scarponi 1976.

form of being are already by nature purely social in character; their properties and modes of efficacy develop only in a social being that is already constituted'. And the author goes on:

> Only with labour does its ontological nature give it a pronounced transition character. It is by its very nature a relationship of interchange between man (society) and nature, and moreover with inorganic nature…as well as organic, and…it characterises above all the transition in the working man himself from purely biological being to social being…. All those determinations which we shall see make up the essence of what is new in social being, are contained *in nuce* in labour. Thus labour can be viewed as the original phenomenon as the model for social being.[2]

Although their first appearance is simultaneous with that of labour, *social life, the first division of labour, language*, etc. find their origin in labour. Labour is constituted as the *intermediary category* that allows the ontological leap from pre-human forms to the social being. It is at the *heart of the process of humanity's humanisation*.[3] In order to understand its essence, we need to see it as both moment of *teleological positing* and *model* of social practice. We can begin with the connections between *labour* and *teleology*.

Labour and teleology

In searching for the production and reproduction of social life through labour and the struggle for existence, the social being creates and renews the very conditions for its reproduction. Labour is, therefore, the result of a *teleological positing* (previously) devised in the consciousness of the social being, a phenomenon that is not present, in essence, in the biological being of other animals. The Marxist distinction between the bee and the architect is well known. Through her capacity of prior ideation, the architect is able to mould an object according to the form she prefers, which is teleologically conceived and impossible for the bee.

Thus, the key ontological category present in the labour-process is announced:

> Through labour, a teleological positing is realised within material being, as the rise of a new objectivity. The first consequence of this is that labour becomes the model for any social practice, …[its] original form as far as being

---

2. Lukács 1980, pp. iv–v.
3. Lukács 1980, pp. v and 1.

is concerned. The simple fact that labour is the realisation of a teleological positing is for everyone an elementary experience of everyday life.[4]

For this reason, Lukács adds, thinkers like Aristotle and Hegel perceived the *teleological character of labour* in all its glory. The problem arises when they elevated teleology to a level that went beyond the sphere of social practice, and transformed it into a universal, cosmological category. In Hegel, for example, teleology became the 'engine of history'.[5]

For Marx, contrary to Aristotle and Hegel, labour is not understood as one of the diverse phenomenological forms of teleology in general, but as the *only point* where the teleological positing can be ontologically proven as an effective moment of material reality. 'We do have to repeat the definition Marx gave to see that all labour would be impossible if it were not preceded by a positing of this kind, one that determined its process at every step.'[6] This allows Lukács to state, 'We can only reasonably speak of social being when we understand that its genesis, its elevation from its basis and its acquisition of autonomy, is based on labour, i.e. on the ongoing realisation of teleological positings.'[7]

Lukács referred to Aristotle in order to understand clearly the complex relations between *teleology* and *causality* with *labour* as the starting point. *Teleology* is present in the very establishment of goals. *Causality* is given by the material reality, by the movement that develops from its bases, even though the teleological act is the trigger. Aristotle distinguishes two components of labour: *thinking* and *producing*. The first, *thinking*, identifies the goal and conceives of the means to accomplish it; the second, *production*, concretely realises the intended goal.

Nicolai Hartmann analytically separates the *first component* (*thinking*) into two acts, giving greater strength to Aristotle's formulation: 1) the *positing of the goal* and 2) *the investigation of the means*. Both are fundamental to understanding the labour-process, particularly in the *ontology of social being*. We can see the *inseparable connection* between teleology and causality, *in themselves* antithetical and, when treated abstractly, mutually exclusive. For *labour*, however, we can see a relation of reciprocity and interaction between teleology and causality.[8]

This relation of reciprocity between teleology and causality derives from the material realisation of a *posited ideality: a previously conceived goal transforms*

---

4. Lukács 1980, p. 3.
5. Lukács 1980, pp. 4–6.
6. Lukács 1980, pp. 8–9.
7. Lukács 1980, p. 9.
8. Lukács 1980, pp. 10–11.

material reality, introducing something qualitatively and radically new in relation to nature. It becomes an activity that is posited.[9] 'Nature and labour, means and end, thus produce something that is in itself homogeneous: the labour process, and finally the product of labour.'[10] Naturally, the search for a purpose, for a teleological positing, is the result of a *human and social need*, but 'in order for it to be a genuine positing of a goal, investigation of the means, i.e. knowledge of nature, must have reached a certain appropriate level; if it has not, then the positing of this goal remains merely a utopian project, a kind of dream, as did flying, for example, from Icarus through to Leonardo and far beyond him'.[11]

Thus, when compared with previous organic and inorganic forms of being, *labour*, in the ontology of being, is a *qualitatively new category*. The teleological act is its key constitutive element 'that founds, for the first time, the specificity of social being'.[12] With labour, the continual realisation of needs, the search for production and reproduction of social life, the consciousness of the social being ceases to be epiphenomenal, unlike animal consciousness that, *ultimately*, remains in the universe of biological reproduction. Human consciousness ceases therefore to be a mere adaptation to the environment and becomes a *self-governing activity* and, in doing so, ceases to be a mere epiphenomenon of biological reproduction.[13] The active and productive side of social being 'makes itself apparent with the positing of the goal of labour'.[14]

Labour, however, 'is not a once only act of decision, but rather a process, a continuous temporal chain of even new alternatives'.[15] This makes it possible for Lukács to state that the development of labour, the pursuit of alternatives present in human practice, rests firmly on choices between alternatives. 'The overcoming of animality by the leap to humanization in labour, the overcoming of the epiphenomenal consciousness determined merely by biology, thus acquires, through the development of labour, a tendency towards a prevalent universality.'[16]

We find here, therefore, 'the ontological genesis of freedom which appears for the first time in reality in the alternative within the labour process.... If we conceive labour in its essential original nature – as the producer of use-values – as an "eternal" form that persists through the change in social

9. Lukács 1980, p. 10.
10. Lukács 1980, p. 13.
11. Lukács 1980, p. 14.
12. Lukács 1980, p. 20.
13. Lukács 1980, pp. 21–2.
14. Lukács 1980, p. 31.
15. Lukács 1980, p. 32.
16. Lukács 1980, p. 35.

formations, i.e. the metabolism between man (society) and nature, it is then clear that the intention that defines the character of the alternative is directed towards a change in natural objects, even though it is induced by social needs'.[17]

Thus, labour is the mediating element between the sphere of necessity and its realisation: it is 'a victory of conscious behaviour over the mere spontaneity of biological instinct when labour intervenes as a mediation between the need and its immediate satisfaction'.[18] In this process of human self-realisation, the progress of the sentient being beyond mere instinct and nature, *labour is configured as the founding ontological reference of social practice*. It is this point that I shall consider below.

Labour as the model of social practice

Labour, understood in its most *general* and *abstract* sense, as producer of *use-values*, is the expression of a metabolic relation between social being and nature. In its basic and limited sense, it is through the act of labour that natural objects are transformed into useful things. Later, within the more developed forms of social practice, parallel to this human-nature relation, interrelations with other social beings develop that are also aimed at the production of use-values. Here, we have the emergence of *interactive social practice*, whose objective is *to convince other social beings to realise a specific teleological act*. This is because the *foundation of intersubjective teleological positing is aimed at action between social beings*.

As Lukács argues, 'The problem arises as soon as labour has become sufficiently social that it depends on co-operation between several people; independent, this time, of whether the problem of exchange-value has already arisen or whether the co-operation is orientated simply to use-value production.'[19] The second form of teleological positing, of the interactive sphere, seeks to act teleologically upon other social beings, something which already occurred in more rudimentary social stages, as in for example the practice of hunting in the Palaeolithic period.[20] In these forms of social practice, the teleological positing is not given by the direct relation with nature, *but it acts and interacts along with other social beings, with a view to realising specific teleological positings*.

These *secondary teleological positings*, with the aim of interrelating with social beings and convincing them, are characterised as more developed and

---

17. Lukács 1980, p. 39.
18. Lukács 1980, p. 41.
19. Lukács 1980, p. 47.
20. Ibid.

increasingly *complex* expressions of social practice, maintaining, as a result, a *greater distance from labour compared to the primary teleological positings*.

At this stage we encounter a problem with language:

> If we want to understand correctly the genesis of these very complicated and intricate interactions, both in their initial rise and in their further development, we must proceed from the fact that everywhere that genuine changes of being take place, the total connection of the complex involved has primacy over its elements.... For word and concept, speech and conceptual thought belong together as elements of a complex, the complex of social being, and they can only be grasped in their true nature in the context of an ontological analysis of social being, by knowledge of the real functions that they fulfill within this complex. Naturally, of course, there is a predominant moment in any such system of interrelations within a complex of being, as indeed in any interaction.... A genetic derivation of speech or conceptual thought from labour is certainly possible, since the execution of the labour process poses demands on the subject involved that can only be fulfilled simultaneously by the reconstruction of the psychophysical abilities and possibilities that were already present into language and conceptual thought, whereas this cannot be understood ontologically without the antecedent requirements of labour, or even the conditions that gave rise to the genesis of the labour process.[21]

With the arrival of speech and conceptual thinking, 'their development must be an incessant and insoluble interaction; the fact that labour continues to perform the predominant moment in no way removes the permanent character of such interaction, but on the contrary, strengthens and intensifies it. It necessarily follows from this that within a complex of this kind, there must be a continuous influence of labour on speech and conceptual thought, and vice versa'.[22]

With the development of more complex forms of social practice – *interactive actions* – these assume a position of superiority over the lower levels, despite the latter remaining the basis for the existence of the former. It is in exactly this sense that Lukács defines them as *secondary*-teleological positings, in relation to the *original* meaning of labour, of the *primary-teleological positings* that have a founding ontological status. The *autonomy* of the teleological positings is thus *relative* to their original structure. The relations between science, theory and labour offer an example: even when science and theory reach the

---

21. Lukács 1980, p. 49.
22. Lukács 1980, p. 50.

maximum-degree of development, of *self-acting* and autonomy in relation to labour, they cannot extricate themselves entirely from their origin, *they cannot entirely abandon their tie to their original base*.[23] However complex and sophisticated, science and theory maintain their ties to the human satisfaction of needs (which are, as we have seen, tied to the dominant system of social metabolism). A relation of attachment to and autonomy from the original base is created.[24] Through labour, an authentic relationship between teleology and causality is established in which the former alters the configuration of the latter and vice versa.

Labour, therefore, is the fundamental, simplest and most elementary form of those complexes whose dynamic interaction is constituted in the specificity of social being. 'Precisely for this reason, it is necessary to point out time and again that the specific features of labour should not be transposed directly to the more complicated forms of social practice.... [L]abour itself materially realises the radically new relationship of metabolism with nature, whereas the overwhelming majority of other more complicated forms of social practice have this metabolism with nature, the basis of man's reproduction in society, as their insuperable precondition.'[25] The more advanced forms of social practice have their original base in the act of labour. However complex, differentiated and distant, they represent an *extension* of and an *advance* on the primary teleological positions, but not an *entirely* autonomous or detached sphere.

In Lukács's words, 'The self-elevation of the earlier forms, the autochthonous character that social being acquires, is precisely expressed in this supremacy of those categories in which the new and more highly developed character of this type of being gains expression as against those on which it is founded.'[26] In the secondary-teleological positings, subjectivity acquires a qualitatively different meaning, in addition to greater complexity. The self-control that emerges initially from labour, in the growing domination over the sphere of biology and spontaneity, refers to the objectivity of this process. There is a new form of interrelation between subjectivity and objectivity, between teleology and causality, within the human and social means of need-fulfilment. Thus, it 'would be as misguided to attempt to derive the more complicated forms of the "ought" from the "ought" in the labour process, by logic for example, as the dualism of their opposition is a false idealist philosophy'.[27]

---

23. Lukács 1980, p. 52.
24. Ibid.
25. Lukács 1980, p. 59.
26. Lukács 1980, p. 67.
27. Lukács 1980, p. 74.

Lukács thus shows how, besides *understanding* the ontological role of labour, the key is also to *grasp* its function in the constitution of social being, a being endowed with autonomy and therefore entirely different from earlier forms of being.[28]

> Hegel, in analysing the act of labour itself, stressed the tool as a moment that is of lasting effect for social development, a mediating category of decisive importance, as the result of which the individual act of labour goes beyond its individuality and is itself erected into a moment of social continuity. Hegel thus provides a first indication of how the act of labour can become a moment of social reproduction. Marx, on the other hand, considers the economic process in its developed and dynamic totality and, in this totality, man must appear as both beginning and end, as initiator and as end-product of the overall process [for] he still composes the real essence of the process.[29]

Labour has, therefore, whether in its *genesis*, in its *development*, or in its being and in its becoming, an ontological intent toward the process of *humanisation of man in its widest sense*. The emergence of more complex forms of human life – the *secondary*-teleological positions that are constituted by moments of interaction between social beings, of which *political practice, religion, ethics, philosophy, art, etc.* are all examples, and that enjoy greater autonomy compared to the *primary*-teleological positions – has its *ontological-genetic* foundations in labour. Rather than *discontinuity and rupture* with labour, they are constituted by a *greater distancing and a more complex extension* (and not just derivation) from labour. However, these more advanced levels of sociability find their *origin* in labour, in the metabolic exchange between social being and nature.[30]

This distance also exists within labour itself. For example, even in the simplest forms of labour there is the beginning of a new form of dialectic between means and ends, between immediacy and mediation, because the satisfaction of needs obtained through labour is a *satisfaction achieved by mediation*. Although cooking or roasting meat is a form of *mediation*, eating it cooked or roasted is something *immediate*. This relationship becomes more complex with the subsequent development of labour, which incorporates a series of mediations between social beings and the immediate ends being pursued. In this process, from its origin, we can notice a differentiation between *mediated and immediate* ends. The expansion of acts of labour brings with it new

28. Lukács 1980, p. 77.
29. Lukács 1980, p. 86.
30. Lukács 1980, p. 99.

elements that, however, do not alter the differentiation present in the act of labour between *mediated and unmediated, mediation and immediacy.*[31]

There is therefore, through labour, a process that simultaneously alters nature and transforms the very being that labours. Human nature also undergoes a metamorphosis as a result of the labour-process, given the existence of a teleological positing and a practical realisation. In Lukács's words:

> the central question of the internal transformation of man consists in his attaining a conscious control over himself. Not only does the goal exist in consciousness before its material realization; this dynamic structure of labour also extends to each individual movement. Labouring man must plan every moment in advance and permanently check the realization of his plans, critically and consciously, if he is to achieve in his labour the concrete optimal result. This mastery of the human body by consciousness, which also affects a portion of the sphere of consciousness itself, i.e. habits, instincts, emotions, etc., is a basic requirement of even the most primitive labour and must therefore give a decisive stamp to the ideas that men forms of themselves.[32]

In the new social being that emerges human consciousness ceases to be a biological epiphenomenon and is constituted as an active and essential component of everyday life. Consciousness is an objective ontological fact.[33] And the search for a meaningful authentic life finds in labour the *primary locus* for its realisation. The very search for a meaningful life is socially undertaken by social beings for their individual and collective self-actualisation. It is a genuinely human category that is not otherwise present in nature.

> Life, birth and death as phenomena of natural life are devoid of meaning.... It is only when man in society seeks a meaning for his life that the failure of this attempt brings in its wake the antithesis of meaninglessness. At the beginning of his life, this particular effect still appears simply in a spontaneous and purely social form. It is only when society becomes so differentiated that a man can individually shape his life in a meaningful way or else surrender it to meaninglessness, that this problem arises as a general one.[34]

---

31. Lukács 1980, pp. 101–2.
32. Lukács 1980, p. 103.
33. Ibid.
34. Lukács 1980, p. 108. Lukács makes many insightful observations about death, the 'soul', dreaming.

To say that a meaningful life finds within the sphere of labour *its first moment of realisation is completely different from saying that a meaningful life is summed up exclusively in labour, which would be completely absurd.* In the search for a meaningful life, *art, poetry, painting, literature, music, the moment of creation, free time,* have a special significance. If labour is *self-determined, autonomous and free,* and therefore *endowed with meaning,* it will be through *art, poetry, painting, literature, music, the autonomous use of free time and freedom* that a social being can be humanised and emancipated in the deepest sense. This, however, leads us to think of the deeper connections that exist between labour and freedom.

Labour and freedom

The search for a meaningful life starting from labour can allow us to explore the connections that exist between labour and freedom. Lukács observes, 'How fundamental labour is for the humanisation of man is also shown in the fact that its ontological constitution forms the genetic point of departure for yet another question of life that has deeply affected men over the entire course of their history, the question of freedom.'[35]

> In a first approximation, we can say that freedom is the act of consciousness which...consists in a concrete decision between different concrete possibilities. If the question of choice is taken to a higher level of abstraction, then it is completely divorced from the concrete, and thus loses all connection with reality, becoming an empty speculation. In the second place, freedom is ultimately a desire to alter reality (which of course includes in certain circumstances the desire to maintain a given situation).[36]

Under certain existing causal nexuses, the decision contains an intrinsic and real moment of freedom:

> It is easy to see how everyday life, above all, poses perpetual alternatives which emerge unexpectedly and must often be responded to immediately at the risk of destruction. In these cases it pertains to the essential character of the alternative that its decision has to be made in ignorance of the majority of components of the situation and its consequences. But even here there is a minimum of freedom in the decision; here too, there is still an alternative, even if, as a marginal case, and not just as a natural event determined by a purely spontaneous causality.[37]

---

35. Lukács 1980, pp. 112–13.
36. Lukács 1980, p. 114.
37. Lukács 1980, p. 116.

In fact, when we conceive of work in its most *simple and abstract* meaning,[38] as creator of use-values, every act of labour has its own teleological positing as a trigger. Without the teleological act, no work (understood as a response to daily life and its vicissitudes) would be possible. The subjectivity that formulates alternatives in the social metabolism between social beings and nature does so 'determined simply by his needs and his knowledge of the natural properties of his object'.[39]

Clearly, again according to Lukács, the content of freedom is essentially distinct in the more advanced and complex forms. The greater the knowledge of the existing and operating causal chains, the more appropriately that knowledge can be transformed into *posited causal chains* and the greater the power of subjects over it, or in other words, the greater the sphere of freedom.[40] The teleological act, expressed through the existence of purpose, is therefore an intrinsic manifestation of freedom within the labour-process. It is the moment of interaction between subjectivity and objectivity, causality and teleology, necessity and freedom.

Thus, for Lukács, the origin of the complex that forms the basis of social being, its *model*, is to be found in the sphere of labour. As shown above, this original structure, created from the act of labour, undergoes fundamental changes when the teleological positings are no longer aimed at the metabolic relation between humankind and nature but at the interactive practice between social beings themselves, to influence their decisions and actions. Faced with this 'second nature', the distances that separate these structures of interaction from those that lead directly to labour are certainly significant. But they were already present in embryo in the most simple social manifestations, to the extent that, rather than talking of dislocation and separation between the different spheres of social being, rather than treating them dualistically, we should instead see a relation of *prolonging and distancing* between labour and the most complex forms of interactive social practice. Through labour, the social being creates himself or herself as a part of humankind: through the process of self-activity and self-control, social being leaps from his or her natural origin based on instincts towards the production and reproduction of himself or herself as a member of *humankind*, endowed with conscious self-control, indispensable on the path to the realisation of freedom.

In Lukács's words, 'If the freedom won in the original labour was necessarily still rudimentary and restricted, this in no way alters the fact that the

38. Marx 1967, vol. 1, pp. 183–4.
39. Ibid.
40. Lukács 1980, pp. 116–17.

most spiritual and highest freedom must be fought for with the same methods as in the original labour',[41] that is, by the domination of the individual action of humankind over nature. It is in precisely this sense that labour can be considered the *model for all freedom*. And the spheres of interactive social practice become the *complex* (and not purely derivative) prolongation of the act of labour.

For this reason, Lukács writes of *primary*-teleological positings, which refer directly to labour and to interaction with nature, and of *secondary*-teleological positings (such as art, literature, philosophy, religion, politics, etc.), which are more *complex and developed than the first* because they assume *interaction between social beings, as interactive and intersubjective practice*, but are constituted as *complexes* that *originate from labour in its primary form*. They are *secondary*, therefore, not in terms of their importance, since the sphere of intersubjectivity is decisive and more complex in contemporary societies, *but in terms of their ontological-genetic* significance. Yet it is not possible to establish a binary, dualistic disjunction between them; rather, for Lukács, between *labour* (*founding* category) and *higher forms of interaction, interactive practice*, there are insoluble nexuses, however great the distances and complexities that arise between these spheres of social being.

This is not, however, a conventional or common understanding of these issues, and theses advocating the loss of centrality of labour have been growing over the last few decades. Amongst these is Habermas's sociophilosophical critique that I shall examine over the following sections.

Habermas's critique of the 'paradigm of labour'

In his analysis of contemporary society, Habermas argues that the *centrality of labour* has been replaced by the *centrality of the sphere of communication or of intersubjectivity*.[42] Without offering a *full reconstruction of his concept of communicative action* (given space-constraints), I shall explore some of the *central*

---

41. Lukács 1980, p. 136.
42. I referred above to the well-known formulation of the author on the prevalence of science as productive force that subordinates and reduces the role of labour in the process of value-creation. Further on in his critique, Habermas states that the development of a theory of communicative action is necessary for an adequate theorisation of social rationalisation, an endeavour that, according to the author, was largely abandoned after Weber (Habermas 1991, p. 7). With rationality being closely related to knowledge in the author's perspective, he adds, however, that 'rationality has less to do with the possession of knowledge than with how speaking and acting subjects *acquire and use knowledge*' (Habermas 1991, p. 8).

elements of Habermas's critique of the 'paradigm of labour'.[43] In order to obtain a general sense of his critique, I shall first offer some words of introduction.

The paradigm of communicative action and the sphere of intersubjectivity

I begin by stating that Habermas's *construct* relativises and diminishes the role of labour in the socialisation of social being, to the extent that in contemporary society it has been replaced by the sphere of *intersubjectivity*, which becomes the privileged moment of social activity. In the author's words:

> The domain of subjectivity is complementary to the external world which is defined by its being shared with others. The objective world is presupposed in common as the totality of facts.... And a social world is presupposed in common as the totality of all interpersonal relationships that are recognised by members as legitimate. Over against this, the subjective world counts as the totality of experiences to which in each instance, only one individual has privileged access.[44]

The categoral nucleus in which subjectivity is developed is given by the concept of *lifeworld*, 'the transcendental site where speaker and hearer meet, where they can reciprocally raise claims that their utterances fit the world (objective, social or subjective) and where they can criticise and confirm those validity claims, settle their disagreements and arrive at agreements. In a sentence: participants cannot assume *in actu* the same distance in relation to language and culture as in relation to the totality of facts, norms or experiences concerning which mutual understanding is possible'.[45]

The concept of lifeworld is analytically similar to the version found in phenomenology.[46] It is a complementary concept to that of communicative action. The latter is based on a co-operative process of interpretation in which participants are simultaneously related to something in the objective, social and subjective worlds, even when they *thematically emphasise only one* of these three components.[47] This co-operative process of interaction, which provides the basis of intersubjectivity, abides by the rule that the hearer recognises and confers validity upon those who speak: 'Consensus does not come about

---

43. I use the English edition *The Theory of Communicative Action* (1991 and 1992), two volumes, translated by Thomas McCarthy. An introduction to Habermas's work can be found in Outhwaite 1994.
44. Habermas 1991, p. 52.
45. Habermas 1992, p. 126.
46. Habermas 1992, p. 135.
47. Habermas 1992, pp. 119–20.

when, for example, a hearer accepts *the truth of an assertion*, but at the same time doubts the sincerity of the speaker or the normative appropriateness of the utterance.'[48] Recognition of the principle of alterity, of validity and understanding between social beings, through subjective interaction, the intersubjectivity that occurs in the lifeworld, assumes a position of centrality in human action. In Habermas's words, *the action-situation is the centre of the lifeworld*.[49]

In the concept of lifeworld, formulated in terms of the theory of communicative action, '[i]n the communicative practice of everyday life, persons do not only encounter one another in the attitude of participants: they also give narrative presentations of events that take place in the context of their lifeworld'.[50] The lifeworld, through the action situation, appears as a reservoir of unshaken and unquestioned convictions that are used by the participants in the communication-process in their interpretative processes of co-operation. Simple elements, therefore, are mobilised under the form of consensual knowledge only when they are relevant to the situation.[51]

The lifeworld's basic constitutive elements are, therefore, language and culture.[52]

> The symbolic structures of the lifeworld are reproduced by way of the continuation of valid knowledge, stabilisation of group solidarity and socialisation of responsible actors. The process of reproduction connects up new situations with the existing conditions of the lifeworld; it does this in the *semantic* dimension of meanings and contents (of the cultural tradition), as well as in the dimensions of *social space* (of socially integrated groups), and *historical time* (of successive generations). Corresponding to these processes of *cultural reproduction, social integration and socialisation* are the structural components of the lifeworld: culture, society, person.[53]

Further:

> I use the term *culture* for the stock of knowledge from which participants in communication supply themselves with interpretations as they come to an understanding about something in the world. I use the terms *society* for the legitimate orders through which participants regulate their memberships in social groups and thereby secure solidarity. By *personality* I understand the

---

48. Habermas 1992, p. 121.
49. Habermas 1992, pp. 119–20.
50. Habermas 1992, p. 136.
51. Habermas 1992, p. 124.
52. Habermas 1992, p. 125.
53. Habermas 1992, pp. 137–8.

competences that make a subject capable of speaking and acting, that put him in a position to take part in processes of reaching understanding and thereby to assert his own identity. The dimensions in which communicative action extends comprise the semantic field of symbolic contents, social space, and historical time. The interactions woven into the fabric of every communicative practice constitute the medium through which culture, society, and person get reproduced.[54]

Communicative actions are not simply 'processes of interpretation in which cultural knowledge is "tested against the world"; they are, at the same time, processes of social integration and socialization'.[55]

The uncoupling of system and lifeworld

The fundamental problem of social theory, according to Habermas, is that of satisfactorily articulating the two strategic categories of 'system' and 'lifeworld', in addition to the *uncoupling* or separation that occurs between them.[56] 'I understand social evolution as a second-order process of differentiation: system and lifeworld are differentiated in the sense that the complexity of the one and the rationality of the other grow. But it is not only qua system and qua lifeworld that they are differentiated; they get differentiated from one another at the same time'.[57] In the systemic analysis Habermas provides, the uncoupling between system and lifeworld is consolidated in the growing complexity of modern society and with the emergence of new levels of systemic differentiation, from which subsystems are formed.[58]

While the *system* includes economic and political spheres aimed at social reproduction, using money and power as means of control, the *lifeworld* is the locus of intersubjective space, where beings are organised in terms of their identities and the values that are born of the sphere of communication. Culture, society and subjectivity, mentioned above, find their universe in the lifeworld. The uncoupling of system and lifeworld can be understood only in so far as the transformations to relations between these are also understood.[59]

Power and money, means of control that developed inside the system, are superimposed upon the interactive system, the communicational sphere. An instrumentalisation and technologification of the lifeworld occurs. With the

---

54. Habermas 1992, p. 138.
55. Habermas 1992, p. 139.
56. Habermas 1992, pp. 151–3.
57. Habermas 1992, p. 153.
58. Habermas 1992, pp. 153–4.
59. Habermas 1992, p. 155.

increase of subsystems, fetishism, as described by Marx, invades and instrumentalises the lifeworld. Habermas characterises this as the *colonisation of the lifeworld*.[60] These phenomena are already constituted as effects of uncoupling between system and lifeworld. The rationalisation of the lifeworld makes social integration possible, through methods that *differ* from those present in the lifeworld, such as language.

For Habermas, capitalism and its modern state-apparatus are configured as *subsystems* that, through the means of money and power, can be distinguished from institutional power, i.e. from the social component of the lifeworld. In bourgeois society, *socially*-integrated areas of action, in relation to *systematically*-integrated areas of action – the economy and the state – assume the forms of private and public spheres, that stand in a complementary relation to one another.[61] 'From the perspective of the lifeworld, various social roles crystallize around these interchange relations: the roles of the employee and the consumer, on the one hand, and those of the client and the citizen of the state, on the other.'[62]

Labour-power undergoes a process of monetarisation and bureaucratisation: 'the capitalist mode of production and bureaucratic-legal domination can better fulfill the tasks of materially reproducing the lifeworld'.[63] The means of power and money can regulate exchange-relations between system and lifeworld only to the extent that the lifeworld adjusts itself, in a process of real abstraction, to the *inputs* that originate in the corresponding subsystem.[64]

As a result of constraints from the system, the instrumentalisation of the lifeworld leads to the reduction and adjustment of the cognitive-instrumental actions of communicative practice:

> In the communicative practices of everyday life, cognitive interpretations, moral expectations, expressions and valuations have to interpenetrate and form a rational interconnectedness via the transfer of validity that is possible in the performative attitude. This communicative infrastructure is threatened by two interlocking, mutually reinforcing tendencies: *systematically induced reification* and *cultural impoverishment*.... In the deformations of everyday practice, symptoms of rigidification combine with symptoms of desolation.[65]

---

60. Habermas 1992, p. 318.
61. Habermas 1992, pp. 318–19.
62. Habermas 1992, p. 319.
63. Habermas 1992, p. 321.
64. Habermas 1992, p. 323.
65. Habermas 1992, p. 327.

The result is both the unilateral rationalisation of everyday-communication, with a 'norm-free reality beyond the lifeworld', and the end of vital tra-ditions.[66] *Reification and desolation begin to increasingly threaten the lifeworld.* Cultural impoverishment in everyday-communicative practice results, there-fore, in the 'penetration of forms of economic and administrative rationality into areas of action that resist being converted over to the media of money and power because they are specialised in cultural transmission, social inte-gration and child rearing, and remain dependent on mutual understanding as a mechanism for co-ordinating action'.[67]

Habermas refers to this as the *colonisation of the lifeworld* where, 'stripped of their ideological veils', the imperatives of the autonomous subsystems invade the lifeworld from outside – *like colonial masters in a tribal society* – and force a process of assimilation upon them.[68] This occurred with the expansion of subsystems regulated by money and power that invade the lifeworld and colonise it, through monetarisation and bureaucratisation. This, in addition to the incorporation of Marx and Weber into his work,[69] constitutes the core of Habermas's critique of the Marxian theory of value in his *Theory of Communi-cative Action*, to which we will turn our attention in the following section.

The colonisation of the lifeworld and Habermas's critique of the theory of value

For Habermas, the *colonisation of the lifeworld* does not allow the unification, as for Marx, of *system* and *lifeworld* in a 'ruptured ethical totality whose abstractly divided moments are condemned to pass away'.[70] Marx 'does move at the two analytical levels of "system" and "lifeworld", but their separation

---

66. Ibid.
67. Habermas 1992, p. 330.
68. Habermas 1992, p. 355.
69. A whole array of authors is mentioned or assimilated by Habermas, more or less critically, such as Parsons, Mead, Lukács and Luhmann among others. However, although the original or the source of Weber's work is amply referred to throughout the work and especially in reference to his theory of modernity, the same procedure is not applied to Marx's work. Especially the section 'Marx and the Theory of Internal Colonization' where Habermas embarks on his criticism of Marx's theory of value, the original or the source is never cited. Reference to his work is always made via other interpretations, such as those of Claus Offe, Georg Lohmann, Lange, Brunkhurst, etc. While the abundant references to Weber are understandable given the weight and support he draws from Weber's theory to support his thesis, the procedure adopted in relation to Marx is strange, not for the scant reference to his works (although also understandable given that leaning on Marx for support for his theory of communi-cative action was not an option), but because of the near absence of any reference, original or secondary, to Marx's work, particularly in the section that refers to him, in clear contrast to the treatment given to Weber's work.
70. Habermas 1992, p. 339.

is not really presupposed in his basic economic concepts, which remain tied to Hegelian logic'.[71] For the author, Marx 'grasp[s] a totality comprising both moments at one blow'[72] according to a logic in which:

> an accumulation process that has broken away from orientations to use value literally amounts to an illusion – the capitalist system is nothing more than the ghostly form of class relations that have become perversely anonymous and fetishized. The systemic autonomy of the production process has the character of an enchantment. Marx is convinced a priori that in capital he has before him nothing more than the mystified form of a class relation.... Marx conceives of the capitalist class so strongly as a totality that he fails to recognize the intrinsic evolutionary value that media-steered subsystems possess. He does not see that the differentiation of the state apparatus and the economy also represents a higher level of system differentiation, which simultaneously opens up new steering possibilities and forces a re-organization of the old, feudal, class relationships.[73]

For Habermas, this mistake by Marx affects and marks his theory of revolution, in the measure in which he conceives of a 'future state' where 'the objective semblance of capital has dissolved and the lifeworld, which has been held captive under the dictates of the law of value, gets back its spontaneity'.[74] This alternative, realised by the industrial proletariat 'under the leadership of a theoretically enlightened avant-garde' must seize political power and revolutionise society. 'System and lifeworld appear in Marx under the metaphors of the "realm of necessity" and the "realm of freedom". The socialist revolution is to free the latter from the dictates of the former.'[75] The elimination of abstract labour, subsumed under the commodity-form, and its conversion into living labour, will create an intersubjectivity of associated producers, 'mobilised' by an 'avant-garde' able to *lead it to the triumph of the lifeworld over the system of deworlded labour-power.*[76]

---

71. Habermas 1992, p. 338.
72. Habermas 1992, p. 339.
73. Ibid.
74. Habermas 1992, p. 340.
75. Ibid.
76. Ibid. Before this critique of Lukács, Habermas makes the same critique of the 'theory of the enlightened avant-garde' (Habermas 1991, p. 364). Without entering into a critique of Habermas's thesis at this stage, it is important to say that there is a vast body of literature that shows that Lukács's argument in *History and Class Consciousness* draws heavily on Lenin's conception of the party. There is also a great deal of literature that subjects to critique the pure and simple identification of Lenin's (and the Lukács of *History and Class Consciousness*) and Marx's theses, which Habermas does without any reservation and in a way that caricatures their positions.

After defending Weber's prognosis against Marx's 'revolutionary expectations', Habermas adds that 'Marx's error stems in the end from dialectically clamping together system and lifeworld in a way that does not allow for a sufficiently sharp separation between the level of system differentiation attained in the modern period and the class specific forms in which it has been institutionalised. Marx did not withstand the temptation of Hegelian totality-thinking; he construed the unity of system and lifeworld dialectically as an "untrue whole".'[77]

This leads to a second weakness in Marx's theory of value, according to the author: 'Marx has no criteria by which to distinguish the destruction of traditional forms of life from the reification of post-traditional lifeworlds.' In addition, 'In Marx and the Marxist tradition the concept of "alienation" has been applied above all to the wage labourer's mode of existence.'[78] Habermas goes on to say that, in the Paris Manuscripts, Marx offered elements for a critique of alienated labour, albeit in a version that 'retained... the more strongly phenomenologically and anthropologically oriented versions of contemporary praxis philosophy'; but it is with the later development of the theory of value and the resulting predominance of abstract labour that 'the concept of alienation loses its determinacy.... Marx speaks in the abstract about life and life's possibilities; he has no concept of a rationalisation to which the lifeworld is subject to the extent that its symbolic structures get differentiated. Thus in the historical context of his investigations, the concept of alienation remains peculiarly ambiguous' since it does not allow the differentiation between 'the aspect of *reification* and that of *structural differentiation of the lifeworld*. For this, the concept of alienation is not sufficiently selective; the theory of value provides no concept of reification, enabling us to identify syndromes of alienation relative to the degree of rationalisation attained in a lifeworld.... In an extensively rationalised lifeworld, reification can be measured only against the conditions of communicative socialisation, and not against the nostalgically loaded, frequently romanticised past of pre-modern forms of life.'[79]

Habermas's third criticism of the *weaknesses* of Marx's theory of value concerns the 'over-generalisation of a specific case of the subsumption of the lifeworld under the system'.[80] Reification should not be confined to the sphere of social labour, since *it can manifest itself both in the public as well as the private realm, in both production and consumption*. By contrast, the theory of

---

77. Ibid.
78. Ibid.
79. Habermas 1991, pp. 341–2.
80. Habermas 1992, p. 342.

value justifies just one channel through which monetarisation of the labour-sphere takes place. In his words, 'Marx was unable to conceive the transformation of concrete into abstract labour as a special case of the systemically induced reification of social relations in general because he started from the model of the purposive actor, who, along with his products, is robbed of the possibility of developing his essential powers.'[81]

Having made these criticisms, the author concludes that Marx did not offer a satisfactory analysis of late capitalism: 'Marxian orthodoxy has a hard time explaining government interventionism, mass democracy and the welfare state. The economistic approach breaks down in the face of the pacification of class conflict and the long-term success of reformism in European countries since World War II, under the banner of a social-democratic program in the broader sense.'[82] Habermas further considers these points in the final pages of *The Theory of Communicative Action*.

It may be necessary to indicate two more aspects of Habermas's critique since they relate directly to the theme of our study. The question of the *pacification of class-conflict* and the connections the author offers between the *theory of value and the thesis of class-consciousness*.

The author considers the first of these questions in the following paragraph:

> [T]he legal institutionalisation of collective bargaining became the basis of a reform politics that has brought about a pacification of class conflict in the social-welfare state. the core of the matter is the legislation of rights and entitlements in the spheres of work and social welfare, making provision for the basic risks of the wage labourer's existence and compensating them for handicaps that arise from the structurally weaker market positions (of employees, tenants, consumers, etc.).[83]

In the chapter in which he outlines his critique of Lukács's concept of reification in *History and Class Consciousness*, Habermas refers to the power of integration of late capitalism:

> [D]evelopments in the United States showed in another way the integrating powers of capitalism: without open repression, mass culture bound the consciousness of the broad masses to the imperatives of the status quo. The Soviet Russian perversion of the humane content of revolutionary socialism, the collapse of the social revolutionary labour movement in all industrial

---

81. Ibid.
82. Habermas 1992, p. 343.
83. Habermas 1992, p. 347.

societies, and the socially integrative accomplishments of a rationalisation
that had penetrated into cultural reproduction.[84]

Under mass-democracy, state-interventionism and the welfare-state that
rapidly developed after World-War II, we find the constitutive elements of
late capitalism that, in Habermas's view, guarantee the pacification of social
conflicts.

This leads him to conclude that, in this conciliatory environment, Marx's
and Lukács's theory of reification 'is supplemented and supported by a
theory of class consciousness.... In the face of a class antagonism pacified by
means of welfare-state measures, however, and in the face of the growing ano-
nymity of class structures, the theory of class consciousness loses its empirical
reference. It no longer has application to a society in which we are increasingly unable to identify strictly class specific lifeworlds.'[85] This is because,
under late capitalism, the class-structure 'loses its historically palpable shape.
The unequal distribution of social rewards reflects a structure of privilege that
can no longer be traced back to class positions in any unqualified way'.[86]

I shall conclude this brief outline of Habermas's critique by saying that his
theory of communicative action 'is not a metatheory but the beginning of a
social theory' with the '"lifeworld" and "system" paradigms' as its central
categorical nuclei.[87] The former, *the lifeworld*, is limited to the sphere of *communicative action*, space of intersubjectivity and interaction *par excellence*. The
latter, the *system*, is predominantly governed by *instrumental reason*, where
the spheres of *labour*, the *economy* and *power* are structured. The disjunction
between these levels, which occurred with the increasing complexity of societies, leads the author to conclude that '[t]he utopian idea of a society based
on social labour has lost its persuasive power... [it] has lost its point of reference in reality'. This occurs because 'emancipated living conditions worthy
of human beings are no longer to emerge directly from the revolutionising
of labour conditions, that is, from the transformation of alienated labour into
self-directed activity'.[88] That is, for Habermas, centrality is transferred from
the sphere of labour to the sphere of communicative action, where the new
nucleus of the utopia is to be found.[89]

84. Habermas 1991, p. 367.
85. Habermas 1992, p. 352. See also Habermas 1991, p. 364.
86. Habermas 1992, p. 348.
87. Habermas 1991, pp. xli–ii.
88. Habermas 1989, pp. 53–4.
89. Habermas 1989, pp. 54 and 68. This conception appears most recently in Méda,
in the form of 'the disenchantment of labour', along the lines of Weber's 'disenchantment of the world'. Méda's proposal, that relativises and minimises the sphere of
labour in contemporary sociability, of the reduction of instrumental reason, is com-

A critical sketch of Habermas's critique

I shall conclude this rather abstract discussion on the centrality of labour with an attempt to question some aspects of Habermas's critique. For its relevance to our study, its intrinsic complexity and the space limitations of this text, I shall focus on the *separation* Habermas makes between *labour* and *interaction* or, using the terminology of *The Theory of Communicative Action*, between *system* and *lifeworld*. This theme is of particular relevance to our investigation. Clearly, we will be providing just a brief initial examination here, to be explored in more detail in further research.[90]

On the basis of the preliminary outline of Lukács's and Habermas's arguments, I understand that *interactive practice*, as a moment of expression of subjectivity, finds its ontological soil in the sphere of *labour*, where the *teleological act* is fully manifested for the first time. Although the sphere of language or communication is a key constitutive element of social being, I cannot agree with Habermas that the communicational sphere constitutes a founding and structuring element in the process of man's socialisation.

As I tried to indicate in my presentation of Lukács's thesis, I understand *labour* to be the *analytical key* to comprehend the more complex teleological positings, those that are no longer guided by the direct relation between humankind and nature, but by the one established between social beings themselves. Labour becomes a central, founding category, the *model of social being*, because it permits the *synthesis* between teleology and causality, from which social being originates. Labour, sociability and language constitute *complexes* that lead to the genesis of social being. As we saw above, labour enables for the first time in social being the advent of a teleological act by interacting with the sphere of causality. *In labour, the social being is revealed*

---

pensated by the increase of the public sphere, the exercise of a 'new citizenship', 'in the increase of social time dedicated to political activity', to the extent to which this is able to structure a social fabric based on autonomy and co-operation (Méda 1997, pp. 220–7). A critical account of the work of Habermas and Weber can be found in Löwy 1998. On important aspects of Habermas's work, see also 'Dossier: Habermas, Une politique délibérative' (*Actuel Marx*, 24, 1998).

90. For this reason, I cannot discuss many issues that could be explored, like the question of the Habermasian distinction between the public and private spheres, of the relation between the state and society, among many others, in which the divergence from Marxian (and Marxist) formulations is greatest. I am also not able to reproduce the critique that I outlined previously, on the relative reduction by Habermas (and also by many critics of the thesis of the centrality of labour) of the abstract and concrete dimensions of labour, a central aspect of the Marxian position. See Antunes 1995a, pp. 75–86, and also 'The Metamorphoses and Centrality of Labour Today', which is included as an appendix to this book.

as subjectivity (through the teleological act and search for goals) that creates and responds to the causal world.

Yet, if labour represents a key moment, language and sociability – fundamental complexes of social being – are intimately related to it, and, as moments of social practice, they cannot be separated from one another. When Habermas transcends and transfers subjectivity and the moment of intersubjectivity to the lifeworld, a distinct and separate universe from the system, the ontologically indissoluble link is broken in his analytical construction.

By introducing an essential analytical distinction between labour and inter-action, between the practice of labour and communicative action, between system and lifeworld, one loses the moment at which the interrelational articulation between teleology and causality, between the world of objectivity and subjectivity, takes place, a vital link in the understanding of social being.

As a result, what appears to be the most daring reformulation by Habermas of Marx's thesis also constitutes its greatest limitation. In Habermas's view, Marx reduces the communicational sphere to instrumental action.[91] In contrast, he overestimates and separates these decisive dimensions of social life, and the loss of this indissoluble bond allows Habermas to give value and autonomy to the communicational sphere. In this sense, then, to talk of colonisation of the lifeworld by the system appears very tenuous, in the contemporary world, when confronted with the totalising power of abstract labour and commodity-fetishism and their reifications in the sphere of communication. And capitalism is, of course, much more than a subsystem.

At an abstract level, Habermas's overestimation occurs with the loss of the relation of distance and extension between labour and interactive practice, which assumes a relational form between spheres that had become dissociated, through the increasing complexity of social life. Whereas for Habermas there is an uncoupling that leads to separation, for Lukács, there is a distancing, a growing complexity and extension that, however, does not break the indissoluble connections between these spheres of sociability, connections that occur as much in the genesis of sociability as in the emancipatory process itself. Habermas, in contrast, through the disjunction he posits as operating as societies grow more complex, confers

---

91. As indicated in Outhwaite 1994, pp. 15–16, who, however, draws on the essential aspects of Habermas's formulation, whom he generously considers to be 'the most important social theorist of the second half of the XX century', who is able to perform a synthesis on modernity that transforms him into a sort of 'Max Weber Marxist' (ibid., pp. 4–5). With a very different reading, Mészáros 1989, especially pp. 130–40, makes a sharp critique of Habermas. Elements of the Habermas–Lukács polemic can be found in Coutinho 1996, especially pp. 21ff.; Maar 1996, especially pp. 48ff.; and Lessa 1997, pp. 173–215.

upon the sphere of language and communication the privileged meaning of emancipation.

Both, therefore, attribute a central role to the sphere of subjectivity. But their treatment of this category is entirely different. For Habermas, the realm of subjectivity is additional to the outside world, while, for Lukács, this separation is meaningless.

Given these considerations, I cannot agree with the analytical separation performed by Habermas – which is the core of his critique of Marx and Lukács – between system and lifeworld, or if we prefer, the sphere of labour and the sphere of interaction. The system does not *colonise the lifeworld* as something external to it. 'Lifeworld' and 'system' are not subsystems that can be separated from one another, but are integral, constitutive parts of the social whole, which Habermas systematically and dualistically separates.

It is precisely because of this disjunction that Habermas's critique of the theory of value begins with the rejection of the notion of *totality* in Marx. If *labour and interaction* are distinct moments in an articulated whole, if between the *primary-teleological positions* and the *secondary-teleological positions*, in Lukács's sense, there is *distancing*, extension and increasing complexity but not *separation*, Habermas's critique of both Marx and Lukács is further undermined. It may be a *complex epistemological construction, but it is devoid of ontological density.*

Habermas's criticism that fetishism and reification in Marx are limited only to the sphere of labour but should also apply to the citizen-consumer also appears without support, unless we reason according to Habermas's *disjunction.* But if this disjunction has no basis, then, again, Habermas's critique is ineffective. If, for Marx, the social whole includes both *labour* and *interactive social practice*, i.e. is not restricted to the sphere of production, then a critique of alienation and fetishism cannot rigidly separate *producer from consumer*, as if these belonged to entirely different spheres. The analytical insights Lukács offers on *estrangement (Entfremdung)* in *The Ontology of Social Being* are, among many other examples, ample developments on the Marxian theory of alienation/estrangement.[92] The same can be said of the sphere of subjectivity, as we shall see in the following section.

Authentic and inauthentic subjectivity

Nicolas Tertulian, in a seminal essay, showed that, in *The Ontology of Social Being*, Lukács constructed:

---

92. See Lukács 1981, p. iv.

a true phenomenology of subjectivity, to make the socio-historical bases of the phenomenon of alienation intelligible. He distinguishes between two levels of existence: humankind in itself and humankind for itself. The first is characterised by a tendency to reduce the individual to his own 'particularity'; the second is the aspiration in search of a *nicht mehr particulare Personlichkeit* [no longer particular personality]. The teleological act (*teleologische Setzung*), defined as original phenomenon, *principium movens*, of social life is divided, for its part, into two distinct moments: the objectification (*die Vergegenständlichung*) and externalisation (*die Entäusserung*).[93]

Stressing the conjunction, as well as the possible divergence between these two moments within the same act, Lukács extols the space of autonomy of subjectivity in relation to the demands of social production and reproduction.... The field of alienation lies in the 'inner space' of the individual, experienced as a contradiction between the aspiration to seek self-determination of personality and the multiplicity of his qualities and his activities, that seek the reproduction of an estranged conjunct/set/complex.[94]

The individual who accepts the immediacy of her condition, imposed by the social *status quo*, and has no aspirations towards self-determinacy, is, for Lukács, an individual in a state of 'particularity', the agent of humankind *in itself, par excellence. It is the moment in which, in Tertulian's brilliant reconstruction, subjectivity experiences conditions of inauthenticity.* The search for a truly human existence implies the will to re-encounter an active, conscious force 'against the imperatives of a heteronomous social existence, the strength to become an autonomous personality'.[95]

Everyday life is not, then, the space *par excellence* of alienated life, but instead, the battlefield between alienation and freedom from alienation. *The Ontology of Everyday Life* offers a number of examples of this battle.[96]

---

93. The parentheses are in the original work of Tertulian 1993.
94. Tertulian 1993, pp. 439–40.
95. Tertulian 1993, p. 440. An exploratory exposition on the concept of person, personality and 'the ontological mode of individuality' in Lukács's *Ontology* can be found in Oldrini 1993. Interacting within a set of concrete conditions, personality, says the author, 'is the result of a social dialectic that links the real bases of the life of the individual, in a "concrete historical and social field"', in which he experiences both conditions of objectification and externalisation. The key for the understanding of the Marxist concept of person and personality is to conceive of it 'in all its complexity, as a social category'. Personality 'is not an epiphenomenon of the environment, the simple result of determinism', nor an 'autarchic force melded into the social whole' (Oldrini 1993, pp. 146–9).
96. Tertulian 1993, p. 440. See my notes on everyday life in the chapter 'Elements for an Ontology of Everyday Life'.

Since 'the phenomena of reification, or, at a more general level, of alienation, are at the heart of Lukács's study, throughout his work',[97] the Hungarian philosopher is able to develop all the potentialities of Marx's reification-thesis, which as we saw above, Habermas mistakenly construes as a *confined* to the sphere of work.

With great philosophical rigour and analytical sophistication, Tertulian develops another idea that is rich in significance: the idea, introduced by Lukács in his mature phase, of the differentiation between *'innocent' reifications* and *'alienating' reifications. Innocent reifications* occur when there is a condensation of activities in an *object*, in a *thing*, entailing the commodification of human energies that function as conditioned reflexes and lead to 'innocent' reifications. Subjectivity is reabsorbed in the functioning of the object, without 'alienation' itself taking place.[98]

'Alienated' reifications occur when subjectivity is transformed into an object, into a *'subject-object* that functions for the self-affirmation and reproduction of an estranged force. The individual self-alienates through the sale of his labour-power, for example, under conditions imposed upon him, or, sacrifices himself to the "consumption of prestige" imposed by the law of the market'.[99]

We can see here the limitations of Habermas's critique of reification in Marx and Lukács, being confined to the sphere of social labour and therefore incapable of incorporating the sphere of consumption. As we saw earlier with Tertulian's analysis, Lukács's treatment of reification is much more complex and fertile, ample and nuanced than Habermas would suggest. It is true that Habermas does not address Lukács's more mature work. But since he criticises Lukács in *History and Class Consciousness* as much as the *entire* Marxian body of work, the limitations he attributes to the (Marxian and Marxist) theory of reification appear unfounded.

The tension and debate around *inauthenticity and authenticity*, between alienation and freedom from alienation – the leitmotiv of Lukács's later work, especially in *The Ontology of Social Being* and the *Prolegomenas* – can be seen in the struggle engaged in by subjectivity to transcend 'particularity' and reach a 'real degree of humanity. The self-determination of personality, which destroys the foundations of reification and alienation, is synonymous with the emancipation of humankind'.[100] This positive alternative for the formation

97. Tertulian 1993, p. 439.
98. Tertulian 1993, p. 441.
99. Ibid.
100. Tertulian 1993, p. 442.

of *being-for-itself* does not rule out, as a possibility, 'the tragic wasting of the subject in the course of battle'.[101]

Perhaps I can conclude these statements by saying that both Lukács and Habermas assign a central role to the sphere of subjectivity in the genesis, development and emancipation of social being. But the treatments that they give to the sphere of subjectivity are completely different. Habermas's construct of intersubjectivity in *The Theory of Communicative Action*, which is based on the disjunction mentioned above, isolates the lifeworld as *a thing-in-itself*, conferring upon it a non-existent separation from the systemic sphere.

In Lukács, on the other hand, in *The Ontology of Social Being*, a fertile relationship between subjectivity and objectivity is developed, *where subjectivity is a constitutive moment of social practice*, in an unshakable interrelationship between the sphere of the subject and the activity of work. It is ontologically inconceivable, in this formulation, to *separate* the sphere of subjectivity from the realm of work, which, as we saw above, with the teleological act intrinsic to the labour-process, gave rise to subjectivity itself in the social act of labour.

For Habermas, in the disjunction he makes from the increasing complexity of social forms, in uncoupling system and lifeworld and the consequent independence of intersubjectivity, it is the sphere of language and communication that assumes emancipatory significance. In Lukács, on the contrary, the links between *subjectivity* and *labour* are indissoluble. Thus, in the *genesis* of social being, its *development* and the process of its own *emancipation*, labour – as founding moment of human subjectivity itself through the continual realisation of human needs, the search for the production and reproduction of social life, the genesis of the consciousness of social being itself – reveals itself as the ontologically essential and founding element.

While, for Habermas, the end of the 'paradigm of labour' is a feasible statement, given his own analytical assumptions, for Lukács, the increasing complexity of society did not erode the original (and essential) meaning of the labour-process, between causality and teleology, between the world of objectivity and sphere of intersubjectivity.

I shall conclude with a final critique: in the context of late capitalism, Habermas's thesis of the *pacification of class-conflicts* is, less than twenty years since its publication, increasingly contentious. Not only has the welfare-state been progressively dismantled in the small number of states in which it existed, but the interventionist state has become increasingly privatised. In this context of transformation, the *limited* empirical basis of support for Habermas's

---

101. Ibid.

argument regarding the pacification of social struggles – the hegemony of the social-democratic project within the labour-movement – is also undermined. And even when this project is successful electorally, it is increasingly distant from the reformist, social-democratic values of the post-war period.

As I attempted to show in the first part of this text, the productive restructuring of capital, neoliberalism and the changes within the state – the loss of its *social interventionism* – were responsible for the crisis of this cycle of *social contractualism*, and there is no concrete evidence of a return, at the dawn of the twenty-first century, to anything similar to the 'golden years of social democracy'. Not in the central countries, and *less still in those countries in a subaltern position in the new international division of labour*. Without the possibility of the continuation of the welfare-state and Keynesianism (limited, in any case, to the small central contingent of European and North-American nations) Habermas's thesis of the 'pacification of social struggles' begins to fall apart. With the erosion of both (and the resulting weakening of social-security systems) throughout recent decades and especially during the 1990s, the *phenomenal and contingent expression of pacification of class-conflict* – to which Habermas wishes to confer a status of determination – is beginning to show signs of decay. What was intended as an illustration of the critique of the 'Marxian inability to comprehend late capitalism' (which Habermas so enthusiastically directed at Marx), appears instead as a weakness of Habermas's *construct*. Once the *conceptual and theoretical deconstruction of labour and the theory of value* has been made, contemporary social logic could legitimate a *negotiated consensus* of the sphere of *intersubjectivity, a relational way of life*. But, by advocating this sequence of events, in the second half of the 1970s, Habermas does not seem to seriously consider that the *political economy of capital and its operational mechanisms* (*amongst which, the theory of value*) could erode the 'bases' of the supposed *pacification of social conflicts* and of a public space capable of undermining the (private) logic of capital.[102]

---

102. At a more sociological level, there has also been a limited attempt to extend the thesis of crisis of the 'paradigm of labour' to the present day. Muckenberger 1997, pp. 46–9, for example, argues that 'this paradigm is concerned with an idea of social well-being based on a collective that shares a lifestyle with profitable work as the basis. This is at the origin of demands for individual substance (both private as well as public). The dramatic change taking place in society is the link between full employment and social well-being – especially in the context of increased structural unemployment. This entails a new mode of exclusion of labour based on a network of social security and threatens all social security systems'. In a very similar way to Offe, the author characterises the 'centrality of work-life' as 'a learning as the first stage, acquisition of skills as the basis for profitable work, solidarity in the workplace as the basis for unionism and conflict-management, understanding and protestant ethic as the main characterstics for the accomplishment of work'. With the crisis of the

Indeed, recent acts of resistance by workers seem to signal the opposite, exemplifying contemporary forms of confrontation between *total social capital* and the *totality of labour*.

There are many examples: the public-sector workers' strike in France in November and December 1995, the greatest workers' movement since May 1968; the South Korean metalworkers' strike of 1997, when around 2 million workers went on strike against government, attempts to introduce flexibilisation and precarious working conditions; in the same year, a strike that brought together 185,000 part-time and full-time workers against United Parcel Services in the US; the dockers' strike in Liverpool, which began in 1995 and lasted more than two years; or even the strike of General Motors workers in the US, in 1998, which gradually slowed down the production-system of the company in many countries.

Previously, in Germany, there were strikes against cuts to the health-service, and, in Spain, a number of national stoppages broke out against the regressive policies of Felipe Gonzales's government. In Canada, there were important strikes during the 1990s, of General Motors workers again, and public-sector workers. The eruption of the unemployed workers' movement in France in 1998 provides another example, with their demands for the redistribution of social wealth amongst the unemployed and the strong potential for the actions to spread to other European countries. We could also mention the important struggle for the reduction of the working day that has mobilised workers in Germany, France and Italy, among others, or even the strikes of Russian miners who were not even paid a salary.[103]

'traditional model of individual and collective reproduction' based on the paradigm of employment, in Germany 'it is increasingly argued that a new society of uncertainty and risk is emerging, at an individual and global level. It is no coincidence that German social theories that are concerned with the question of individualisation are the "risk society" or the "new uncertainty".... Given the existence of a clear reduction in forms of social integration and cohesion based on the centrality of work-life, social synthesis will be increasingly adapted to one that is debated, organised and controlled publicly'. In an era in which destructive capital privatises and increasingly controls spaces that were once public, the weakness of the above argument is clear.

103. It is a shame that Robert Kurz, a very interesting author responsible for one of the most damning critiques of capitalism and its destructive effect, is incapable of understanding the new configurations of class-struggle, which are not the last battles, but the forms of confrontation between work as a whole and total social capital, between the working class in its various cleavages and the personifications of capital. Although his critique of European trade-unionism is largely vivid and true – 'trade-union protest...does not seriously imagine...even the outline of an alternative system...' – Kurz has, on the other hand, great difficulty grasping class-movements that transcend the sphere of traditional trade-unionism. He sees them as the expression of the 'old class-struggle' that has been overcome, which 'can only be the immanent formal movement of the capital-relation, but not the movement

And this is not to mention the Los Angeles riots of 1992, the Chiapas rebellion in Mexico or the rise of the Landless Workers' Movement (MST) in Brazil, in addition to the countless, often confrontational strikes (general and partial) that have taken place in Argentina, Ecuador, Mexico, Brazil, etc., among many other forms of rebellion that have taken place across the world in recent years. These examples do not constitute evidence of the integration, of the *pacification of social conflicts*, as Habermas suggests, but, instead, reveal a scenario of increasing instability and social confrontation between capital and labour.[104]

---

that can overcome the capitalist relation'. And, in doing so, he is imprisoned in the denunciation of the contemporary destructive chaos, devoid of subjects. See Kurz 1997, especially the essay that gives the book its title. A very different treatment of the issue can be found in Joachim Hirsch: '[A] social revolution in a deepest sense will come into action only when the political apparatus, along with the basic structures of society, are transformed. And those changes are the basis of the whole process. This refers to forms of work and the division of labour, the relationship between society and nature, gender-relations that impact the family-structure (which, as we know, is the foundation of women's oppression), the sphere of everyday life and the dominant models of consumption as well as social norms and values. This is a more difficult process, often painful and, above all, extraordinarily long and slow. It cannot be ordered or imposed by decree by the state. To do so requires an independent social organisation, which should enable human beings to express and develop their experiences, agree and disagree, to formulate common goals and to impose themselves against the ruling apparatus, create common goals and give them power against the state and capital' (Hirsch 1997, pp. 67–8).

104. I am not able to discuss this in detail here, but the literature I use includes Ellen Wood, 1997a; Singer 1997; Soon 1997; Fumagalli 1996; Petras 1997; and McIlroy 1996, among others already mentioned throughout this book.

Chapter Nine

Elements towards an Ontology of Everyday Life

In the previous chapters, I have sought to show that the importance of the category *labour* lies in it constituting the *original*, *primary* source of the realisation of social being, the *model of human activity*, the basic ontological foundation of human 'multi-facetedness'.

At this abstract level, it seems unnecessary to say that I am not referring here to *waged, fetishised or estranged labour*, but to labour as creator of *use-values*, labour in its *concrete* dimension, as *work*, as 'an eternal nature-imposed necessity, without which there can be no material exchanges between man and Nature', in Marx's well-known phrase.[1]

If labour, in capital's social-metabolic order, takes on a necessarily waged, abstract, fetishistic and estranged form (given capital's imperative to produce exchange-values for the reproduction of capital), this concrete historical dimension of wage-labour cannot, however, be *eternalised* or taken *ahistorically. In an emancipated society, in which mediations of the 'second order' created by capital's system of social metabolism have been overcome, the free association of workers – their self-activity, their full autonomy and their real control over the act of labour – is the ontological foundation for their condition to 'be free and universal'*, as described in Marx's Paris Manuscripts. The real and autonomous power over the labour-sphere and sphere of reproduction finds its corollary in the *free and*

---

1. Marx 1967, vol. 1, pp. 42–3 and 183–4.

autonomous sphere of life outside of work, where *free time* is real, self-determined and no longer constrained by the rules of the market, by the necessity to consume exchange-values (materially and immaterially).

With this as our starting point, it goes without saying how problematic it becomes to advocate the end of the *centrality of labour*. As we saw earlier, the so-called 'crisis of the society of abstract labour' cannot be identified as being *either the end of wage-labour within capitalism* (an elimination that is ontologically bound to the elimination of capital itself) or the end of *concrete labour*, understood as the foundation of the initial *prototype* of human activity and multifacetedness. To do this is effectively to ignore, in its necessary and essential dimension, the Marxist distinction between *concrete* and *abstract* labour, resulting in serious analytical misunderstandings.

Labour is, therefore, a real moment of positing of human ends, *endowed with an intrinsic teleological dimension*, and, as such, it represents *an elementary experience of everyday life*, in the answers it offers to society's needs and requirements. To recognise the essential role played by labour in the *genesis* and *self-creation* of *social being* brings us straight to the decisive quality of *everyday life* as the starting point for the being-for-themselves of human beings. In the following pages, I shall sketch some preliminary elements that constitute an *ontology of everyday life*.

Reference to the sphere of *everyday life* is essential to go beyond the sphere and activity of spontaneous, contingent and immediate consciousness, to forms of consciousness that manifest more emancipated, free and universal values. Nicolas Tertulian refers to this as the process of emergence of *authentic subjectivity* as opposed to manifestations of *subjectivity* characterised by *inauthenticity*.[2]

In reference to the sphere of everyday life, Lukács makes a decisive contribution:

> Society can only be understood in its totality, in its evolutionary dynamic, when it is able to understand everyday life in its universal heterogeneity. Everyday life constitutes the objective-ontological mediation between the simple spontaneous reproduction of physical existence and the highest forms of conscious genericity[3] precisely because here, in an uninterrupted form, the most heterogeneous constellations result in the two human extremes appropriated by social reality, particularity and genericity occur in their

---

2. Tertulian 1993, pp. 439ff.
3. The category of 'genericity' is a free translation of the German *Gattungsmäßigkeit*. This category appears in the 'Labour' chapter of Lukács's *Ontology of Social Being* – more precisely in the penultimate paragraph of the chapter – as 'the species character in human being' (Lukács 1980, p. 135).

immediate dynamic interrelation. As a result, research into this sphere of life can also shed light on the internal dynamic of development of the genericity of human beings, in order to make those heterogeneous processes – that in society create realisations of genericity intelligible.[4]

Thus, the understanding of the socio-historical genesis brings us back to the universe of daily life. This is because 'the being of each society arises from the totality of such actions and relations' once 'genericity that is realised in society cannot be mute, as in the ontological sphere of life that is reproduced merely biologically. The history of society shows that this going beyond mute, biological genericity is objectified in the highest forms, of science, philosophy, art, ethics, etc.'[5]

Therefore the interrelations and interactions between the material world and human life meet in the universe of daily life, in this sphere of being, its 'mediation zone', able to overcome the abyss between being-in-itself, marked by relative silence, and being-for-itself, the space of a life that is more authentic and free. This is because:

> the essence and historical-social functions of everyday life would not generate interest if this were considered to be a homogeneous sphere. However, precisely because of this, precisely because of its immediate foundation in human beings' economic-particular modes of reacting to the challenges of life that social existence presents...everyday life possess an extensive universality.... Thus, everyday life, the immediate form of human genericity appears as the basis for all the spontaneous reactions of human beings in relation to their social environment, where human beings appear to act in an often chaotic way. Yet, for this reason precisely, it holds within it the totality of modes of reaction, obviously not as pure, but as chaotic-heterogeneous manifestations. As a result, whoever wishes to understand the real historical-social genesis of these reactions, will be obliged to investigate this zone of being in detail.[6]

The journey from being-in-itself to being-for-itself certainly cannot ignore the forms of *mediation* present in *social and political praxis*. But, the reference to *daily life* and its connections with the *world of labour* and *social reproduction* is essential when we seek to understand some of the key dimensions of social being. The connections that exist between the practical and historical-ontological actions and the more authentic spheres of human genericity, such

---

4. This is a translation of the Portuguese version of Lukács's 'Prefácio' to *The Sociology of Everyday Life*, by Agnes Heller (Lukács 1987, pp. 11–12).
5. Lukács 1987, p. 10.
6. Lukács 1987, pp. 10–12.

as ethics, philosophy, art, science, the higher forms of social praxis, find their *ontological base* in the *heterogeneity of everyday life*, in its immediate and spontaneous activities and become, as a consequence, the starting point of the process of humanisation of social being. This is because 'whilst in normal everyday life each decision that is not completely routine is taken in an atmosphere of innumerable ifs and buts, in such a way as to rarely offer any judgement on the totality nor on its confrontations, in revolutionary situations and their preparatory processes, this negative infinity of particular questions is condensed into few central questions that, however, are presented for the majority of people as problems that point to the destiny of their lives, that, in contrast to "normal" everyday life, assume the quality of a question formulated with clarity that must be answered with clarity'.[7]

An ontology of everyday life is certainly very different from the cult of the contingent element, from the *phenomenological* defence of everyday life, that consumes, without the complex mediations, all the possibilities of the human species. Everyday life, in the contingent and phenomenological understanding, would be the ultimate expression of human possibility, losing the essential Marxist (and Lukácsian) differentiation between being-in-itself and being-for-itself. This approach is very distant from the one I am developing. Yet, I also do not think it is possible, as many vulgar readings of Marx have done (and still do), to ignore the decisive ontological sphere that is present in everyday life and fail to perceive it as integral and central, especially if we seek to understand the forms of conscience of the *social-being-that-lives-from-labour* as it moves from the forms closest to immediacy, from being-in-itself, to the authenticity of the forms of being-for-itself.[8]

---

7. Lukács 1981, vol. 2, p. 506.

8. Studies of class-consciousness in the social sciences and history are, for the most part, empirical descriptions or accounts, more or less sophisticated, of how the working class acted (or acts), generally in keeping with its sphere of contingency. At the other extreme, we find, especially in philosophical studies, a frequently idealised and ahistorical construction of the working class, in a reading that is misleading in the opposite direction. The exaggerated polarisation between false and true consciousness present in Lukács's *History and Class Consciousness* is an example of this. In studies of class-consciousness, the greatest challenge lies in trying to grasp both the dimension of empirical consciousness, of everyday-consciousness and its forms of manifestation (which Mészáros referred to as contingent consciousness), as well as trying to understand what the other possibilities for collective action might be, ones closer to a more complete, less fragmented and commodified understanding of the social whole as well as the interrelationships between these levels. In a nutshell, how class actually worked and how it could have worked, what other possibilities existed in the real concrete historical conditions in which the study takes place. It is a difficult challenge for which Lukács, in *The Ontology of Social Being*, by reclaiming the dimension of everyday life, is able to offer core-analytical elements that are far superior to the ones present in *History and Class Consciousness*. See, for example, Mészáros 1986, Chapter 2.

Chapter Ten

Working Time and Free Time: towards a Meaningful Life *Inside* and *Outside* of Work

I would like to conclude with some observations that I believe are central to the question of *working time and free time*, given the importance of this issue in contemporary sociability.

On the connections between *work* and *free time* in *Capital*, Marx offers the following synthesis:

> In fact, the realm of freedom actually begins only where labour which is determined by necessity and mundane considerations ceases; thus in the very nature of things it lies beyond the sphere of actual material production. Just as the savage must wrestle with Nature to satisfy his wants, to maintain and reproduce life, so must civilized man, and he must do so in all social formations and under all possible modes of production. With his development this realm of physical necessity expands as a result of his wants; but, at the same time, the forces of production which satisfy these wants also increase. Freedom in this field can only consist in socialized man, the associated producers, rationally regulating their interchange with Nature, bringing it under their common control, instead of being ruled by it as by the blind forces of Nature; and achieving this with the least expenditure of energy and under conditions most favourable to, and worthy of, their human nature. But it nonetheless still remains a realm of necessity. Beyond it begins

that development of human energy which is an end in itself, the true realm of freedom, which, however, can blossom forth only with the realm of necessity as its basis. The shortening of the working-day is its basic prerequisite.[1]

The reduction of the working day (or weekly working *time*) has been one of the most important demands of labour, representing a mechanism by which to contrast this with the extraction of surplus-labour by capital, from the Industrial Revolution through to the contemporary flexible accumulation of Toyotism. From the advent of capitalism, the reduction of the working day has been central to workers' struggle, the *basic prerequisite-condition*, as Marx observed, for an emancipated life.[2]

Nowadays, this idea has even greater weight, because it has come to be, *contingently*, an important tool (although, when considered in isolation, rather limited) in *minimising* the structural unemployment that affects vast numbers of workers. But it goes beyond the sphere of immediacy since the discussion around the reduction of the working day represents a *decisive starting point rooted in the realm of everyday life* for, on the one hand, an important reflection on *time, working time and control over working and living time*[3] and, on the other, the possibility for a *meaningful* life *outside* of work to flourish.

As Grazia Paoletti observed, in the introduction to the collection of articles referred to above:

> The question of time…implies the possibility of control over the life of individuals and the organisation of society, of working time and capitalist production in urban life.… [I]t implies a conflict over the use of time, both in the quantitative and qualitative sense, as well as the different priorities in the conception of social organisation: it is, ultimately, a battle of *civility*.[4]

In the struggle for the reduction of the working day (or time), it is possible to see resistance against both forms of oppression and labour-exploitation, in addition to contemporary forms of estrangement that occur outside of the productive world, in the sphere of material and symbolic consumption, the reproductive sphere outside of (productive) labour. Both the oppressive control of capital in working time as well as capital's oppressive control during living time are articulated in this struggle.

---

1. Marx 1967, vol. 3, p. 820.
2. Ibid.
3. See, for example, Paoletti (ed.) 1998, with different contributions on the significance of the struggle for the reduction of working time to 35 hours in Italy and elsewhere in Europe.
4. Paoletti (ed.) 1998, p. 34.

A clarification may be important in this discussion: the reduction of the working *day* does not necessarily imply the reduction of working *time*. As João Bernardo argues, 'A worker today, who performs complex activities and works seven hours a day, works for a much longer real time than a worker of another era who worked 14 hours a day but whose work was much less complex. The formal reduction of the working hours corresponds to an increase in the real time of labour spent during this period.'[5] Something similar takes place if, after the reduction *by half* of the working day, the intensity of the operations previously performed *doubles*. As such, the struggle for the *reduction of the working day* also implies a decisive struggle for the control (and reduction) *of the oppressive time of work*, because the formal reduction of hours can correspond to 'an increase in the real time of labour spent during this period'.[6] As for many other categories, *temporality* is also a socio-historical construction. In the words of Norbert Elias:

> As long as there have been human beings...life followed the ever recurring course from life to death. The compulsive nature of this course and the sequence of its phases did not depend on the will or consciousness of the human beings. But the ordering of the sequence in the form of years was only possible once people had developed for their own purposes the regulative symbol of the year.
>
> The social need for time measurement in ancient societies was far less acute and pervasive than in the more highly organised states of modern times, not to mention the present-day industrial state. In conjunction with a shift towards increased differentiation and integration, in many modern societies a particularly complex system of self-regulation has developed within individual people as regards time. The external, social compulsion of time, represented by clocks, calendars or timetables, possesses to a high degree, in those societies, the characteristics which promote the formation of individual self-constraints. The pressure of these external constraints is relatively unobtrusive, moderate even, and without violence, but it is at the same time omnipresent and inescapable.[7]

This raises another important issue: a meaningful life *outside* of work presupposes a meaningful life *inside* work. It is not possible to make *fetishised, estranged wage*-labour compatible with *(genuinely) free time*. A life deprived of meaning inside work is *incompatible* with a meaningful life outside of work.

---

5. Bernardo 1996, p. 46.
6. Ibid.
7. Elias 1998, pp. 22–3.

In some form, the sphere outside of work will be *tarnished* by the *disaffection* present in working life.[8]

Since the global system of capital today even reaches into the domain of *life outside work*, the *de-fetishisation of consumer-society* is inextricably linked to the *de-fetishisation of the mode of production* of things. It is necessary therefore to relate *decisively* the campaign for *free time* to the struggle against the logic of capital and the ubiquity of *abstract labour*. Without this, demands remain subordinated to the prevailing order, based on the view that they can be achieved through *consensus* and *interaction*, without addressing the foundations of the system or affecting the interests of capital, or worse still, the struggle against capital and its system of social metabolism is abandoned for a *resigned* social practice.

This would entail *civilising* capital, achieving the *utopia of fulfilment*, of the *possible*, seeking to achieve 'free time' through *consensus* – at the height of the Toyotist era, the era of flexible accumulation, deregulation, tertiarisation, casualisation, structural unemployment, the dismantling of the welfare-state, the cult of the market, a destructive society of material and symbolic consumption, in sum, of the radical (de-)sociabilisation of the present world.

It would be, as Dominique Méda argues (strongly influenced by Habermas), in a spirit of *disenchantment with the world* and consequently *disenchantment with work* (within which, the author recalls, *the utopia of the work-society would have lost its persuasive force*) to advocate 'the imposition of a limit on instrumental rationality and the economy, and the construction of spaces aimed at the real development of a public life, for the exercise of a new citizenship, reducing both individual time dedicated to work and increasing social time dedicated to activities that are, in fact, political, ones that are actually able to structure the social fabric'.[9]

In this vein, the (positive) expansion of public spaces has the (also positive) corollary of the reduction of working activity. But its *greatest* limitation – and not its only one – is the attempt to *restrict* and *limit*, but not *destroy* and *counterpose itself radically and antagonistically* to, capital's social-metabolic order.[10]

---

8. Antunes 1995a, p. 86.

9. Méda 1997, pp. 220–7.

10. Not to mention the fact that these arguments are often, in the vast majority of cases, marked by a strong *Eurocentrism* that does not reflect and therefore does not incorporate the *totality of labour*. To imagine them applying to Asia, Latin America, Africa, 'limiting the development of instrumental reason' and 'increasing public space', is surely an abstraction that is stripped of any effectively emancipatory significance. A more critical reflection is offered by Mazzetti 1997. Its greatest limitation, however, also becomes clear when we consider the *totality of labour* as opposed to *total social capital*, since, in this way, it becomes necessary to think of labour *as including the so-called Third World*, which is made up (with China) of more than two-thirds of the *working class*.

From this resigned position to one that lives with capital, the distance is not insurmountable.

A meaningful life in all aspects of social being can only arise with the demolition of the barriers that exist between *working time* and *non-working time* in such a way that, from a meaningful, self-determined, *vital activity – which is beyond the hierarchical division that subordinates labour to capital in force today* and which rests, therefore, upon entirely new foundations – a new sociability can develop. A sociability woven by *social and freely associated individuals* (men and women), in which art, philosophy, time that is really free and restful, in accordance with the most authentic aspirations that arise within everyday life, enable the realisation of an identity between the individual and the human race in all its diversity. *In entirely new forms of sociability, then, where freedom and necessity realise one another.* If labour becomes meaningful it will also (and *decisively*) be through art, poetry, painting, literature, music, free time, leisure, that a social being can attain humanisation and emancipation in their fullest sense.

We can draw some conclusions from the considerations made above. *Firstly*, the fight for the reduction of the working *day* or working *time* must be at the heart of labour's struggles today, on a global scale. The world of labour must fight for the reduction of labour with a view to minimising the brutal structural unemployment that results from the destructive logic of capital and its system. It must fight for *the reduction of working hours or working time in order to halt the proliferation of the huge numbers of precarious and unemployed workers.* To the just slogan *less work for all* we should therefore *add* another which is *no less important: Producing what? And for whom?*

Secondly, the right to work is a necessary demand *not because fetishised, estranged, waged work is valued and glorified* (which must be eradicated with the end of capital), but because to be *outside of labour*, in the current form of capitalism, particularly for the masses of workers who live in the so-called Third World (who make up two-thirds of humanity), who are *completely* deprived of social security, represents an even greater *disempowerment, disaffection and brutalisation* than for those experienced by the *class-that-lives-from-labour*. But it is essential to note that, even in the so-called First World, unemployment and precarious forms of labour are becoming increasingly intense, processes that are aggravated by the gradual collapse of the welfare-state. *Therefore, even in these countries, the right to work along with the reduction of working hours and working time is a demand capable of responding to the real, daily needs of the working class.*

However, this struggle for the *right to reduced working time and the increase of time outside of work* (so-called free time) without the reduction of salary – which is, incidentally, very different from the flexible working day which does not oppose the logic of capital – must be closely related to the struggle against the system of social metabolism of capital that converts 'free time' into consumption time *for capital*, where individuals are compelled to 'improve their skills' in order better to 'compete' in the labour-market, or to exhaust themselves in *fetishised* consumption that is entirely deprived of meaning.

Instead, if the basis of collective action were radically aimed at forms of (de-)sociabilisation of the world of commodities, *the immediate struggle for the reduction of working hours or time* becomes *entirely compatible* with the *right to work* (with reduced hours and without a reduction in salary).

Thus, the immediate struggle for the reduction of working hours (or time) and the fight for employment, instead of being mutually exclusive, are necessarily *complementary*. And social endeavour for *meaningful work* and for an *authentic life outside of work*, for *disposable time* for work and *genuinely free and autonomous time* outside of work – both, therefore, out of the oppressive *control* of capital – become essential elements in the construction of a society no longer regulated by the system of social metabolism of capital and its mechanisms of subordination. In the concluding pages, I shall indicate the basic social foundations for a new system of social metabolism.

Chapter Eleven
Foundations of a New Social-Metabolic Order

The potential for a new authentic and meaningful life, at the dawn of the twenty-first century, highlights the urgent need for the construction of a new system of social metabolism, a new *mode of production* based on *self-determined activity,* based on *disposable time (to produce socially-necessary use-values), on the realisation of socially-necessary labour in contrast to hetero-determined production (based on the exclusive use of surplus-time for the production of exchange-values for the market and the reproduction of capital).* I shall outline in more detail these elements in the foundation of a new social-metabolic order.

The core-constitutive principles of this new life are to be found in the establishment of a social system in which: 1) *the meaning of society is entirely directed towards the satisfaction of human and social needs;* 2) *the exercise of labour is synonymous with self-activity, free activity based on disposable time.*

As we saw in the first chapter, the system of capital, stripped of any significant human-societal orientation, became a system of control where *use-value* was totally subordinated to *exchange-value,* to the reproductive necessities of *capital itself.* For this to occur, *a structural subordination of labour to capital* took place with the resulting hierarchical social division based on fetishised wage-labour. The vital functions of individual and social reproduction were radically altered, with the establishment of a set of reproductive functions – which Mészáros calls 'second order mediations'[1] – in which gender-relations, in addition to material and symbolic production (such as art), were subordinated to the imperatives of valorisation and capital-reproduction. Michael Löwy calls this:

> [t]he venal (mercantile) quantification of social life. Capitalism, regulated by exchange-value, the calculation of profits and the accumulation of capital, tends to dissolve and destroy all qualitative values: use values, ethical values, human relations, human feelings. Having replaces Being, and only subsists the monetary payment – the *cash nexus* according to the famous expression of Carlyle which Marx takes up.[2]

The use-value of socially-necessary goods became subordinated to their exchange-value, which came to control the logic of capital's social metabolism. The basic productive functions and the *control* of this process were radically separated between those who *produced* and those who *controlled*. As Marx stated, capital separated workers from the means of production, between the *snail* from its *shell*,[3] widening the gap between production to meet human social necessities and production to meet the self-reproduction needs of capital.

As the first *mode of production* to create a logic that does not consider real social necessities as a priority, it marked a radical change from previous systems of social-metabolic control (of production primarily to meet the necessities of *human* reproduction). Capital established a system geared to its own self-valorisation that is *independent of the real reproductive needs of humanity*.

Thus, the return to a social logic aimed at meeting the needs of individuals and society is the first and deepest challenge of humanity in the new century. As Mészáros argues, 'The imperative to go beyond capital as a social metabolic control, with its almost forbidding difficulties, is the shared predicament of humanity as a whole.'[4]

Or, in Bihr's words:

> the mode of capitalist production as a whole, by submitting nature to the abstract imperatives of capital-reproduction, engenders the ecological crisis. In the universe of capitalism, the development of productive forces is transformed into the development of the destructive forces of nature and men. From a source of wealth it becomes a source of impoverishment, in

---

1. Mészáros 1995, p. 117.
2. Löwy 1999, p. 67.
3. Marx 1967, vol. 2, p. 359.
4. Mészáros 1995, p. 492.

which the only recognised wealth is not use-value, but the abstraction that is value. And, in this same universe, the power conquered by society is converted in the growing impotence of that society.[5]

The second social imperative is to transform labour into free self-activity, with a basis in *disposable time*. This entails that society's new structure must reject the dichotomous separation between *necessary working time* for social reproduction and *surplus working time* for the reproduction of capital.

A society will only have meaning and effective emancipation when its vital functions, controlled by its system of social metabolism, are, according to Mészáros, genuinely exercised autonomously by associated producers and not by an external body that controls these functions.[6] The only conceivable way, from the perspective of labour, is through the general adoption and creative utilisation of disposable time as an orienting principle of societal reproduction.[7] Still, according to Mészáros, 'From the standpoint of living labour it is perfectly possible to envisage disposable time as the condition that fulfils some vital positive functions in the life-activity of the associated producers [...], provided that lost unity between need and production is reconstituted at a qualitatively higher level when compared to the previous historical relations between the snail and its shell.'[8]

Although disposable time, from the perspective of capital, is conceived of as something to be exploited in the interest of its own expansion and valorisation,[9] from the perspective of living labour, it appears as the condition by which society can meet its real social needs and wants and develop a subjectivity endowed with meaning both *inside* and *outside* of work. This is because free time will be devoted to engaging in self-determined acts of labour, 'autonomous activities, external to the money-commodity relation',[10] that negate the totalising relation of the *commodity-form* and oppose, therefore, *a society that produces commodities*.[11] Social logic governed by disposable time presupposes a real articulation between subjective availability and the autonomous determination of time with authentic human social-reproductive, material and symbolic needs.

---

5. Bihr 1991, p. 133. Decisive analysis of the connections between the ecological crisis and the destructive logic of capital, a task that is essential today, can be found in Bihr 1991, Chapter 5; in Mészáros 1995, especially Chapters 15 and 16; and in Vega Cantor 1999, pp. 167–200.
6. Mészáros 1995, p. 494.
7. Mészáros 1995, pp. 573–4.
8. Mészáros 1995, p. 574.
9. Ibid.
10. Kurz 1997, p. 319.
11. Ibid.

Engagement in autonomous labour, having eliminated the use of surplus-time for the production of commodities as well as *destructive and superfluous production-time* (spheres that are controlled by capital), will rescue the *constructive significance of living labour* from the *destructive significance of abstract labour under capital*. This is because, under the system of social metabolism of capital, the labour that *constructs* capital *deconstructs* social being. The *wage-labour* that gives meaning to capital generates an *inauthentic subjectivity* in the act of labour. In a superior form of sociability, labour, in *restructuring* social being, *will have deconstructed* capital. And *self-determined* labour that will make capital *meaningless*, will establish the social conditions for an *authentic* and emancipated *subjectivity* to arise, giving a new *meaning to labour*.

Theses that espouse the *end of the centrality of labour* and its replacement by the *communication and intersubjective spheres* are undermined when set against a *comprehensive and wide-ranging conception of labour* that includes both its *collective* and *subjective* nature, the sphere of *productive* and *unproductive, material* and *immaterial* labour, the forms it assumes through the *sexual division of labour* and the *new configuration of the working class*, etc. This broader notion entails that the thesis of the centrality of labour in the constitution of contemporary society be revisited and re-established.

Moreover, rather than the replacement of *labour* by *science*, or *production of exchange-values* by the *communication- and symbolic* sphere – the replacement of *production* by *information* – today we can observe the greater *interrelation and interpenetration* between productive and unproductive activities, manufacturing and services, manual and conceptual activities, production and scientific knowledge.

We can, therefore, understand the *form of being* of the working class if we conceive of the heterogeneous and complex nature of *social labour* today, which includes both a minority of qualified workers in modern, computerised industry in production- and service-sectors, and a majority of wage-workers who experience more intense forms of labour-exploitation through part-time, temporary, outsourced, subcontracted work.

Finally, I have sought to show that the form assumed by the society of *abstract labour* itself – through the creation of a mass of workers rejected by the productive process – led to the *appearance* of the loss of centrality of labour in contemporary society. Yet, to understand the changes under way in the world of labour, we are obliged to go beyond appearances. In so doing, I have sought to show that the meaning given to the act of labour by capital is entirely different to the meaning that human beings can confer onto it.

Appendices

Appendices to the Second Edition

Appendix I

Ten Theses and a Hypothesis on the Present (and Future) of Work[1]

I – *The twentieth century and labour-degradation in the society of the automobile*

The twentieth century stands out as the century of the automobile. It was based on timed, homogeneous production, at a controlled pace, that would give the consumer a choice between a black Model T Ford and another black Model T Ford. The production-line that was conceived of for serial, rigid piecework was designed for mass-production and therefore mass-consumption, with the gradual increase of workers' salaries.

This productive system spread throughout the industrial and service-sectors (McDonald's was also designed in line with this model) and its corollary was brilliantly expressed in the classic Charlie Chaplin film *Modern Times*: the degradation of unilateral, standardised, piecemeal, fetishised, commodified and robotic labour. As a consequence, workers were treated like animals (the 'trained gorillas' that Frederick Taylor talked about), commodified and even subjected to domination over their sexuality.[2]

1. This paper is part of the research-project 'Where is the World of Work Heading?', developed with the support of CNPq. A first draft was published in da Silva (ed.) 2007, to be published in Spanish by Clacso.
2. Gramsci 1974, p. 166.

As well as being regulated, labour in Taylorist and Fordist society was mechanised, piecemeal, manual, dehumanised and, ultimately, alienated.

This was the dominant scenario until the early 1970s, when a structural crisis of the productive system took place which, to a certain extent, is still under way today as the vast and global process of productive restructuring has still not been completed.

Thus, throughout these transformations, the *Taylorist and Fordist* firm began its demise. It was necessary therefore to implement new mechanisms and forms of accumulation that could offer solutions to the crisis that was under way, especially after the social struggles that took place in 1968 in France, or in the 'hot autumn' in Italy, in 1969, both of which sought the social control of production.

Capital's process of restructuring took on various forms: in Sweden (in Kalmar), in the north of Italy (so-called 'Third Italy'), in the US (in California), in the UK, in Germany and in many different countries and regions. The most significant of these was the Toyotist experiment in Japan. Capital needed to guarantee *accumulation*, but accumulation of an increasingly *flexible* kind. The result was the so-called flexibilised and *lean-production* firm.

This structural transformation was aided by the success of neoliberalism, when a new set of prescriptions, a new ideological design, emerged to replace the welfare-state. A new set of practices began to develop that were intimately linked to the productive restructuring taking place on a global scale.

II – *Lean engineering in the microcosm of production*

The process of productive restructuring was based on what the dominant ideology called *lean production*, that is, the lean enterprise, the 'modern enterprise' that constrains, restricts, represses and limits living labour and increases its techno-scientific machinery, which Marx called *dead labour*. It redesigned the production-plant quite differently to the Taylorist/Fordist plant, vastly reducing the living labour-force while increasing productivity. It re-territorialised and even de-territorialised the productive world and revolutionised *space* and *time*.

The results are ubiquitous: severe unemployment, structural instability of labour, lower wages, the loss of rights, etc. There has been an expansion of what Juan Castillo called *organisational lyophilisation*, a process whereby *living labour* is increasingly replaced by *dead labour*.[3]

---

3. Castillo 1996a.

The new, 'freeze-dried', lean firm required a new type of labour: something different from those once known as workers and now mystifyingly called 'collaborators'. What were the contours of this new type of labour?

It should be more 'versatile' and 'multifunctional', of a different kind from the one developed in the Taylorist and Fordist company. The kind of labour that is increasingly sought after is no longer defined by *Taylorist* or *Fordist* specialisation, but is based on 'multifunctional de-specialisation', on 'multi-functional labour', expressing the *enormous intensification of the pace, timing and process of labour*. And this has been occurring both in the industrial world and in the services, not to mention in agriculture, blurring the traditional division between the agricultural, industrial and service-sectors.

Besides the use of machines, the world of work has also experienced an increase in *immaterial* labour, in the field of communications, advertising and marketing, fields belonging to the society of the logo, of the symbolic and of the superfluous. It is this discourse that business refers to as the 'knowledge-society', a discourse that is present in Nike's designs, in Microsoft's software-development, in Benetton's new range, etc., and is the result of the *immaterial* labour that is articulated and integrated with *material* labour, and that expresses contemporary forms of value.[4]

Public services such as health, energy, education, telecommunications, pensions, etc. have also suffered an intense period of restructuring and been subjected to the maxim of *commodification*, profoundly affecting public-sector workers.

The results are clear: forms of labour-extraction have intensified, tertiarisation has increased and *notions of time and space have also been transformed* and this has greatly altered the way that capital produces commodities, be they material or immaterial, physical or symbolic. A single concentrated business can be replaced by several small units interlinked through a network, with a much lower number of workers and much greater production. Telematic work, internet-work and home-based work have flourished amidst the most diverse forms of precarious labour.[5] The repercussions upon the organisational, valorative, subjective and ideological-political map of the world of work are evident.

Stable labour has become, therefore, (nearly) virtual. We are witnessing the erosion of regulated contract-work that was dominant in the twentieth century and are experiencing its replacement by tertiarisation, various kinds of flexibilisation, part-time work, different forms of 'entrepreneurialism',

---

4. Antunes 1995a and 2005.
5. Huws 2003.

'co-operativism', 'voluntary work', third-sector work, etc., examples of what Luciano Vasapollo referred to as *atypical work*.[6]

The emergence of co-operatives is interesting since they were originally conceived of as instruments of workers' struggle against unemployment and labour-despotism. Today, in contrast, capital has created false co-operatives as a means of destabilising labour-rights even further. Employer-'cooperatives' are the opposite of worker-cooperatives in that they actually destroy labour-rights and increase the precarious conditions of work of the working class. Entrepreneurialism is another case in point, presenting itself as a hidden form of wage-labour and providing fertile ground for the proliferation of distinct forms of *wage-, working-time, functional or organisational flexibilisation*.

Amidst this scenario of *structural precarisation of labour*, capital is demanding that national governments dismantle social legislation that protects labour. And flexibilisation of labour-law entails the further increase of measures of overtime-extraction, of forms of precarisation and the destruction of the social rights fought for by the working class ever since the industrial revolution in England and post-1930 in the case of Brazil. All this has taken place at the height of techno-scientific advance, destroying many (unfounded) optimistic expectations for the future, because despite the informational advances, the world of informality has vastly expanded.

III – *The information era and the epoch of labour-informalisation*

There is, therefore, another contradiction within the contemporary (de-)sociability of global and financial capital: it appears that, the stronger the ideology and practice of the so-called 'modern enterprise', the greater the rationalisation of its *modus operandi*, and the more companies focus on 'competencies', 'qualifications', 'knowledge'-management, etc., the higher the level of labour-degradation (in the sense of the loss of ties and the erosion of regulation and contracts) for a significant portion of male and female workers.

At the *top*, we find super-qualified workers who operate in the sphere of information- and communication-technologies; at the base, we find increasing levels of precarisation and unemployment, both of which are structural. Between the two extremes, we find a hybrid-mix whereby the super-qualified worker of today can find herself unemployed or in precarious employment tomorrow, both scenarii being on the rise in the world of global capital.

By appropriating the cognitive, intellectual dimension of labour – a key trait of modern capitalism – capital has increased the forms and mechanisms

---

6. Vasapollo 2005.

of value-creation. In this way, it has also increased the means of control and subordination of the subjects of labour, using even 'more coercive mechanisms, renewing primitive forms of violence, since [paradoxically] companies also need the greater subjective and social co-operation and "involvement" of the worker'.[7] Rather, then, than the end or loss of importance of the labour theory of value, there has been a qualitative change and increase in the forms and mechanisms of labour-extraction.

The slogan adopted by Toyota at the Takaoka plant and printed on the flag that waves outside its premises is symptomatic of this transformation: 'Yoi kangae, yoi shina' ('Good thoughts mean good products').[8] But it is worth remembering that attempts to encourage worker-'involvement' and implement flexibilisation have also met with resistance from the workers, as illustrated in the protest of 1,300 workers organised by unions against outsourcing.[9]

Similarly, it is no coincidence that Manpower – a transnational company using the outsourcing of labour on a global scale – is a symbol of employment in the US:

> [Manpower] builds partnerships with clients in over 60 countries, ... more than 400 thousand clients from various sectors like trade, industry, services and promotion.... Manpower is prepared to serve its customers with high added-value services, such as: hiring and managing temporary staff; recruitment and selection of permanent professional staff for all areas; trainees and internships programs, outsourcing projects and contact centre services; HR management (Total HR) and hiring highly specialized professionals.[10]

As a result, the prevalence of *instrumental reason* assumes the form of widespread *social irrationality* and introduces a fundamental and ardent challenge: the deconstruction of this ideology and practice is the condition according to which *labour* and, therefore, humanity can become genuinely meaningful and bring to an end the destructive process of *labour-dehumanisation* that has been in place since the start of the Industrial Revolution.

The evidence is strong: at the height of the era of the *computerisation* of labour, of the *mechanical and digital* world, we are encountering the *epoch of labour-informalisation*, of outsourced, precarious, subcontracted, part-time, *sub-proletarian workers*.

---

7. Bialakowsky 2003, p. 135.
8. *Business Week*, 18 November 2003.
9. *Japan Press Weekly* 2004.
10. Manpower Brazil, <www.manpower.com.br>.

While in Brazil's recent past, the working class only experienced marginal levels of informality, today more than 50 per cent of the working class finds itself in this condition (here, informality is understood in a broad sense), deprived of rights, outside of the social protection safety-net and with no work-permit. Widespread unemployment, severe precariousness, sharp falls in wages, increasing loss of rights: these are the most common features of our working class, signalling a new century characterised by heated clashes between the social forces of labour and the totality of global social capital.

IV – The twenty-first century: between the continuity and superfluousness of labour

There is another pendular movement affecting the working class. On the one hand, *fewer* men and women find work *and* work *very hard* – at a pace and intensity similar to that of the early days of capitalism, at the genesis of the Industrial Revolution – reducing stable work, the heir of the industrial phase of capitalism of the early-twentieth century. Since, however, capital cannot *completely* eliminate living labour, it has been able to reduce it in some areas at the expense of increasing it in others, as can be seen in the growing appropriation of the cognitive dimension of work and, at the same time, in the increase of unskilled, precarious work. Here we find, therefore, the *perennial* aspect of labour.

On the backswing of the pendulum, *more* men and women are finding *less stable work,* travelling the world in search of any job and representing an increasing trend towards labour-precarisation across the globe, from the US to Japan, from Germany to Mexico, from the UK to Brazil, with rise of structural unemployment as the most virulent expression of this trend. In China, for example, a country that is growing at an astonishing pace – given the peculiarities of a late industrialisation that combines a surplus-, hyper-exploited labour-force with industrial-informational machinery – the industrial proletariat has also decreased, as a result of the techno-scientific progress under way. According to Jeremy Rifkin, between 1995 and 2002, China lost more than 15 million industrial workers.[11] For this reason, the Chinese Communist Party and its government are alarmed at the leap in social protests that have increased tenfold in the last few years, reaching around 80,000 actions in 2005. A similar process is taking place in India and in many other parts of the world, including Latin America.

---

11. 'Return of a Conundrum', *The Guardian*, 2 March 2004.

Taylorist/Fordist work from the era of the automobile has decreased, but the world of the *class-that-lives-from-labour* has expanded. This brings us to contemporary forms of value.

V – *The growth of abstract-intellectual labour and new forms of value (the interconnections between material and immaterial labour)*

With the conversion of *living labour* into *dead labour*, from the moment when software enables the informational machine to perform activities that belong to human intelligence, we can observe what Lojkine vividly referred to as the *objectification of cerebral activities in the machinery*, the transferral of intellectual and cognitive knowledge from the working class to the informational machinery.[12] This transferral of intellectual capacities, which are converted into the language of machinery by computers, emphasises the transformation of *living labour* into *dead labour*.

Thus, the overlap between *material* and *immaterial* labour is increased, since we are not only experiencing a vast expansion of precarious labour, but also the significant growth of labour carrying a greater intellectual dimension, in more computerised industrial activities as well as in the service- and communications-sectors, among many others.

In this way, *immaterial labour* expresses the informational sphere of the commodity-form: it is the expression of the *informational* content of the commodity and displays the transformations of labour inside large companies and in the service-sector where direct manual labour is being replaced by labour carrying a greater intellectual dimension. *Material* and *immaterial* labour and the increasing overlap between the two are, therefore, centrally subordinated to the logic of the production of commodities and capital.

We fully agree here with J.-M. Vincent, when he observes:

> [T]he value-form of labour itself is metamorphosed. It increasingly assumes the value-form of abstract intellectual labour. The intellectual labour-force produced inside and outside production is absorbed as a commodity by capital that incorporates it to give new qualities to dead labour.... Material production and the production of services increasingly require innovation, becoming as a result more and more subordinated to a growing production of knowledge that is converted into commodities and capital.[13]

---

12. Lojkine 1995a.
13. Vincent 1993, p. 121.

The new phase of capital, in the era of the 'lean enterprise', re-transfers *know-how* to labour, but does so having increasingly appropriated itself of its *intellectual* dimension, of its cognitive capacities, *and seeks* to involve more and more profoundly the subjectivity present in the world of work. However, the process is not limited to this aspect since part of the *intellectual knowledge* is transferred to the computerised machines that, in turn, become more *intelligent and reproduce a portion of the activities transferred to them by the intellectual knowledge of labour.* Since the machine cannot entirely eliminate human labour, it requires a greater *interaction* between the subjectivity that labours and the new intelligent machine.

And, during this process, the *interactive involvement* further increases the *estrangement and alienation of labour*, expanding modern forms of *reification*, distancing it even further from the exercise of what Nicolas Tertulian, in the tradition of Lukács, referred to as an *authentic and self-determined subjectivity.*[14]

Therefore, rather than the replacement of labour by science, or even the substitution of the production of values for the sphere of communication, the replacement of production by information, what we are witnessing in the world today is a greater *interrelation*, a greater *interpenetration* between productive and unproductive activities, between factory- and service-activities, between executive and conceptual activities, that have grown in the context of the productive restructuring of capital. This leads to the need to develop a broader notion of the *form of being of labour* in contemporary capitalism, and not to its negation.

However, theories that advocate the prevalence of immaterial labour today (with the resulting disproportionate value attached to it) seem mistaken. For our part, instead, we would argue that the forms of immaterial labour express the distinct modalities of living labour that are necessary for the contemporary valorisation of value. During the phase of execution in which scientific knowledge is directly mixed with executive knowledge, the *creative power* of living labour assumes both the form of material labour (which is still dominant) and the *tendency* towards the *modality* of immaterial labour.[15]

Being neither the only nor the dominant modality, immaterial labour – and here we find another typically Eurocentric aspect of these theses – is converted into *abstract-intellectual labour. This increasingly intangible immaterial labour is placed into the prevalent logic of material accumulation, in such a way that the measure of value is given once again by the average social time of an increasingly complex job, and immaterial labour is assimilated into the new phase of value-production, into*

---

14. Tertulian 1993.
15. Antunes 2005.

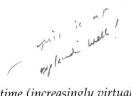

the new forms of time (increasingly virtual) and space. Therefore, rather than the breakdown of the law of value, the increasing intertwinement of material and immaterial labour reflects a fundamental new element in understanding the new mechanisms of the theory of value today, in the context of the logic of financialisation.

Earlier, we mentioned the case of Manpower, a transnational company that outsources its labour-force across the world. We also saw that what is intangible for many, is clearly quantifiable for Toyota. Finally, it is important to highlight that *immateriality* is a tendency, whilst *materiality* is prevalent, especially when we consider capitalism on a global scale, structured according to the (new) international division of labour, in which – it is worth reminding ourselves – two-thirds of the human labouring force is to be found in the Global South. The rise of China in the last decade (or India), a country anchored to a vast surplus labour-force, to the use of informational technology and a network of transnational companies – alongside the socio-technical control of workers – is leading to an immeasurable exploitation of the labour-force and, consequently, a significant increase in value undermining (empirically and theoretically) the theory of the loss of importance of living labour in the production of value. Further, the examples of China and India are evidence of the fragility of theses that defend the predominance of immaterial labour as a form of *overcoming* or *inadequacy* of the law of value.

From the intensified labour of Japan to the *contingent labour* of the US, from the immigrants who migrate to the advanced West to the underworld of labour in Asia, from the *maquiladoras* of Mexico to the precarious workers across western Europe, from Nike to McDonald's, from General Motors to Ford and Toyota, from call-centres to Walmart workers, we can observe different modalities of living labour, at the top and at the base, all necessary in some way for the expansion of the new modalities of value-creation.

VI – *Postindustrial society and interpenetration of sectors in the era of financialisation*

We have seen that global productive restructuring across industry and services as a result of the new international division of labour required a number of transformations in the socio-technical organisation of production and labour-control, in terms of both the re-territorialisation and de-territorialisation of production, among others. This has taken place during a period of globalisation and financialisation of capital, in which the independence of the three traditional economic sectors (industry, agriculture and services) has become obsolete as their activities have become increasingly interconnected – key examples are *agro-industry, the service-industry* and *industrial services*. It is important to note (even for the political consequences of this thesis) that recognising sectoral interdependence is very different from defending the *'postindustrial society'* thesis, a concept which is laden with political implications.

VII – *Labour's multiple transversalities: gender, generation and ethnicity*

The world of work is experiencing a sharp increase in the contingent of female workers, who represent 40 per cent or sometimes more than 50 per cent of the labour-force in some advanced countries, and have been absorbed by capital through the provision of part-time, precarious and unregulated work. Recently, in the UK for example, female workers were the majority of the labour-force (in 1998). However, it is known that the increase in female workers is indirectly proportional to their wages and rights, since the wage-inequality experienced by women contradicts their increased participation in the labour-market. Women's remuneration rates are substantially inferior to their male counterparts' and the same occurs with respect to their rights and working conditions.

In the *sexual division of labour* that capital establishes in the *factory-space*, generally conceptual activities or those based on *intensive capital* are performed by male labour, while those requiring fewer qualifications, that are more elementary and often based on *intensive labour* are destined to female labour (and often also to male and female immigrant- and black workers). This is not to mention the double work of women in the world of production and reproduction, both of which are indispensable for capital.[16]

With the sharp rise of the *new informal proletariat*, of the manufacturing and service-sector sub-proletariat, new jobs are performed by immigrant-labour, such as the *Gastarbeiters* in Germany, the *lavoratori in nero* in Italy, the *chicanos* in the US, eastern-European immigrants (Polish, Hungarian, Romanian, Albanian workers) in western Europe, the *dekasseguis* of Japan, Bolivians in Brazil, *brasiguaios* in Paraguay (Brazilian workers), etc. It is worth recalling that the riots in Paris in late 2005 brought to the fore the rich connections between work, unemployment, precarisation, immigration, generations, etc.

The question of generation concerns the exclusion of young and old workers from the labour-market: the young find themselves joining the ranks of the unemployed and later, when they reach the age of 35 or 40, once made redundant, they again have great difficulty finding a new job.

---

16. Pollert 1996.

At the same time, over the last few decades there has been the precocious inclusion of children in the labour-market, especially in middle-industrialising and subordinate countries such as in Asia or Latin America, but it also affects many advanced countries. Although this trend has been in decline, it is still significant and hard to measure, especially in countries such as China, India and Brazil.

There are, therefore, deep cleavages and transversalities today between stable and precarious workers, men and women, young and old, national and immigrant, black, white and Asian, qualified and unqualified, 'included' and 'excluded', representing what I refer to as the *new morphology of labour*. This brings us to our next thesis.

VIII – *Tracing a new morphology of labour*

In contrast to theses that advocate the end of labour, our challenge is to understand the *new morphology* of labour, of which the most distinguishing feature is multifacetedness, resulting from the significant transformations that have shaken capital in recent years.

This *new morphology* stretches from classic industrial and rural workers, who are in a process of relative decline (which is unequal if the North and South are compared), to service-sector wage-earners, the new contingents of outsourced, subcontracted, temporary male and female workers in a process of expansion. The *new morphology* is already experiencing the simultaneous retraction of the Taylorist/Fordist industrial working class and the expansion, in line with the logic of Toyotist flexibilisation, of the new modalities of labour, such as telemarketing and call-centre workers, *motoboys* who die on the road, office-workers employed in banks, fast-food workers, young supermarket-workers, etc. These workers are a constitutive part of those social forces of labour that Ursula Huws refers to as the *cybertariat, the new proletariat of the cybernetic era that experiences (nearly) virtual work in a (very) real world*, to borrow from the evocative title of the author's book.[17] There, she discusses the new configurations of labour in the digital, informatics and telematics era, the new workers who oscillate between the vast *heterogeneity* (of gender, ethnicity, generation, space, nationality, qualification, etc.) of their *form of being* and the impulse towards *homogenisation* that results from the precarious condition of their diverse occupations.

---

17. Huws 2003.

XI – *The erosion of the hierarchy of labour-representation organisations*

If the impulse towards labour-flexibilisation is a requirement for increasingly globalised capital, the responses of the world of work need to be configured at an increasingly international to global scale, carefully articulating the nexus between national and international action. As the era of globalisation of capital has grown more intense in the most recent decades,[18] we are also moving towards the internationalisation of social struggles of labour-forces that have swelled with the mass of unemployed workers across the world.[19] In Argentina, for example, we can observe new forms of social confrontation such as the uprisings of unemployed workers, the *piqueteros*, who block off roads to stop the circulation of goods (with clear repercussions for production) and brand the country with the scourge of unemployment. Or even, the growth of workers' struggles around 'reclaimed' factories that were occupied during the height of the Argentinian recession in early 2001, which has resulted in around 200 companies now being under workers' control. Both were decisive responses to Argentinian unemployment and they signal the emergence of new forms of social labour-struggles.

Other significant experiments include the unrest in France at the end of 2005, with riots led by immigrants (without or with very little work), the destruction of thousands of cars (symbol of the twentieth century) and the impressive demonstrations in early 2006 when students and workers waged a joint struggle against the First Employment Contract (CPE).

This new morphology of labour cannot fail to impact on the organisations that represent labour. Hence, the profound crisis affecting political parties and trade-unions. While some analysts envisage the demise of these class-organisations, here we limit ourselves to observing that a *new morphology of labour* also entails a *new design of the forms of social and political representation of labour-forces*. If Taylorist and Fordist industry is a thing of the past (at least, as a trend), how can we assume a vertical trade-unionism can represent the new composite world of work?[20] And further, what does it mean today to be a *distinct, class-based political party* (Marx), when many are still rooted in either social democracy heavily bound by neoliberalism, or the vanguardism that was typical of the twentieth century?

A conclusion emerges, in the guise of a hypothesis: today we should recognise (and even celebrate) the *erosion of hierarchy* within class-organisations.

---

18. Chesnais 1996a and 1996b.
19. Bernardo 2004.
20. Bihr 1991.

The old maxim that first come the parties, then the unions followed by, at the bottom, social movements, is no longer reflected in the real world and among social struggles. Most important today will be that social, union- or political movement that understands the *roots* of our social ills and structures and which issues are *vital*. And to do so, *to be radical*, it will be essential for it to understand the new morphology of labour, as well as the complex workings of capital.

X – *The pendulum of labour*

Ever since the ancient world and its philosophy, labour has been understood as the expression of life and degradation, creation and unhappiness, vital activity and slavery, social happiness and servitude. Labour and toil. Moment of catharsis and martyrdom. At times its positive meaning was emphasised, at others its negative traits. In *Works and Days* by Hesiod, an ode to work, the author did not hesitate to observe that 'there is not dishonour in labour, but idleness is dishonour'.[21]

With human development, labour became *travail*, which word originates from *tripalium*, an instrument of torture, moment of punishment and suffering. In contrast, idleness became part of the journey towards human realisation.

Christian thought, throughout its long and complex path, prolonged the controversy, conceiving of labour as martyrdom and salvation, a certain shortcut to heaven, a pathway to heaven. At the end of the Middle-Ages, with St Thomas Aquinas, labour was considered a *moral act worthy of honour and respect*.[22]

Weber, with his *positive work-ethic*, assigned once more to pursuing a trade the path to salvation, in heaven and on earth, labour as *the very purpose of life itself*. The prevalence of trades was therefore sealed under the command of the world of commodities and money, replacing the realm of rest, leisure and idleness.

Whether as *Arbeit, lavoro, travail, trabajo, labour or work*, the society of labour reached modernity and the world of commodities. Hegel wrote beautifully about the *dialectic of the master and the slave*, showing that the master only becomes such through the other, the slave.[23]

It was, however, with Marx that labour achieved full synthesis: to labour was the eternal necessity to maintain the social metabolism between

---

21. Hesiod 1990, p. 45.
22. See Neffa 2003, p. 52.
23. Hegel 1966, pp. 113–18.

humankind and nature. Yet, under the empire (and fetish) of the commodity, this *vital activity was transformed into imposed, extrinsic and external, forced and compulsory activity.* Marx's reference to factory work is well known: 'Its alien character emerges clearly in the fact that as soon as no physical compulsion or other compulsion exists, labour is shunned like the plague.'[24]

This pendular movement, at once duplicitous and contradictory – that is in fact the expression of a real *labour-dialectic* – has confirmed the place of human *labour* as a key question in our lives. And, throughout the twentieth century, waged and fetishised labour has grown more than ever before, assuming the shape of alienated and estranged work.

XI – *A new system of social metabolism: self-determination and available time*

The construction of a new system of social metabolism,[25] of a new *mode of production and life*, based on *self-determined activity* (to produce socially-necessary use-values) and on *the realisation of socially-necessary labour in contrast to hetero-determined production* (based on surplus-time for the exclusive production of exchange-values for the market and the reproduction of capital), is imperative in the world of today.

There are therefore, two vital principles:

1) social meaning will primarily be derived from meeting real human and vital social needs, be these material or immaterial; and
2) the exercise of labour, stripped of the forms of alienation and estrangement associated with it through capital, will be synonymous with self-activity, i.e. free activity, based on disposable time.

With the logic of capital and its system of social metabolism, the production of socially-necessary use-values was subordinated to the exchange-values of commodities; in this way, basic productive functions, as well as the control over this process, were radically separated between those that *produce* and those that *control*. As Marx observed, capital operated the separation between workers and means of production, between the 'snail and its shell',[26] driving deeper the wedge between production aimed at meeting human social needs and the reproductive needs of capital.

As the first *mode of production* to establish a logic that does not take real social necessities into consideration – but instead only the need to reproduce

---

24. Marx 1975, p. 274.
25. Mészáros 1995.
26. Marx 1967, vol. 2, p. 359.

capital to a greater and greater degree – a *mode of production was established that is remote from the self-reproductive needs of human beings.*[27]

The other essential social principle is given by the transformation of labour into *vital, free, self-activity,* based on *disposable time.* This entails rejecting the disjunction between *necessary labour-time* for social reproduction and *surplus labour-time* for the reproduction of capital. The latter must be radically uprooted.

The exercise of autonomous labour – once the expenditure of surplus-time for the production of commodities has been eliminated, along with *destructive and superfluous* production-time (spheres that are controlled by capital) – will reclaim the *formative meaning of living labour,* against the *destructive meaning of abstract labour given by capital.*[28] This is the case under capital's social-metabolic order, where labour that *forms* capital *destroys* the social being. Under a new form of sociability, by contrast, *social labour, by meeting authentic human and societal needs, will destroy capital* – giving new *meaning* both to life *within* work as much as life *outside of* work.

Achieved by? What means?

27. Mészáros 2002.
28. Antunes 1995a.

Appendix 2

Labour and Value: Critical Notes[1]
On André Gorz's Recent Work

A discussion of André Gorz's work is a difficult endeavour, especially given the breadth of his work, its numerous phases and periods, and its originality, oscillations, continuities and discontinuities. Although I have read some of his books, I would not attempt a critical analysis of his voluminous and dense production, something more suitable for a specialist on Gorz's writing. Instead, I shall simply raise a few controversial issues on his intellectual work that I believe deserve some critique.

Gorz's reflections constitute a vast, creative and original body of work, and have often been provocative, an invitation to debate, which I show in *Adeus ao Trabalho?* (*Farewell to Work?*), where I offer a critique of *Farewell to the Working Class* (1982). It is also necessary to recognise that Gorz dedicated himself intensely to the study of labour and achieving the arduous task of understanding its transformations and metamorphoses.

In this text, we will attempt a *critique of the critique,* even if just as an introduction, and focus on three key questions in Gorz's work and his polemic against Marx: his understanding of the category of *labour,* his critique of the concept of the *proletariat,* and the modern meaning he ascribes to the *theory of value.* We shall refer to *Metamorphoses of Labour* and *The Immaterial,* returning from time to time to *Farewell to the Working Class* and interviews with the author.

I

André Gorz understands that the modern idea of *labour* is a creation of capitalism, of its industrial phase, and therefore a synonym of waged, fetishised and alienated labour. This is clearly presented in the first pages of *Farewell to the Working Class* and also reiterated in *Metamorphoses of Labour.*

In his words, 'what we call "labour" is an invention of modernity', generalised under industrialisation, distinct from 'doing', 'work' and 'self-production'.

---

1. This text was originally published in *Estudios Latinoamericanos, Mexico City, Nueva Época*, no. 21, January–June 2008, Cela/UNAM; and in Josué Pereira da Silva and Iram Jácome Rodrigues (eds.) 2006, *André Gorz e Seus Críticos*, São Paulo: Annablume.

It is 'an activity performed in the *public* space, solicited, defined and recognised as useful beyond ourselves and for this reason, it is remunerated'.[2]

The contemporary notion of work, according to the author, 'only arises, effectively, with manufacturing capital. Until then, i.e., until the XVIII century, the term "labour" (*arbeit, lavoro, travail*) designated the toil of servants and day labourers, producers of goods for consumption or necessary services for survival'.[3]

A fierce critic of the 'unjustified utopia' formulated by Marxism, Gorz also observes that 'in Marx there already was an enormous contradiction between the admirably insightful theory and phenomenological descriptions of the relation of the worker to the machine: the separation of the worker from the means of production, the product, the science embodied in the machine. Nothing in the description justified the theory of "attractive labour"'. The key question, for Gorz, becomes therefore freedom *from* work. And it is from here that he builds his *construct*, structured by the struggle for free time, for a citizen's wage and for new forms of autonomy.

With firm roots in the work of authors such as Hannah Arendt, Gorz *unilateralises* labour, as a moment of *negativity par excellence*, devoid of any freedom or creativity. However, on this critical point, his analysis does not convince and his phenomenological (not ontological) understanding of labour is unable, in our view, to capture the complex processes operating in reality, its movements of positivity and negativity, creation and servitude, humanity and inhumanity, self-constitution and undoing, that are present in the *whole* history of labour.

As mentioned in my earlier work,[4] in the *philosophy of labour*, the labouring act has been understood as expression of both life and degradation, creation and unhappiness, vital activity and slavery, social happiness and servitude.

While Hegel wrote beautifully about the *dialectic of the master and the slave*, showing how the master *only becomes master* through the other, the slave, it was Marx who demonstrated that, at the same time as labour is *eternally necessary to maintain the social metabolism between humanity and nature*, it is also, in the fetishised world of the commodity, an *imposed, extrinsic and external* activity, at once *forced and compulsory*, of an intensity such that *if they could, workers would shun work as they would the plague*.[5]

---

2. Gorz 2003, p. 12.
3. Gorz 2003, p. 24.
4. Antunes 2005.
5. Marx 1975, p. 274.

This is because, in Marx's view, while, at its genesis, labour is an expression of a *vital activity*, in its concrete historico-social reality, it undergoes a metamorphosis under the constraints of the 'second nature' mediated by capital and becomes alienated and fetishised. Therefore, *concrete labour*, which creates socially useful things, is subordinated to *abstract labour*, which is waged and estranged.

However, in this first critical note, it is important to observe that, rather than a *unilateralisation* of labour, there is in Marx a recognition that labour is the vivid expression of a contradiction between positivity and negativity, since, depending on the way of life, of production and social reproduction, the labouring act can both create and subordinate, humanise and demean. It is as much instrument of freedom as source of slavery. It can both emancipate and alienate. *This depends, in essence, on the shape of social relations of production.* This has been the case throughout human history, well before the advent of capitalism.

It is by capturing in theory this complex and contradictory nexus that Marx is able to demonstrate that labour, while transforming nature, transforms human nature itself. Therefore, to *unilateralise it* entails ignoring its double, contradictory nature, its multiple meanings, the real source of its richness (and also misery). And the *unilateralisation* of this complex process impedes, rather than aids, Gorz's understanding of its movement.

Thus, a fully meaningful life can only exist with the *demolition* of the barriers that exist between *working time* and *non-working time*. In this way, from a vital meaningful activity, from self-determined labour directed at the creation of socially useful goods – beyond the hierarchical division that subordinates labour to capital that is in force today, and therefore, upon entirely new bases – a new form of sociability based on *disposable time* can be developed.

In other words, a new form in which ethics, art, philosophy, genuinely free time, in line with more authentic aspirations that arise within everyday life, can encourage the development of entirely new forms of sociability. But it is good to remember that this can only occur with the rupture of the destructive logic of capital that presides over contemporary (de-)sociability.

There is another point that should be addressed in this critique of Gorz. If, for the author, labour is the *realm of necessity in want of freedom par excellence*, it is good to recall Lukács's *The Ontology of Social Being* and his magnificent essay in *History and Class Consciousness*, in which labour, at the same time as being the space of commodification and reification, is also the *model of human activity*, *ultimate* moment of *teleological positing*, of the conscious act that seeks purpose. For this reason, labour also expresses the first moment of freedom. It is through the labouring act that one can choose between multiple or distinct alternatives. And, in so doing, a moment of freedom emerges, albeit a preliminary one. In Lukács's words:

> The fundamental question of labour for the humanisation of man is also present in the fact that its ontological constitution marks the genetic starting point for another vital question that profoundly affects humanity in the course of its history, the question of freedom. Its ontological genesis also originates in the sphere of labour.[6]

It is clear that the freedom content referred to here is essentially different in more advanced and complex forms of sociability. However, the teleological act, expressed through the collocation of purpose, is an act of choice, a manifestation of freedom inside the process of labour. It is a real moment of interaction between subjectivity and objectivity, causality and teleology, necessity and freedom.[7]

Further, 'If the freedom won in original labour was necessarily rudimentary and restricted, this does not alter the fact that even the most spiritual and elevated freedom has to be obtained through the same methods that exist in original labour'[8] through the power of individual human action over the sphere of nature. It is exactly in this sense that labour can be considered the preliminary moment of freedom.

Therefore, *unilateralising* labour and reducing it to its exclusively negative dimension is not a viable analytical path to take.

II

The notion of *proletariat* that Gorz attributes to Marx seems very problematic. According to him, 'Marx, since 1846, conceives of the proletariat as a potentially universal class, *uninvested of any particular interest*, and therefore, susceptible to seizing power in its hands and rationalising the social process of production'.[9]

He goes on: 'The main utopia of this conception is that the proletariat is destined to realising the unity of the real as the unity of Reason: individuals that are without *any interest* or any particular trade will end up uniting with the *universal aim of making mutual collaboration rational and voluntary*, and together, they will produce, in common, a world that belongs to them entirely: nothing

---

6. Lukács 1980, pp. 12–13.
7. Lukács 1980, pp. 116–17.
8. Lukács 1980, p. 136.
9. Gorz 2003, p. 32 (my italics).

will exist independently of them [the only entities able to realise the] *triumph of the unity of Reason.'*[10]

In fact, Gorz is repeating here the same misunderstanding present in *Farewell to the Working Class*, in which he attributes to Marx an interpretation shaped more by vulgar Marxism than by Marx and that does not stand up to a more rigorous analysis of the Marxist notion of the proletariat and its potential.

This deserves some clarification: Marx showed the transformative possibilities of the proletariat with a complex analysis that articulated elements of materiality (the role of the labour-force in the creation of value) with elements of subjectivity of the proletariat that could arise to a greater or lesser extent depending on the context of class-struggle. The example of the Paris Commune, typical of that time, confirms rather than undermines the Marxist position.

Therefore, Marx captured both the *revolutionary potentiality* of the working class as much as its *contingency*, immediacy or reformism. We may recall his (and Engels's) observations about the *labour-aristocracy*. In other words, in contrast to Gorz's reading, the working class, for Marx, could operate as much in the space of *contingency* as engage in emancipatory struggle. However, its *potentiality* could enable it to assume, in special situations, a clear revolutionary dimension. And this is supported in the strength of the labour theory of value and in the reality of class-struggle. There is, therefore, no sacralisation that can undermine Marx's theory.

As a prisoner of abstract criticism, Gorz found himself unable to advance an understanding of the *new morphology* of the working class today, its possibilities and limitations. Even if we put to one side the serious inaccuracy of claiming an indeterminate *non-class of non-workers* (present in *Farewell to the Working Class*), Gorz greatly impoverished the Marxist conceptualisation of the proletariat.

Hindered by a *unilateralisation* that conceives of labour as brimming with negativity and tied to an apparent *positive work-ethic* (common to Weber and absent in Marx), Gorz is able to relate his increasing discrediting of the potential of the working class (or the proletariat) with an apparent *sacralisation* of the Marxist concept of the proletariat. This connection allowed the author – Eurocentrically – to 'justify' his *disenchantment* with the potential of workers today.

In contrast to theories that advocate the end of work and the potential of the working class (or the modern proletariat), our task is to understand what can

---

10. Gorz 2003, p. 36 (my italics).

be referred to as the *new morphology* (of labour and the working class). This ranges from industrial and rural workers, in a process of decline especially in the northern countries, to the service-sector proletariat, the new contingents of outsourced, subcontracted, temporary male and female workers whose numbers are *increasing on a global scale*.

Recent events in France with the tumult between immigrants (with little or no work), students and workers (the struggle against the First Employment Contract (CPE)) are symptomatic.

III

No less controversial are André Gorz's reflections on the notion of labour-*immateriality*. Influenced by 'human-capital' theories and others that defend the intangibility of 'value' generated by immaterial labour, Gorz moves towards the idea that 'labour is no longer measurable according to pre-established standards and norms'.[11]

Unlike the automaton – mode of labour in the era of machinery – 'post-Fordist workers, in contrast, must enter into the process of production with the entire cultural baggage they acquired during leisure activities, team sports, conflicts, disputes, musical, theatrical activities, etc. It is in these activities outside of labour that their vitality, their ability to improvise, to co-operate are developed. It is their vernacular knowledge that the post-Fordist enterprise puts to work and exploits'.[12]

In this way, again according to the author, *knowledge becomes the most important source of creation, since it is at the heart of innovation, of communication and of creative and continually renewable self-organisation.* This leads to the conclusion that 'the work of living knowledge *produces nothing that is materially palpable.* It is, above all in the network economy, the work of the person whose job is to produce the activity itself'.[13]

The intangibility of this form of work comes to the surface:

> Knowledge, unlike social labour in general, cannot be translated and measured in simple abstract units. It is not reducible to a quantity of abstract labour that it would be the equivalent, the result or product of. It covers and designates a wide range of *heterogeneous capabilities*, i.e. without *a common standard*, amongst which judgement, intuition, aesthetic sense, level of education and information, the ability to learn and to adapt to

---

11. Gorz 2005a, p. 18.
12. Gorz 2005a, p. 19.
13. Gorz 2005a, p. 20 (my italics).

unexpected situations: capacities that are also operated by heterogeneous activities that range from mathematical calculus to rhetoric and art, to the ability to convince an interlocutor; from techno-scientific research to the invention of ethical norms.[14]

The conclusion, therefore, is clear:

The heterogeneity of so-called 'cognitive' labour activities, of the immaterial products that they create and the capacities and knowledge they imply, makes both the value of the labour-force or its products unmeasurable. Work evaluation scales become a web of contradictions. The impossibility of standardising all the parameters for the services required results in futile attempts to quantify its qualitative dimension, and set performance indicators calculated almost by the second, that do not account for the 'communicational' quality of the service required by others.[15]

He continues, outlining the consequences of this mode of labour in terms of the law of value:

The crisis of the measurement of labour-time inevitably engenders a crisis in the measurement of value. When the socially necessary labour-time for production is uncertain, this uncertainty cannot but have repercussions on the exchange-value of what is produced. The increasingly qualitative, unmeasurable character of labour puts the relevance of notions of 'surplus-labour' and 'surplus-value' into question. The crisis of the measurement of value calls into question the definition of the essence of value. It puts into question, as a consequence, the system of equivalences that regulates commercial exchange.[16]

The immeasurability of value becomes, therefore, the new *ruling indeterminacy*. That which is a tendency – immaterial labour generated by knowledge and the cognitive dimension – becomes, for Gorz, *dominant* and even *determining*, a methodological mistake that hinders a full understanding of the new modalities of the law of value.

A convergence can be seen, therefore, between Gorz's formulation and Habermas's outdated theory of *science displacing value and making living labour superfluous*:

With computerisation and automation, *labour has ceased to be the principal productive force* and salaries have ceased to be the principal cost of production. The organic composition of capital (i.e. the relation between fixed capital

---

14. Gorz 2005a, p. 29.
15. Ibid.
16. Gorz 2005a, pp. 29–30.

and working capital), has rapidly increased. Capital has become the predominant factor of production. Remuneration, reproduction, continuous technical innovation of fixed, material capital require far higher financial means than the cost of labour. The latter is currently frequently less than 15 percent of the total cost. The distribution between capital and labour of the 'value produced' by companies leans increasingly in favour of the former.... Wage-earners are obliged to choose between the deterioration of their working conditions and unemployment.[17]

Value without measure, labour without surplus-labour – the collapse and immeasurability of value-theory is inevitable, strengthened now by the thesis of the immateriality of labour.

From our perspective, however, forms of immaterial labour express the distinct modalities of living labour that are necessary for the valorisation of value today. During the stage in which scientific knowledge and knowledge derived from labour are mixed even more directly, the *creative power* of living labour assumes the (still dominant) form of material labour as well as the *tendential modality* of immaterial labour.

This is owing to the fact that the very creation of advanced informational machinery is achieved through the active interaction between the (intellectual) knowledge of workers operating the computerised machine, transferring part of their attributes to the new equipment that resulted from this process, *objectifying subjective activities, and adding new dimensions and configurations of the theory of value.*

A more complex labour-force is thus configured, at once multifunctional and consistent with the phase of the lean, flexibilised and Toyotised enterprise, and which is exploited in an even more profound and sophisticated way, materially and immaterially, than under Taylorism/Fordism.

Therefore, rather than the redundancy of the law of value, recognition of the growing overlap between material and immaterial labour as a consequence of the increase of activities carrying greater intellectual weight – both amongst more computerised industrial activities as in the service- and communication-sectors – is fundamental for our understanding of the new mechanisms of the law of value.

A clear example of this tendency is the propaganda used by the transnational company Manpower that we saw earlier. Another is Toyota, which we can deduce from the slogan 'Good thoughts mean good products' printed at the entrance to the Takaoka factory.[18] Undoubtedly, the Japanese

---

17. Gorz 2005b (my italics).
18. *Business Week*, 18 November 2003.

manufacturer (as well as Manpower) knows how to *quantify* and *account for* the surplus-value extracted from its qualitative labour.

Thus, rather than rendering the labour theory of value redundant, the law undergoes a qualitative alteration that strengthens it and gives vitality to capital, both during the process of valorisation as much as in its assault on the world of labour. Rather than a reduction or loss of relevance of the labour-theory of value, it undergoes a substantive transformation as a result of the increased forms and mechanisms of capital-creation and -valorisation, a process still deeply shaped by the increase in the forms and mechanisms of surplus-labour extraction.

Therefore, immaterial labour (or non-material labour as Marx referred to it in Chapter VI (unpublished)) expresses the *informational sphere of the commodity-form*,[19] it displays the changes to labour inside large industrial and service-sector enterprises endowed with advanced technology, that are subordinated to the logic of commodity- and capital-production. They are forms of *abstract (intellectual) labour* and not of its finitude.

Finally, it is important to add that *immateriality* is a tendency, while *materiality* is still largely prevalent, especially when we consider globalised capital, its (new) international division of labour in which, it is worth repeating, two-thirds of working people are to be found in the global South. Chinese exploitation over the last decade (not to mention India), built upon a vast surplus labour-force and the incorporation of informational technology, embedded with forms of socio-technical control of the workers, has brought about a disproportionate exploitation of the labour-force and, as a result, the sharp expansion of value, undermining (empirically and theoretically) the theory of the redundancy of living labour in value-production. It also severely weakens the theory of the immateriality of labour as a form capable of *overtaking* or *rendering redundant* the law of value.

From intensified labour in Japan to *contingent labour* in the US, from the immigrants who reach the West to the sub-world of labour in Asia, from the Mexican *maquiladoras* to the precarious workers across the whole of western Europe, from Nike to McDonald's, from General Motors to Ford and Toyota, from call-centre workers to Walmart employees, it is possible to see that the *inferno of labour* displays the distinct modalities of living labour that are needed for the creation of value.

---

19. Vincent 1993 and 1995.

One last comment: from a recent interview with André Gorz,[20] the author mentions a number of important points, such as the way growth is measured exclusively by capital and the market, and his rejection of capitalism by stating that a 'subversive logic' is imperative to dismantle it. These formulations, in some way, remind us of Gorz's more critical and radical writings, where we find more common ground.

---

20. Gorz 2005b.

Appendices to the First Edition

The Crisis of the Labour-Movement and the Centrality of Labour Today[1]

In recent decades, particularly after the mid-1970s, the world of work has encountered perhaps its most critical period since the emergence of the working class and the workers' movement. The constitutive elements of this crisis are complex, as during this time a number of dramatic transformations have taken place that have had profound consequences for the world of work and especially the labour- and trade-union movement.

In this article, I shall indicate what I consider to be some key elements for a comprehensive under-standing of this *crisis*. A more detailed and precise exploration of these elements is not possible given the breadth and complexity of the issues in question. An initial theorisation, however, is essential since this crisis has affected both the *materiality* of the working class, its *form of being*, as well as the spheres of subjectivity, politics, ideology, values and ideals that guide its actions and concrete practice.

I begin by saying that, during this period, we have experienced a *structural crisis of capital* that has afflicted all capitalist economies from the early 1970s. Its impact has been so profound that it has led capital, according to Mészáros, 'to material practices

---

1. First published in Amin et al., 1998.

of the *extended destructive self-reproduction* of capital, raising the spectre of global destruction, rather than accepting the positive restrictions needed within production for the satisfaction of human need'.[2] Among many other consequences, it has led capital on a vast process of restructuring aimed at the recovery of its cycle of reproduction that, as we will see below, has strongly impacted on the world of work.

A second key element in the understanding of the reasons for the ebbing of the labour-movement lies in the fall of the socialist states of Eastern Europe and the USSR, spreading within the world of work the false idea of the 'end of socialism'.[3] Although the long-term consequences of the fall of Eastern Europe are positive (because there is the possibility of resuming a socialist project of a new kind, upon entirely new bases, that rejects, among other harmful aspects, the Stalinist thesis of 'socialism in one country' and recovers the central aspects of Marx's formulation), in the short term, large contingents of the working class and the labour-movement have accepted and even assimilated the damaging and misguided notion of the 'end of socialism' and the end of Marxism. Further still, another consequence of the end of the misleadingly named 'socialist bloc' has been the brutal erosion of the rights and social conquests of workers in capitalist countries, strengthened by the professed 'elimination' of the socialist threat in today's world.

With the collapse of the traditional Left of the Stalinist era, there has been an acute *process of political and ideological social-democratisation of the left* and, as a result, its subordination to the order of capital. This *social-democratic accommodation* has strongly affected the trade-union and parliamentary Left, with repercussions within the working class. Left-wing unionism, for example, has turned ever more frequently to the institutionalisation and bureaucratisation that are also characteristic of trade-union social democracy.[4]

It is important to add that, with the spread of neoliberalism at the end of the 1970s and the ensuing crisis of the welfare-state, there has also been a process of regression of social democracy itself, which began to function in a very similar way to the neoliberal agenda. *Neoliberalism began to dictate the ideology and programme to be implemented by capitalist countries, firstly in the centre and not long after in the subordinate countries.* This entailed productive restructuring, accelerated privatisation, the reduction of the size of the state, fiscal and monetary policies in line with the global organs of capitalist hegemony such as the IMF and the World Bank, the dismantling of workers' social rights, heavy attacks on left-wing unions, the dissemination of subjectivism and extreme

---

2. Mészáros 1995.
3. See Kurz 1992.
4. Bernardo 1996.

individualism of which 'postmodern' culture is an expression, outright ani-
mosity towards any socialist proposal opposed to the values and interests of
capital, etc.[5]

It is clearly a *complex process*, which can be summarised as follows:

1) there has been a *structural crisis of capital* with a *profoundly depressive effect*
   that has exacerbated its destructive traits;[6]
2) the postcapitalist experience of the USSR and Eastern-European countries
   came to a close, after which important parts of the Left accelerated further
   their process of social-democratisation;[7]
3) this process took place over a period in which social democracy itself also
   underwent a crisis; and
4) the economic, social and political project of neoliberalism has spread,
   strongly affecting the world of work in a number of dimensions.

Given the scope and intensity of the *structural crisis*, capital has sought
to respond through a number of mechanisms, ranging from the expansion of speculative and financial activities, to the *replacement* or *blending* of
Taylorist and Fordist patterns of production with various forms of 'flexible
accumulation'[8] or so-called Toyotism, or the Japanese model. This last point
is of central importance, since it relates to *transformations in the process of
production* of capital, where several changes have occurred, the understanding of which is crucial as we move from the twentieth to the twenty-first
century. Here, as Marx signalled, it is necessary 'to appropriate the material
in detail, to analyse its different forms of development, to trace out their
inner connexion'.[9] I shall indicate a few of the issues that strike me as most
relevant.

In recent years particularly, as a response of capital to the crisis of the 1970s,
changes in capital's productive process have intensified as a result of technological advances, forms of flexible accumulation and alternative models to
Taylorism/Fordism such as the Toyotist or 'Japanese model'.[10]

These transformations derived, on the one hand, from inter-capitalist competition and, on the other, from the need to control the labour-movement and

---

5. See Harvey 1992; and Sader 1997.
6. Mészáros 1995; and Chesnais 1996a.
7. Magri 1991.
8. Harvey 1992.
9. Marx 1967, vol. 1, p. 19 – 'Afterword to the Second German Edition of *Capital*'.
10. See Amin (ed.) 1996.

class-struggle, profoundly affecting the working class and its trade-union movement.[11]

In essence, this form of flexibilised production seeks the worker's total adherence to and internalisation of capital's project. It is as a form of what I have elsewhere called *manipulative involvement* taken to the extreme,[12] in which capital seeks the consent and participation of workers inside the firm, to enact a project that is conceived of and designed along exclusionary foundations. It is a form of *alienation* or *estrangement* (*Entfremdung*) that, unlike Fordist despotism, leads to an even deeper internalisation of capital's ideals, intensifying the expropriation of labour's *know-how*.

What are the most important consequences of these transformations in the production process and in what way do they affect the world of work? Briefly:

1) a reduction in manual, factory-based, concentrated labour typical of Fordism and of the phase of expansion known as social-democratic regulation;[13]

2) a sharp increase in various forms of *sub-proletarianisation or labour-precarisation*, as a result of the growth of part-time, temporary, subcontracted and tertiarised labour, *which has increased on a global scale in the Third World as well as in the central countries*;[14]

3) a significant increase in female labour among the working class, on a global scale. This increase has been particularly prevalent within the sphere of precarious, subcontracted, tertiarised and part-time work, where pay is generally low;

4) a dramatic increase in moderate-wage earners, especially in the service-sector which initially grew substantially but has also been experiencing increasing unemployment due to the introduction of new technologies;

5) the exclusion of young and 'old' (around 45 years of age and over) workers from the labour-market in central countries;

6) the intensification and super-exploitation of labour, with the use of migrant-labour and increasing use of child-labour, under criminal conditions, across many parts of the world, especially Asia, Latin America, etc.;

---

11. Bihr 1991; Gounet 1991 and 1992; Murray 1983; McIlroy 1997.
12. Antunes 1995a.
13. Beynon 1995; Fumagalli 1996.
14. Bihr 1991; Antunes 1995a; Beynon 1995.

7) the exponential growth of structural unemployment, which, along with precarious labour, affects around 1 billion workers, around one-third of the world's workforce; and

8) an expansion of what Marx called *combined social labour* in the process of exchange-value creation,[15] whereby workers in different parts of the world participate in the productive process. This, obviously, does not signify the end of the working class but its use in more precarious, intensified and diversified ways.

As a result, the working class has become even more *fragmented, heterogeneous and complex*. It has become better qualified in various sectors, such as the steel-industry, where there has been a relative *intellectualisation* of labour, but *de-skilled* and *more precarious* in others, such the automotive industry, where the toolmaker no longer has the same status and a whole array of roles such as quality-inspectors, printers, miners, port workers, naval construction-workers, etc. have disappeared.[16] On the one hand, there is a minority of 'polyvalent and multifunctional' workers, able to operate digital machines and even transform themselves into what Marx called, in the *Grundrisse*, *supervisors and overseers of the productive process*.[17] On the other hand, there is a precarious, unqualified mass that is now affected by structural unemployment.

These transformations have created a working class that is even more differentiated: workers who are qualified/unqualified, in the formal/informal market, men/women, young/old, stable/precarious, immigrants/nationals, etc. In contrast, however, to the opinions of those who advocate the 'end of the central role of the working class' in today's world,[18] the greatest challenge for the class-that-lives-from-labour, at this turn of the century, is to strengthen the bonds of *class-belonging* that exist across the different segments that make up the world of work. These bonds must span from those who exert a central role in the process of exchange-value creation to those who are on the margins but who, as a result of the precarious condition in which they exist, constitute potentially rebellious social contingents against capital and its forms of (de-)socialisation. It is a prerequisite in order to oppose the brutal structural unemployment that affects the world on a global scale and that is the clearest example of the destructive and nefarious character of contemporary capitalism.

---

15. Marx 1994.
16. Lojkine 1995a.
17. Marx 1974.
18. Habermas 1989; Gorz 1990a; and Offe 1989.

A full understanding of the crisis that affects the world of work therefore must take into account this set of problems that have had a direct impact on the labour-movement, affecting both the *political economy* of capital as much as its *political and ideological* spheres. Clearly, the form the crisis has taken has depended on the *economic, social, political and ideological transformations* that have taken place in different degrees in the globalised world. For a detailed analysis of what is taking place in the world of work in each country, the challenge is to try to articulate an analytical framework that is able to combine the overarching, *universal* tendencies of capital and the labour-process with the *particularities* of each country. But it is essential to recognise the wide range of transformations and changes that have affected the working class. Uncovering and understanding these changes is an absolute priority if we are to rescue a class project that is able to confront the monumental challenges present at the end of this century.

Capitalism, and, more broadly, a *social logic driven by capital's metabolic system of control*,[19] has been unable to eliminate the multiple forms and manifestations of *estrangement* or *alienation* of labour. Instead, in many cases, as the more explicitly despotic dimension of Fordism has diminished, there has been a process of intensification and greater internalisation to the benefit of a 'manipulative involvement' associated with Toyotism, or the Japanese model.

If *estrangement* is understood, as Lukács suggested, as the existence of social barriers that impede the development of individuality towards human multifacetedness and emancipation, contemporary capital, to the extent that it is able to realise human capacities through technological and informational advances, makes the phenomenon of *estrangement* grow. This is due to the fact that, for the *class-that-lives-from-labour*, technological development does not necessarily promote the development of a meaningful subjectivity, but on the contrary, can even 'disfigure and degrade the human personality'. At the same time that technological development can lead to 'a direct increase in human capacity', it can also 'in the process, sacrifice individuals (and even whole classes)'.[20]

The pockets of poverty in the so-called First World, the explosive rates of structural unemployment, the elimination of various professions in the world of work due to improved technology aimed *primarily at the creation of exchangevalues* and extreme forms of precariousness, are just some of the most flagrant

19. Mészáros 1995.
20. Lukács 1981, p. 562.

examples of the social barriers that prevent, under capitalism, the search for a meaningful and emancipated life for the social being who works. Of course, this is yet more stark in the Third World, where two-thirds of the human workforce work in even more precarious conditions.

As contemporary forms of *estrangement* reach beyond the sphere of production into the sphere of *consumption*, the space *outside* of work, so-called *free time*, is, broadly speaking, *time that also submits to the values of the system that produces commodities and its* material and immaterial *consumption-needs*.[21]

In this scenario, what are the alternatives?

First, it is necessary to alter the logic of social production: production should be primarily driven by *use-values* and not by *exchange-values*. We know that humankind would have the conditions to reproduce itself socially, on a global scale, if destructive production were eliminated and if social production were driven not by the logic of the market but by the production of *socially useful things*. With a few hours of work each day, the world could reproduce itself in a non-destructive way, establishing a new system of social metabolism.

Second, the production of *socially-necessary things* should have *disposable time*, not *surplus-time*, as the criterion that presides over contemporary society. In this way, social labour, endowed with a greater human and social dimension, would lose the fetishised and estranged character that it manifests today and, besides enabling self-activity, it would open up the possibilities for meaningful free time beyond the sphere of work. Also because there can be no real *free time* built upon *objectified* and *estranged* labour, the *free time* that exists today is time to consume commodities, whether material or immaterial.

The starting point to instilling a new societal logic is to develop a profound, contemporary critique of the (de-)sociabilisation of humanity, both in its concrete forms as well as in the fetishised representations that exist today, as the necessary condition of overcoming the crisis that has afflicted the world of work in the last few decades of the twentieth century.

---

21. Antunes 1995a; and Bernardo 1996.

APPENDIX 2

The New Proletarians at the Turn of the Century[1]

The title of this conference, 'Proletarians of the World at the Turn of the Century: Struggles and Transformations', is very suggestive and inspires a range of questions that can help us understand the new configuration of the world of work today and of the 'new proletarians of the world'. I think it is possible to raise a number of issues that can at least identify the *workers, the proletarians of the world at the end of the twentieth century.* They are certainly different from the proletariat of the mid-nineteenth century, but they are certainly neither on the way to extinction if we examine the world from a global perspective.

It is very strange that, as the number of workers who live by selling their labour-power has been increasing on a global scale, so many authors have waved *farewell to the proletariat,* have defended the notion of the *loss of centrality of the labour-category,* or the end of human emancipation through labour. What I shall show here is a path that runs contrary to these tendencies that are so misleading.

Workers today, though not identical to those of the middle of the last century, are neither on the *route to extinction* as, in different ways, authors such as Gorz, Offe, Habermas and, more recently, Dominique Méda and Jeremy Rifkin, among many others, have argued.

I shall therefore argue against these authors with an analysis that seeks to understand what the proletarians of the world today are, or, as I referred to them in *Adeus ao Trabalho? (Farewell to Work?), the-class-that-lives-from-labour,* the class of those who live by selling their labour. I should clarify, firstly, that I do not intend to introduce a new concept, but instead to attempt to characterise the expansion of and understand the *proletariat today, workers today.* As is well known, Marx ended *Capital* when he was beginning his conceptual formulation of the classes. He wrote a page and a half, a text that would certainly have offered a more systematic, detailed treatment of the social classes, and particularly of the working class.

Marx (and also Engels) very often defined the working class and the proletariat (generally as synonymous). Engels's book *The Condition of the Working*

---

1. Transcript of a presentation given at a conference to launch edition no. 5 of *Lutas Sociais,* a publication of the postgraduate social-sciences studies-programme at PUC-SP. This text was first published in *Lutas Sociais,* no. 6, PUC-SP, 1999.

Class in England could have also been called *The Condition of the Proletariat in England*. 'Proletarians of the world, unite!' is often translated as 'Workers of the world, unite!'. Or further, 'The emancipation of the proletariat must be the work of the proletariat' is translated as 'The emancipation of the workers must be the work of the working class itself'. Marx and Engels used the notion of workers and the proletariat almost interchangeably. It might be possible to say that, in Europe in the mid-nineteenth century, workers were predominantly industrial proletarians.

So: our first task is to try to understand what the working class is *today*, what the proletariat is *today*, in the broadest sense of the term, not limiting our understanding of workers or 'proletarians of the world' *exclusively* to industrial proletarians. I would say that the proletariat or the working class today, which I have referred to as the *class-that-lives-from-labour*, includes *all wage-earners, men and women who live by selling their labour-power and who are dispossessed of the means of production*. This Marxian and Marxist definition is, I believe, entirely *pertinent*, as indeed is the essence of Marx's formulation, for thinking of the working class today.

In this sense, I would say that the working class today has, at its core, the workers whom Marx called *productive workers*, especially in Chapter VI (unpublished) and in numerous passages in *Capital* that discuss the *idea of productive labour*. Thus, I would say that the working class today is not restricted to direct manual workers but includes social labour, collective labour that sells its labour-power in exchange for a wage, as a whole. But its core is composed of *productive workers who, as Marx explained, directly produce surplus-value and who also directly participate in the process of capital-valorisation*. The working class holds its central role in the process of production of surplus-value in the process of commodity-production, in the most advanced factories where the level of interaction between living labour and dead labour, between human labour and technology, is at its most advanced.

It constitutes the central nucleus of the modern proletariat. The products made by Toyota, Nissan, General Motors, IBM, Microsoft, etc. are the result of the interaction between living and dead labour, however much authors such as Habermas argue that abstract labour has lost its structuring force in contemporary society. If abstract labour (the use of physical and intellectual energy, as Marx described in *Capital*) no longer has this position, how are Toyota's cars produced, who creates IBM's computers, Microsoft's programs, General Motors' and Nissan's cars, etc., to cite just a few examples from the transnational corporations?

However, it is also important to see that the working class today also includes *unproductive workers*, again in Marx's understanding of the term – those whose forms of labour are used as services, both for public use, such as traditional public services, and for capital's use. Unproductive labour is labour that does not directly participate as a live element in the process of capital-valorisation and surplus-value creation. This is why Marx differentiates it from productive labour that participates directly in the process of surplus-value creation. Unproductive workers are, according to Marx, those whose labour is consumed as a *use-value* rather than those whose labour creates *exchange-value*.

At the turn of the century, the working class includes the broad array of wage-earners in the service-sector who do not directly create value. This field of unproductive labour is rapidly expanding under contemporary capitalism, even though some aspects of it are in retreat. For example, in industry, there is a visible tendency towards the reduction, and, in some cases, elimination, of unproductive labour, which is instead performed by the productive worker. This worker, in the era of globalised capital, becomes even more exploited and we see an intensification of the exploitation of the labour-force. Many unproductive activities are disappearing, i.e. those that capital can eliminate. But those unproductive activities that capital can eliminate are also those that it created, transferring many to the realm of productive workers.

Unproductive workers, therefore, as creators of anti-value in the capitalist labour-process, live similar experiences to those of productive workers. They belong to what Marx called 'overhead costs of production' that are, however, completely vital to the survival of the capitalist system.

Therefore, I would argue, first, that the world of work is today made up of, as Marx believed, both productive and unproductive labour. What is needed is to try to understand what constitutes both productive and unproductive activity today.

We will now examine another set of problems: given that all productive labour is waged but not all wage-labour is productive, a contemporary understanding of the working class *must include all wage-earners*. The working class today is much broader than the industrial proletariat of the nineteenth century, even though the modern industrial proletariat constitutes the fundamental *core* of wage-earners, *the productive worker*. It includes workers engaged in material or immaterial activities, manual work, operating in the advanced modern factories and those exercising 'intellectualised' activities (although far fewer) whom Marx referred to as 'supervisors or overseers of the productive process' (*Grundrisse*).

In the picture I am presenting, *I would argue that the central role is still held by what we would call productive labour, the social and collective labour that creates exchange-values, that generates surplus-value.*

However, a *broad* notion of the working class today seems to me important and decisive in order to comprehend the meaning of the *form of being* of this class and, in this way, offer a critique of those who defend the thesis of the end of the working class – if we wish to do a *critique of the critique*.

Offe, for example, in what became a seminal essay, 'Labour as a Key Sociological Concept?', attributed the loss of centrality of labour to, among other issues, the fact that manual labour no longer carries with it a work-ethic. Yet, since when was labour considered central by Marx because it was endowed with an ethic? This argument would be meaningful for Weber, but not for Marx. The working class, for the latter, is ontologically decisive because of the fundamental role it exercises in the process of value-creation. It is due to the very materiality of the system, *and the subjective potentiality that this entails*, that its role is central. Thus, Offe's critique concerning the decentralisation of labour (in fact, a Weberian critique of a Weberian thesis, that of the prevalence of the *positive work-ethic*), for Marx – and for a Marxian reflection – is not relevant. Marx has a profoundly *negative vision of and is deeply critical of wage-labour, of fetishised labour*. In the Paris Manuscripts, Marx says that *if he could, the worker would run from work as he would from the plague*.

To think of proletarians or workers of the world today implies also thinking of those who sell their labour-power in exchange for a wage as including the rural proletariat that sells its labour-power to capital, the so-called day labourers of agro-industrial regions. This rural proletariat that sells its labour-power is also a constitutive part of workers today, of the *class-that-lives-from-labour*.

Workers at the end of the twentieth century also include – and this strikes me as a decisive blow to the thesis of the loss of importance of the world of work – on a global scale, from Japan to Brazil, from the US to Korea, from England to Mexico and Argentina, the precarious proletariat. This is what I referred to in my book *Adeus ao Trabalho?* (*Farewell to Work?*) as the *modern sub-proletariat* of manufacturing and services, characterised by part-time, temporary, precarious work, by service-sector work, fast-food workers, etc. The British sociologist Huw Beynon referred to them as *hyphenated workers*: workers in part-time, precarious, hourly-paid work. The British film *The Full Monty* shows, with a great deal of irony, a little of what it is to be an English worker in a period of industrial decline. It is a comedy that sensitively portrays the harsh living conditions of unemployed British wage-earners, of precarious workers. They find work in supermarkets, for example, earning £3–4 per hour; today they have work, tomorrow there is none, the day after tomorrow there might be, but they never have any rights. This is the part-time sub-proletariat, *a precarious proletariat with regard to its working conditions and one deprived of minimal labour-rights*.

This is the 'modern' version of the proletariat of the nineteenth century. If in a minority of sectors we can find a more 'qualified and intellectual' proletariat (in the sense that capital confers upon it), in the majority the expansion, on a global scale, of the precariousness of work has been much more intense. As an example, we might think of the female workers at Nike in Indonesia who work about 60 hours per *week* and receive $38 per *month* producing thousands of trainers and not earning enough at the end of the month to buy even one pair.

As you may know, according to the ILO, today there are more than 1 billion working men and women who are either precariously employed, underemployed or unemployed. The human force of labour is discarded with the same ease as a disposable syringe. This is what capital does and thus has access to an enormous mass of workers who already form part of structural unemployment, of a monumental industrial reserve-army which is growing everywhere. This trend is intensified by the destructive logic of capital that has been much easier to perceive in the last 20 to 30 years. This is due, on the one hand, to the insidious rise of neoliberal *ideology* and *practice* and, on the other, to a social fabric that has conformed to the new configuration of capitalism, the phase of productive restructuring of capital, in which, especially since the structural crisis that began in the 1970s, Toyotism and other experiments in deregulation, flexibilisation, etc. have made their mark on the capitalist world.

But it is clear that the *class-that-lives-from-labour*, the working class today, the *new proletarians of the end of the twentieth century*, are not managers of capital (as João Bernardo referred to them) – those who constitute a portion of the dominant class because of the important role they play in the control and management of capital. The high-level executives who control the process of capital-valorisation and reproduction within companies and receive very high salaries are part of the hierarchical control-system, a fundamental part of capital's social-metabolic order, as Mészáros described it, the system of social metabolism that hierarchically subordinates labour to the control of capital. The managers of capital are, of course, not wage-earners and are clearly excluded from the working class.

My description of the working class also clearly excludes small entrepreneurs because they hold – even if on a smaller scale – the means of production, and it also excludes those who live from interest and speculation. Therefore, a comprehensive understanding of the working class today entails an understanding of the entire set of social beings who live by the sale of their labour-power, who are wage-earners and are deprived of the means of production. This is the synthesis of the working class I outline in *Adeus ao Trabalho?* (*Farewell to Work?*): a more heterogeneous, complex and fragmented class.[2]

---

2. Alain Bihr's book also traces the most important characteristics of the European proletariat today.

In the second part of this presentation, I would like to outline some of the main empirical characteristics of the working class today.

The first trend that has been developing in the world of work today is the reduction in manual, factory-, stable workers that were typical of Taylorism/ Fordism. This proletariat has declined worldwide, in different ways depending on the country and its position in the international division of labour. The Brazilian industrial proletariat for example, between the 1960s and late 1970s, grew enormously. The same took place in Korea, to give another example. But, here, I shall focus on the last twenty years in the central countries and particularly in the last decade for subordinate industrialised countries such as Brazil. The ABC region in the São Paulo hinterland of Brazil has little more than 110–120,000 metalworkers today, compared with around 240,000 in 1980. Then, Campinas (in the same region) had around 70,000 metalworkers but today has around 37,000 secure workers. As you may remember, in the past, a company such as Volkswagen used to say it was important because it had more than 40,000 workers. Today they have fewer than 20,000 workers, yet they produce much more. In other words, today the 'achievement and vitality' of a capital is measured in a factory that produces more with fewer employees.

You might say, therefore, that André Gorz was right when he predicted the *end of the proletariat*. By this line of argument, what is in decline is tending towards disappearance. But there is a second, decisive trend (that Gorz himself perceived, since he is a talented social scientist despite failing to treat the problem analytically). This second trend – which is very important because it counteracts the first one – *is the one marked by the huge expansion of wage-labour and the precarious proletariat on a worldwide scale*. In the last few decades, at the same time as there has been a reduction in secure jobs, there has been an explosive increase in the number of male and female workers in temporary wage-labour. This is a powerful manifestation of this new segment of workers who constitute the working class today, an expression of the *new proletariat*.

A third tendency is that there has been a large increase in female labour, in industry but especially in the service-sector. In the UK, for example, there are more female workers than male workers. In various European countries, around 40–50 per cent of the labour-force is female. This is because, the more part-time work increases, the more it will be performed by female workers.

This trend has important ramifications. I am not able to treat this issue in great detail but its consequences are vast. Firstly, the incorporation of women into the labour-market is certainly an important step in the *partial* emancipation of women, as previously this access was marked much more by male labour. Yet, and this strikes me as key, capital has reconfigured a new *sexual division of labour*. Areas where there is a greater use of *intensive capital*, of more advanced machinery, are dominated by men. And areas of greater *intensive labour*, where there is an even greater exploitation of manual labour, are populated by women. Studies on this topic, such as the work of British researcher Anna Pollert, highlight this trend. And when it is not women, it is black people, when it is not black people it is immigrants, when it is not immigrants it is children, or all of these at once!

And, if the working class is as much female as it is male, socialism will not be built by the male working class alone. Unions cannot be male-only; the emancipation of humankind from the oppression of capital must be a liberation from all forms of oppression. In addition to capital's forms of class-oppression, gender-oppression is pre-capitalist, it endures through capitalism and will continue post-capitalism, *if this form of oppression is not radically eliminated from relations between social beings, between men and women*. Emancipation from capital and gender-emancipation are constitutive moments of a *process of emancipation of humanity against all forms of oppression and domination* – the revolt of black people against white racism, the struggle of immigrant-workers against xenophobic nationalism, of homosexuals against sexual discrimination, among many other cleavages that oppress social beings today. I would say that, in order to think of the question of human emancipation and the *central struggle against capital*, these elements are crucial. There are thus many emancipatory struggles.

Of course, the working class has always also been female. But it was predominantly female in certain productive sectors, such as the textile-industry. Today, it is predominantly female in many areas, in different industries and especially in part-time work. As capital perceived that women perform multiple activities, in domestic work and outside of the home, it used and intensely exploited this polyvalence of female labour. It already exploited female labour inside the domestic space, in the sphere of reproduction, and extended this exploitation to manufacturing and the service-sector. It is even more important therefore to articulate *class*-actions around *gender*-actions.

A fourth trend is that there has been a dramatic expansion of moderate-wage earners in the banking, tourism- and, more generally, service-sectors. They are the new proletarians, experiencing an increasingly acute degradation of work, as I mentioned earlier.

A fifth trend is that there has been a pronounced exclusion of the young and the 'old' (in the sense given to them by destructive capital). Young people are those who once finishing their studies find no place in the labour-market. Young Europeans, North Americans and Brazilians no longer have a guaranteed place in the labour-market. In Europe, the only guarantee is the risk of unemployment. And those older than 40 years of age, considered 'old' by capital, once unemployed, are frequently not able to return to the labour-market. They take on informal, part-time jobs. Think of the jobs that have disappeared: quality-inspectors, for example, no longer employed in factories. Will an individual who has worked as a quality-inspector for 25 years and is made redundant be able to return to another plant with a new profession or will the factory hire a young worker who is willing to take on a variety of activities and multitask, and who can be paid much less than what the quality-inspector earned? The answer is clear. Tragically, he will be a new recruit to the vast industrial reserve-army.

In contrast, therefore, to visions of the *end of work*, it seems clear that capital has been able, on a global scale, to augment the spheres of wage-labour and labour-exploitation with different forms of precariousness, underemployment, part-time work, etc. The essence of Toyotism, as Satoshi Kamata stated in his book *Japan in the Passing Lane* (a classic report about Toyota, which the author describes as the 'factory of despair'), is the minimisation of 'waste'. Metaphorically speaking, if the worker breathes and while she is breathing there are moments in which she is not producing, she should be urged to *produce while breathing and breathe while producing and never breathe without producing*. If the worker could produce without breathing, capital would allow this, *but to breathe and not produce, no*. In this way, Toyota was able to reduce 'down time' and 'waste' by 33 per cent.

This is how the Japanese automotive industry went from producing a negligible amount of cars in 1955 compared with the US (only 69,000 units compared with 9.2 million in the US) to overtaking that production twenty years later. It forced production up. Japanese capitalists would call North-American capitalists and say: 'Your workers are slow, your production-system is slow, you need to learn from us'; also because, they would argue, 'We learned from you, Toyotism is not an original Japanese creation, it was inspired by the North-American model of supermarkets, the textile-industry, etc'.

Therefore, what we are seeing is not the *end of work* but the return to very high levels of labour-exploitation, of *intensification of the time and rhythm of work. Recall that the working day can even be reduced as the pace intensifies*. And this is exactly what is occurring nearly everywhere: a greater intensity, a greater exploitation of the human force that labours. At the other end of the labour-process, the production-units at the cutting edge – which are clearly a minority, when one considers *work as a whole* – there are, of course, more 'intellectualised' forms of immaterial labour (in the sense given to them by capital). All of this, however, is very different from talk of the end of work.

What is also clearly visible today is what Marx referred to as *socially combined labour*. He would say: it does not matter if the worker is more intellectualised, if she is a manual labourer, if she is at the centre or on the fringes, the important thing is for her to contribute to the creation of values, to the *valorisation of capital* and this process of creation is the result of a socially combined labour, as he explains in Chapter VI (unpublished) which I quote here from memory. And, if it is actually *subsumed* by capital, if it participates directly in the process of valorisation of that capital itself, then it is productive labour.

The working class – the 'workers of the world at the turn of the century' – is more exploited, more fragmented, more heterogeneous and more complex, even in terms of its productive activity: it is made up of workers using, on average, four, five or six machines. They have no rights, their work is *meaningless*, in accordance with the destructive nature of capital whose metabolic relations not only degrade nature and lead the world to the brink of environmental catastrophe, but also increase the vulnerability of the human force that labours, with unemployment and underemployment and increasing levels of exploitation.

I cannot agree, therefore, with the thesis of the end of work and less still with the end of *labour's* revolution. Emancipation nowadays is fundamentally a revolution *in* work, *of* work and *by* work. But it is a more arduous social challenge, since it is not easy to reclaim the meaning of *class-belonging* that capital and its forms of domination (including the powerful sphere of culture) are intent on masking and concealing.

Of course, under Taylorism/Fordism, workers were not homogeneous: there were always male workers, female workers, young workers, old workers, qualified and unqualified workers, national and immigrant-workers, etc., i.e. multiple cleavages within the working class. Clearly there was also tertiarisation then (in general, restaurants, cleaning, public transport, etc. were tertiarised). There has been, however, a dramatic expansion of this process that has qualitatively affected it, increasing and intensifying the already existing cleavages.

Unlike Taylorism/Fordism (which, it is important to remember, is still in existence in many parts of the world, albeit in a hybrid-form), under Toyotism, in its Japanese version, the worker becomes her own despot, as I showed in *Adeus ao Trabalho?* (*Farewell to Work?*). She is encouraged to self-incriminate and self-punish, if her production does not reach the so-called 'total quality' (this mystifying deceit of capital). She works in a team or production-cell and, if she does not turn up to work, she will be covered by the other members of the team. This is the ideal of Toyotism. According to this logic, resistance, revolt and refusals are completely rejected as attitudes that are against the 'good performance of the company'. This led a well-known scholar, Coriat, to say – in praise – that Toyotism leads to an *encouraged involvement*. I would rather characterise it as *manipulated involvement*. It is a real moment of *estrangement* or, if you prefer, of labour-alienation but taken to the extreme, internalised into the 'soul of the worker', leading her to think only of productivity, of competitiveness, of how to improve the performance of the company, her 'other family'. To give a basic example: how many steps in the day can a worker reduce to do her job? Each step that has been cut, in an hour, represents so many steps in a day. So many steps in a day equates to so many steps in a month. And so many steps in a month equates to so many steps in a year. Each stage represents so many extra items produced, *creating an infernal circle of disaffection and dehumanisation in work: the worker does the thinking for capital*. This is what Toyotism and forms akin to it seek to achieve.

And there is another important question: Taylorism and Fordism adopted a linear model whereby scientific management *elaborated* and the manual labourer *executed*. Toyotism, however, understood that the *intellectual knowledge* of the worker is much greater than Taylorism or Fordism believed, and that it was important to allow the *intellectual knowledge of labour to blossom* and for this, also, to be appropriated by capital. Jean-Marie Vincent, among others, called this the phase of *abstract intellectual labour*. In my formulation it is the moment in which the expenditure of energy, to recall Marx, is the expenditure of intellectual energy, which Toyotist capital takes ownership of in a much more profound way than Taylorism/Fordism ever did. This is the only reason that capital allows workers to 'not work' for a period each week (of about one or two hours) during which they can discuss in quality-control circles. It is in these moments that the ideas of those who realise production flourish – going beyond the standards set by scientific management – and Toyotist capital knows how to appropriate expertly this intellectual dimension of labour that emerges on the factory-floor and that Taylorism/Fordism despised.

Clearly, this process that expands and becomes more complex in *sectors at the cutting edge of production* (that cannot be generalised), results in smarter machines, which in turn need more 'qualified' workers better able to operate computerised machinery. And in the process, new, more intelligent machines perform activities previously performed exclusively by humans, leading to a process of interaction between differentiated living labour and more computerised dead labour. Which led Habermas to argue, in my view mistakenly, that science was becoming the main productive force, replacing – and with this eliminating – the relevance of the labour-theory of value. On the contrary, I believe there is a new form of interaction between living labour and dead labour: there is a process of *technologification of science* that, however, cannot eliminate living labour, even though it can reduce it, change it, fragment it. However, the tragedy of capital is that it cannot definitively subsume living labour and cannot, therefore, eliminate the working class. My aim in this presentation was to understand a little of the nature of this working class today.

APPENDIX 3

The Metamorphoses and the Centrality of Labour Today[1]

The world of work, as a result of transformations and metamorphoses that have unfolded over recent decades in the advanced countries and their repercussions in industrialising countries, has lived through a double-edged process: on the one hand, there has been a *de-proletarianisation* of industrial, manufacturing labour in the advanced-capitalist countries. In other words, there has been a reduction in traditional industrial labour. On the other, there has been a significant *sub-proletarianisation* of labour, as a result of the numerous forms of part-time, precarious, tertiarised, subcontracted, informal labour and so on. Labour has therefore become more *heterogeneous, complex and fragmented*.

Empirical evidence presented in various studies has led me to reject the thesis of the suppression or elimination of the working class under advanced capitalism, especially when we observe the spread of multiple forms of precarious labour. Moreover, a significant portion of the *class-that-lives-from-labour* is firmly rooted in medium-industrialised countries such as Brazil, Mexico, India, Russia, China and Korea, among others, where this class has a central role in the productive process.

Instead of *farewell to the proletariat*, we have an ample, differentiated array of groups that compose the *class-that-lives-from-labour*.[2]

The 1980s saw profound transformations in the world of work in the advanced-capitalist countries, in its participation in the productive structure and in its forms of representation by trade-unions and political parties. The changes were so profound that it is possible to talk of a *class-that-lives-from-labour* undergoing its most severe crisis of the century during this time, one that affected not just its *materiality* but also its *subjectivity* and, in the intimate relations between these, its *form of being*.

In this decade, we have seen a great technological leap, in which automation and organisational changes have invaded the factory-space, positioning themselves within labour-relations and relations of capital-production. The world of production is undergoing a whole range of different experiences. Taylorism and Fordism are no longer the only forms and they have blended with other productive processes (neo-Fordism and neo-Taylorism), and

---

1. First published in *Actuel Marx*, 24, 1998.
2. See Antunes 1995a.

in some cases have been altogether replaced, as the Japanese experience of Toyotism has shown.

New labour-processes are emerging, where timed piecework has been replaced by flexibilised production, with new forms production adapted to the logic of the market. New modes of industrial devolution are being tried out and new standards of workforce-management are being sought, of which the 'total-quality processes' are a clear example, not just in Japan but in several advanced-capitalist countries and across the industrialised Third World. Toyotism penetrates, blends with or even substitutes Taylorist/Fordist practices.[3] We are witnessing transitional forms of production that even as they unfold are having a severe impact on labour-rights. These have become deregulated and flexibilised in order to provide capital with the instruments it needs to adapt to this new phase.

These transformations, completed or still unfolding depending on the different social, economic, political, cultural and ethnic conditions of the countries in which they have been applied, penetrate deeply into the traditional manufacturing workforce. The crisis profoundly affects the sphere of consciousness, the subjectivity of workers, their forms of representation, of which unions are an expression.[4] What have been the main consequences and the ones that deserve further reflection? Is the *class-that-lives-from-labour* disappearing?

Firstly, there are multiple processes under way: on the one hand there has been the de-proletarianisation of industrial, manual labour, especially (but not only) in the advanced-capitalist countries. On the other hand, there has been a powerful process of sub-proletarianisation, which can be seen in the part-time, precarious, temporary labour that is a feature of what is known as 'the dual society' in advanced capitalism. There has been a significant 'tertiarisation' of labour in various productive sectors, as well as a dramatic increase in wage-labour in the service-sector; there has also been a significant heterogenisation of labour, of which the growing participation of female workers in the working world is an expression. In sum, there has been a process of de-proletarianisation of manual and industrial labour, and labour has become more heterogeneous, sub-proletarianised and precarious. A reduction in traditional manufacturing labour has accompanied an increase in the size of the class-that-lives-from-labour.

---

3. On this issue, see, among others, Murray 1983; Harvey 1992; Coriat 1992; Gounet 1991 and 1992.

4. See Antunes 1995a; Beynon 1994; Fumagelli 1996; McIlroy 1997.

I would like to give some examples of these trends, of this variegated process within the world of work. I begin with the question of the de-proletarianisation of manual, industrial labour. Take France, for example: in 1962 the number of industrial workers was 7,488,000, in 1975, it reached 8,118,000 and in 1989 it fell to 7,121,000. While in 1962 it represented 39 per cent of the active population, by 1989 it had fallen to 29.6 per cent.[5]

We could say that in the important western-European industrialised countries, the number of effective workers active in industry represented about 40 per cent of the active population in the beginning of the 1940s. Today, its proportion is situated at around 30 per cent. It is foreseen that it will be reduced to 20 per cent or 25 per cent in the beginning of the next century. These figures show a clear reduction in the manufacturing proletariat in the advanced-capitalist countries, as a result of both the recession and especially as a result of automation, robotics and multiple flexibilisation processes.[6]

In parallel to this trend, the heterogeneity and complexity of the class-that-lives-from-labour has also significantly increased, given the sub-proletarisation of labour that can be observed in part-time work, precarious work, etc. To give an example: during the period from 1982 to 1988, while in France there was a reduction of 501,000 full-time jobs, there was an increase of 110,000 part-time jobs.[7] In other words, a number of Western-capitalist countries saw a decline in full-time jobs at the same time as they experienced an increase in forms of sub-proletarianisation, exemplified by part-time, precarious and temporary workers.

Gorz adds that approximately 35–50 per cent of the active British, French, German and American population is unemployed or employed in precarious, part-time work – a clear illustration of the dual society.[8]

A significant portion of the increase in the sub-proletarianised labour-force is made up of women. Of the 111,000 part-time jobs created in France between 1982 and 1988, 83 per cent were filled by female labour. We can say that the female contingent has grown in a number of countries where the female labour-force represents, on average, 40 per cent or more of the labour-force as a whole (see the British case, above).

Similarly, there has been an intense increase of waged work in the service-sector, which has led to the claim that in 'research on structure and tendencies in the development of the highly industrialised Western societies we find

---

5. Bihr 1990 quoted in Antunes 1995a, p. 42; and Bihr 1991, pp. 87 and 108.
6. Gorz 1990a; Antunes 1995a; Beynon 1995.
7. Bihr 1990 quoted in Antunes 1995a, p. 44; and Bihr 1991, pp. 88–9.
8. Gorz quoted in Antunes 1995a, p. 43; and Gorz 1990a and 1990b.

more frequently its characterisation as a "service-society". This is in relation to the absolute and relative growth connected to the "service-sector".[9]

Meanwhile, there are other important consequences that result from the 'technological revolution'. Alongside the quantitative reduction of the traditional labour-force, there has been a qualitative reduction in the form of being of labour. The reduction in variable capital as a function of the increase in constant capital – or, in other words, the replacement of living labour by dead labour – offers the opportunity of converting the worker into a supervisor or regulator of the production-process, as mentioned in the *Grundrisse*. However, for Marx, the law of value made it impossible for this tendency to be fully effective under capitalism.

Therefore, under the impact of technology there is a possibility within the labour-process, characterised by the intellectualisation of labour in the process of value-creation, which is achieved through socially combined labour. This allowed Marx to state:

> Since with the development of the *real subsumption of labour under capital* or the *specifically capitalist mode of production* it is not the individual worker but rather a *socially combined labour capacity* that is more and more the *real executor* of the labour process as a whole, and since the different labour capacities which cooperate together to form the productive machine as a whole contribute in very different ways to the direct process by which the commodity, or, more appropriate here, the product, is formed, one working more with his hands, another more with his brain, one as a *manager*, *engineer*. or technician, etc., another as an *overlooker*, the third directly as a manual worker, or even a mere assistant, more and more of the *functions of labour capacity* are included under the direct concept of *productive labour*, and their repositories under the concept of *productive workers*, workers directly exploited by capital and altogether *subordinated* to its valorisation and production process. If one considers the *total worker* constituting the workshop, his *combined activity* is directly realised materially (*materialiter*) in a *total product* which is at the same time a *total quantity of commodities* and in this connection it is a matter of complete indifference whether the function of the individual worker, who is only a constituent element of this total worker, stands close to direct manual labour or is far away from it.[10]

This shows that, even today '[t]he understanding of the development and self-reproduction of the capitalist mode of production is quite impossible

---

9. Offe and Berger 1991, p. 11.
10. Marx 1994.

without the concept of the *total* social capital...similarly, it is quite impossible to understand the manifold and thorny problems of nationally varying as well as socially stratified labour without constantly keeping in mind the necessary framework of proper assessment: namely the irreconcilable antagonism between *total* social capital expansion and the *totality* of labour'.[11]

Clearly, this antagonism is particular to local socio-economic circumstances, to the position of each country in the global structure of capital-production and the relative maturity of global socio-historical development.

Thus, to talk of the suppression of labour under capitalism seems to lack empirical or analytical foundation entirely, especially when we consider that two-thirds of the workforce is in the industrialised and middle-income Third World (including China), where the trends we have highlighted are particularly sharp.

What appears to be taking place, instead, is a quantitative transformation (reduction in the number of traditional workers) and a bipolar qualitative change: at one extreme, there is in some sectors a more highly qualified worker who becomes 'supervisor and overseer of the production process'; at the other extreme, there has been dramatic deskilling in some sectors and reduction in others, such as the mining and steel-industries. There is therefore, a metamorphosis in the world of labour, which varies from sector to sector, establishing a contradictory process that enhances skills in some industries and deskills in others.[12] Hence, the world of work has become more complex, heterogeneous and fragmented.

We can thus observe, on the one hand, a real process of intellectualisation of manual labour; on the other, conversely, a de-qualification and even sub-proletarianisation, visible in precarious, informal, temporary, etc. labour. While we can say that the first trend is more coherent and compatible with technological progress, the second has been a constant in contemporary capitalism and its destructive logic, proving not only that the workforce is not on its way to extinction, but also, crucially, that it is not possible to envisage, not even in the very distant future, the elimination of the *class-that-lives-from-labour*.

II

Having made these considerations, in the second part of this text, I shall examine the arguments of those critics of the 'work-' or 'labour-society' and present an analytical framework to understand this debate. What do we mean by crisis of the 'work-society'? Is there uniformity in this critical analysis?

---

11. Mészáros 1995, p. 891.
12. Lojkine 1995a.

In contrast to those authors who defend the loss of centrality of the category of labour in contemporary society, the current trend – whether in the direction of the greater intellectualisation of industrial labour or the increase of qualified labour or the de-qualification or sub-proletarianisation of labour – does not lead to the conclusion that labour has lost its centrality to the commodity-producing society. Although there has been a quantitative reduction (with qualitative consequences) in industrial production, abstract labour plays a decisive role in the creation of exchange-values. Neither the reduction of physical labour-time in the production-process, nor the reduction of direct manual labour and the increase in more intellectualised labour, negate the law of value, when we consider labour in its totality as socially combined labour, the collective worker as the expression of multiple combined activities.

When we speak of a crisis in work, it is absolutely necessary to specify which aspect we are considering: whether it is a crisis of the society of abstract labour[13] or whether it is a crisis of concrete labour, as a structural element of the social exchange between human beings and nature.[14] In the first case – the crisis of abstract labour – there is a differentiation to make that is decisive and which has been somewhat neglected. The issue here is: is contemporary society driven by the logic of capital, by the system of commodity-production, or not? If the answer is affirmative, the crisis of abstract labour can only be understood as a reduction in living labour and an increase in dead labour.

The line of argument that *minimises* and, in some cases, actively negates the prevalence and centrality of capitalist logic in contemporary society is, for many authors, the basis of their rejection of the central role of labour, both in its abstract form, that creates exchange-values – claimed to be no longer decisive today – as much as in its concrete form, since this would no longer be relevant in the structure of an emancipated society and a meaningful life. Whether because it qualifies as a postindustrial and postcapitalist service-society, or because it is governed by a tripartite institutional logic led by the concerted action of capital, the workers and the state, or driven less by trade, more contractual or, even, consensual, our contemporary society is supposedly no longer centrally ruled by the logic of capital.

I believe that without this essential distinction between concrete and abstract labour, when we bid farewell to labour, we commit the serious analytical error of considering as unitary a phenomenon that has a dual dimension.

It does not seem possible to think of human society without social labour as the creator of use-values, as the form of interchange between social beings

---

13. As argued by Kurz 1992.
14. As argued by Offe 1989; Gorz 1990a and 1990b; Habermas 1989; and Méda 1997, among many others.

and nature. If it were possible to envisage, beyond capital, the elimination of the abstract-labour society – which would of course be articulated along with the end of a commodity-producing society – it would be ontologically distinct from assuming or conceiving of the end of labour as a useful activity, as a vital activity, as a founding element, a model of human activity. In other words, it is one thing to conceive, with the end of capitalism, of the end of abstract labour, of estranged labour; it is another altogether to conceive of the elimi-nation, in the sphere of human sociability, of concrete labour, which creates socially useful things and, in doing so, transforms their own creators. Once we conceive of labour without this dual form, we can only identify it as syn-onymous with abstract labour, estranged and fetishised labour. This leads, at best, to imagining a society of 'free time', in some sense, but one that cohabits with existing forms of estranged and fetishised labour.

Our hypothesis is that, notwithstanding the increased heterogeneity, com-plexity and fragmentation of the working class, the possibilities for human emancipation can still be socially viable if they originate primarily from the world of work; a process of simultaneous emancipation *of* labour, *in* labour and *by* labour. This revolt and confrontation does not exclude or even sup-press others that are equally important. But, as we live in a society that pro-duces commodities and exchange-values, labour-revolts have a central status. The entire broad array of wage-earners in the service-sector, plus 'tertiarised' workers, informal workers, domestic workers, unemployed and underem-ployed workers, can be added to the workers who produce directly, and thereby, acting as a class, constitute the social sector endowed with the great-est anti-capitalist potential. Similarly, the environmental movement, the femi-nist movement and many others have greater vigour when they are able to articulate their particular, authentic demands with the denunciation of the destructive logic of capital (in the case of the environmental movement) and the fetishised and estranged character of the human species when ruled by the social logic of capital (in the case of the feminist movement).[15] This out-come depends, of course, on the socio-economic realities of each country and its position in the international division of labour, as well as the subjectivity of the social beings who live by labour, their political, ideological and cultural values.

Thus, instead of declaring the end of labour or of the working class, there is another more pertinent question: in the conflicts led by workers and socially excluded groups the world over, is it possible to detect a greater role and potential amongst the more qualified strata of the working class, those living

---

15. See Antunes 1995a; Mészáros 1995; and Bihr 1991.

under 'stable' conditions, and who therefore participate to a greater extent in the process of value-creation? Or, conversely, is the more fertile base for action to be found precisely among the most marginalised, sub-proletarianised strata? We know that the more qualified, more intellectualised workers who evolved along with technological development could have (at least objectively) greater anticapitalist potential, given the central role they play in the creation of exchange-values. Paradoxically, it is these more qualified segments that suffer the process of manipulation inside the productive space more acutely. They thus experience, at a subjective level, more involvement and subordination at the hands of capital, with Toyotism constituting the best expression of this manipulation. Recall the 'Toyota Family' motto in the early 1950s: 'Protect the company to protect your life'.[16] On the other hand, some portions of more skilled workers are also susceptible, especially in advanced-capitalist countries, to actions of neocorporatist inspiration.

In contrast, the broad array of precarious, part-time, temporary and unemployed workers that I refer to as the sub-proletariat, by being further (or even excluded) from the process of value-creation, would have, at a material level, a less important role in anticapitalist struggles. Yet, the condition of dispossession and marginalisation of these subjects has the potential to position them as social subjects capable of bolder actions, since they have nothing more to lose in capitalist society. Their subjectivity could be, therefore, more prone to rebellion.

The recent strikes and social uprisings that took place in the advanced-capitalist countries in the early 1990s are important examples of the new forms of social confrontation against capital. Examples of these include: the riots in Los Angeles, the Chiapas revolt in Mexico, the emergence of the Landless Workers' Movement in Brazil, widespread strikes such as the public-sector workers' strike in France in November–December 1995, the long strike of the Liverpool dockers from 1995 to 1998 or the strike of around 2 million metal-workers in South Korea in 1997 against the casualisation and flexibilisation of work. Again, the strike of the United Parcel Service workers in 1997, with 185,000 strikers, united both full-time and part-time workers.[17]

These actions, among many others, often brought together different strands of the class-that-lives-from-labour and are important examples of the new confrontations against the destructive logic that presides over contemporary society.

---

16. Antunes 1995a, p. 25.
17. See Petras 1997; Dussel 1995; and Soon 1997.

We know that these different manifestations of estrangement have affected not just the arena of production, but even more so the sphere of consumption, of time outside of work, making free time increasingly subjected to the values of the system of commodity-production. The social being who labours must have just enough with which to live, but must be constantly induced to want to live in order to have or dream of new products, vastly reducing the necessities he or she is in need of.[18]

In contrast to those who argue that the social phenomenon of estrangement (*Entfremdung*, or 'alienation' as it is often referred to) has lost significance in contemporary society, we believe that the changes under way in the labour-process have not eliminated the basic conditions of this phenomenon, making the actions that originate in the workplace against estrangement and fetishisation still enormously relevant in contemporary society.

III

If we conceive of the current form of labour as an expression of *social labour* that is more *complex*, more *socially combined*, and even more *intense* in its pace and processes, I also cannot agree with theses that minimise or even ignore the process of exchange-value creation. In contrast, our argument is that the society of capital and its *law of value* are increasingly *less* in need of *stable* labour and *more* in need of *part-time*, tertiarised labour, which is increasingly becoming a constitutive part of the process of capitalist production.[19]

But, precisely because capital cannot eliminate *living labour* from the process of value-creation, it has to increase *the use and the productivity of labour in order to intensify the forms of extraction of surplus-value in an ever shorter period of time.* Therefore, it is one thing to *have the imperative need to reduce the variable dimension of capital and the resulting necessity to increase its constant dimension. It is another, entirely different thing to imagine that by eliminating living labour capital can continue to reproduce itself.* The reduction of the stable proletariat, heir of Taylorism/Fordism, the increase of *abstract intellectual labour* within modern production-plants and the general increase in forms of precarious, part-time, tertiarised labour that have proliferated in the 'era of the flexible firm' and de-verticalisation of production, *are strong examples of the force of the law of value.* As Tosel remarks, because capital has a strong element of waste and exclusion, it is the very 'centrality of abstract labour that produces the non-centrality of labour, present in the mass of workers excluded from living

---

18. Heller 1978, pp. 64–5.
19. This issue is discussed in more detail in Chapter 7 of this book.

labour' that, once (de-)socialised and (de-)individualised by being expelled from work, 'desperately try to find forms of individuation and socialisation in isolated spheres of non-work (training, charity and services)'.[20]

Following on from my argument, I also cannot agree with the thesis of the transformation of science into the 'leading productive force', replacing labour-value, which is assumed to have become defunct.[21] This argument ignores the importance of the complex relations between value-theory and scientific knowledge. In other words, it ignores that 'living labour, in conjunction with science and technology, constitute a complex and contradictory unity under the conditions of capitalist developments', since 'the tendency of capital to give production a scientific character is counteracted by capital's innermost limitations: i.e. by the ultimately paralysing, anti-social requirements "to maintain the already created value as value", so as to contain production within capital's limited foundation'.[22]

This is not to say that the labour-theory of value does not recognise the increasing role of science, but that science's development is anchored to the material base of the relations between capital and labour and cannot overtake them. And it is as a result of this structural constraint, which *frees* and even *compels* science's expansion to increase the production of exchange-values *but prevents a qualitative leap by society towards a society that produces useful goods within the logic of disposable time*, that science cannot become the leading productive force. A prisoner of this material base, rather than the *scientisation of technology* there is, as Mészáros suggests, a process of *technologification of science*.[23] The ontological prisoner of a material soil structured by capital, science cannot become its principal productive force. It *interacts* with labour, because of the pressing need to participate in the process of capital-valorisation. *It does not override value, but is an intrinsic part of its mechanism.*

Furthermore, scientific knowledge and knowledge derived from labour are directly combined in the contemporary world *without the former subsuming the latter*. A number of experiments, amongst which the Saturn-project of General Motors is an example, failed when they tried to automate the productive process *ignoring* labour. Intelligent machines cannot replace workers. Rather, their use requires the intellectual labour of the worker whose interaction with the computerised machine transfers part of the worker's new intellectual attributes to the new machine that results from this process. A complex interactive process between labour and productive science is thus established which

20. Tosel 1995, p. 210.
21. Habermas 1975.
22. Mészáros 1989, pp. 135–6.
23. Mészáros 1989, p. 133.

cannot lead to the extinction of labour. This feedback-system compels capital to find *an even more complex, multifunctional labour-force, to be exploited in an even more intense and sophisticated manner*, at least in those productive sectors where there is a greater technological presence.

With the transformation of *living labour* into *dead labour*, from the moment in which, through new software, computerised machinery begins to perform activities that are characteristic of human intelligence, we can see a *process of objectification of cerebral activities in the machinery*, a transferral of intellectual and cognitive knowledge from the working class to the computerised machinery.[24] This transferral of intellectual capacity to the machinery, knowledge that is converted into the language of the machinery, underlies the transformation of *living labour* into *dead labour*.

Another of capital's trends during the phase of productive restructuring concerning the relation between labour and value has been that of *reducing the levels of unproductive labour within the factory*. The elimination of various functions such as *supervision, inspection, middle-management, etc.*, a central element under Toyotism and the modern capitalist firm based on lean production, seeks to transfer and incorporate into *productive* labour-activities that were once performed by *unproductive* workers. By reducing unproductive labour through its incorporation into productive labour, capital is no longer bound to a set of workers who do not directly participate in the process of value-creation.

Besides the reduction of unproductive labour, there is also a trend towards an increasing overlap between *material* and *immaterial* labour. We are witnessing the growth of intellectual labour in industries with a smaller presence of computerised machinery as well as in the services- and communications-sectors, among others. The growth of service-sector work, in areas that are not directly productive but that often perform activities that are *closely tied* to productive labour, is another important element in our understanding of the broader notion of labour in the contemporary world. Since, in the techno-scientific world, the production of knowledge is an essential part of the production of goods and services, we can say that 'workers' ability to increase their knowledge…has become a decisive characteristic of labour in general. It is not an exaggeration to say that the labour-force is increasingly an intelligent force able to react to changing production and unexpected problems'.[25] The expansion of forms of *immaterial labour* is therefore another characteristic of the post-Taylorist system of production, since the productive system is

---

24. Lojkine 1995a, p. 44.
25. Vincent 1995, p. 160.

increasingly in need of research-, communication- and marketing activities to obtain advance information from the market.[26] There is, in the realm of productive and service enterprises, an increase in the number of activities referred to as *immaterial*.

Thus, immaterial labour expresses the power of the informational dimension of the commodity-form: it is the expression of the *informational* content of the commodity, displaying the transformations of labour in large enterprises and in the services, where direct manual labour is being replaced by more intellectual labour.

In our interpretation, the new dimensions and forms of labour have increased the array and complexity of working activities and the advancement of immaterial labour is an illustration of this trend. Both *material* and *immaterial* labour, in the increasing overlap that exists between them, are, however, subordinated to the logic of production of commodities or capital. As intellectual activity has grown within production:

> the very value form of labour has changed. It increasingly assumes the value-form of abstract intellectual labour. The intellectual labour-force produced both inside and outside of production is absorbed as a commodity by capital that incorporates it to bring new qualities to dead labour.... Material production and the production of services increasingly require innovations and are, as a result, gradually more subordinated to a growing knowledge-production that is converted into commodities and capital.[27]

Thus, as mentioned above, *labour-estrangement* [*Entfremdung*] is essentially preserved. Although less apparent because of the narrower separation between elaboration and execution and the less rigid hierarchies within firms, the subjectivity that emerges in post-Fordist factories and productive spaces is the expression of an *inauthentic* and estranged *existence*. Besides workers' *knowledge*, which Fordism expropriated and transferred to scientific management and the sphere of elaboration, the new phase of capital expressed by Toyotism re-transfers *know-how* to labour but it does so while increasingly appropriating for itself its *intellectual* dimension, its cognitive capacities, seeking to involve worker-subjectivity in a more profound and intense way. Yet, this process is not limited to this alone, since a part of *intellectual knowledge* is transferred to the computerised machinery, which become *more intelligent, reproducing some of the activities transferred to them by the intellectual knowledge of labour*. Since machines cannot eliminate human labour, they need a higher

---

26. Lazzarato 1993, p. 111.
27. Vincent 1993, p. 121.

level of *interaction* between the subjectivity that works and the new intelligent machine. And, in this process, the *interactive involvement* increases *labour-estrangement* even more, increases modern forms of *reification*, and creates an even greater distance between subjectivity and the pursuit of an authentic and self-determined daily life.

If this estrangement persists and becomes even more complex in the activities at the cutting edge of production – among the supposedly more 'stable' and integrated portion of the workforce that performs *abstract intellectual labour* – the picture is even more intense among the more precarious strata of the human labour-force, who are deprived of their rights and experience instability on a daily basis through work that is part-time, temporary, etc. Under conditions of absolute separation from labour, estrangement undergoes a *loss of unity* between labour and leisure, means and ends, public life and private life, among other forms of disjunction between the elements of unity in the 'work-society', resulting in 'a historical process of disintegration, a movement towards the disunity of opposites...towards increasing antagonism, deepening contradictions and incoherence'.[28] From the Los Angeles riots in 1992 to the revolts of the unemployed in France that have been increasing since 1997, we are witnessing many demonstrations against estrangement by those who have been expelled from the world of work and consequently prevented from living a life endowed with meaning. At the most intellectualised pole of the working class, which exercises *abstract intellectual labour*, the forms of reification have a particular, more complex form (*more 'humanised' than its dehumanising essence*) because of the new forms of 'engagement' and interaction between living labour and computerised machinery. Amongst those who are most penalised by the precariousness and exclusion of labour, reification takes on a form that is *directly* more dehumanising and brutal. These constitute contemporary estrangements under capitalism, differentiated in their effects but affecting the *class-that-lives-from-labour* as a whole.

I conclude, therefore, by saying that rather than the replacement of labour by science, or even the replacement of the production of values by the sphere of communication, what we are experiencing in the world today is greater *interrelation* and *interpenetration* between productive and unproductive activities, between manufacturing and service-activities, between execution and conception, which in a context of capital's productive restructuring are generating post-Taylorist/Fordist processes of production. A broader understanding of labour can allow us to understand the role it plays in contemporary sociability at the dawn of the twenty-first century.

---

28. Ramtin 1997, pp. 248–9.

APPENDIX 4

Social Struggles and Socialist-Societal Design in Contemporary Brazil[1]

Contemporary capitalism's configuration over the last few decades has accentuated its destructive logic, profoundly affecting the world of work. The capitalist pattern of accumulation, under Taylorism and Fordism, has been increasingly altered, mixed with and even replaced by flexibilised and unregulated forms of production, of which so-called flexible accumulation or the Japanese model/Toyotism are examples.

Fordism/Taylorism is understood as the expression of a productive system and its respective labour-process that dominated a large part of capitalist industry for much of the twentieth century, based on mass-homogeneous production. It was characterised by the *combination* of *Fordist-serial production* with *Taylorist timekeeping*, as well as being based on piecemeal and fragmented labour, with a clear demarcation between *elaboration* and *execution*. From this productive and labour-process based on concentrated, vertical large industry, the *mass-worker* emerged, the collective worker of strongly hierarchical large enterprises.

The welfare-state, which supported the social-democratic model and provided the political, ideological and contractarian apparatus for Fordist production in various central countries, has also been undermined by anti-social neoliberal deregulation and privatisation. With its material base in the productive restructuring of capital, the neoliberal project has led to the reorganisation of production in various capitalist countries. Moving increasingly close to the neoliberal agenda, different social-democratic countries in the West have shown great compatibility with the project and even defended it. From Felipe Gonzales to Mitterand, and Tony Blair's New Labour in the UK, the exhaustion of the classic social-democratic project is evident as it has undergone a transformation into a programme that incorporates basic elements of neoliberalism with an ever thinner layer of social-democratic contractarianism.

Against this background, the process of capitalist recovery that began in post-World-War II Japan emerged as a set of prescriptions applied with increasing vigour from the mid-1970s, a *capitalist* attempt to resolve the

---

1. First published in *Crítica Marxista*, 7, 1998.

structural crisis that was unfolding in the main central capitalist countries. Having resulted in a strong return to capitalism in Japan, Toyotism represented the most structured productive solution offered by capital and a possible remedy for the crisis. Toyotism, or the 'Japanese model', can be understood, in essence, as a form of labour-organisation born in the Toyota-factory in Japan after World-War II that diverges (more or less widely) from Fordism in the following ways:

1) it is production more directly tied to shifts in demand;
2) it is heterogeneous, it is based on teamwork, with a multiplicity and flexibility of functions, on the reduction of unproductive activities *within the factory and on the* increase and diversification *in the intensity of forms of labour-exploitation*; and
3) *it is premised on the* principle of *just-in-time*, the best possible use of the production time, and uses the *kanban*-system of signs to control the replacement of parts or stocks, which, under Toyotism, must be kept to a minimum. Whilst, in the Fordist factory, around 75 per cent was produced inside the factory, in the Toyotist factory around, 25 per cent is produced in the factory. It gives the process of production a *horizontal* form and transfers a large part of what was previously produced in the factory over to 'tertiaries'.

'Total quality' takes on an important role in the productive process. Quality-control circles (QCCs) have proliferated, made up of groups of workers who are encouraged to discuss the work and performance, in order to improve the productivity and profits of the firm. In fact, it is the new form used by capital to appropriate the *intellectual know-how* of labour. *Taylorist despotism* is thus combined with labour-*manipulation*, with the 'involvement' of workers, *through an even deeper process of internalisation of alienated (estranged) labour*. The worker is obliged to think and act *by* capital and *for* capital, intensifying (rather than dissipating) the subordination of labour to capital. In the West, the implementation of QCCs has been varied, depending on the specificities of the countries in which they have been applied.

This *specific development path of contemporary Japanese capitalism* presented itself as a viable alternative for capital in the West, to be adapted depending on the particularities of each country and the Fordist model already in place. Building on different experiences of capital – from the Japanese path to the experiences in the US (California), from northern Italy to the Swedish experience, among many others, *but with the Toyotism as its most daring project –*

capital redrew its productive process, blending new elements with its previous Fordist productive model.[2]

As these trends developed – trends that represent capital's responses to its own *structural crisis* characterised by its continual depressive tendency[3] – capital's destructive logic has intensified. The more inter-capitalist competitiveness increases, the worse are its consequences, of which two are particularly virulent and cruel: the destruction and/or precarisation, without precedent throughout the modern era, of the human labour-force, of which *structural unemployment* is the main example; and the increasing degradation of the relation between human beings and nature – environmental destruction – that results from a social logic aimed primarily at the production of commodities and the valorisation of capital.

Severe destructiveness is, ultimately, the deepest expression of a structural crisis that highlights contemporary forms of (de-)socialisation: the destruction of the human labour-force; the destruction of social rights; the brutalisation of swathes of men and women who live through the sale of their labour-power; the increasing relation between production and nature that creates a vast 'throw-away society', disposing of what served as packaging for commodities and keeping the wheels of capital's reproductive circuit spinning.

In this setting, characterised by the three poles – NAFTA, Europe and Asia (with the US still hegemonic within NAFTA, Germany at the helm of the European Union, and Japan in the lead within Asia) – as one pole is strengthened, the others are weakened. As they expand into parts of the world that are of interest and co-administer and manage crises, they create even more destruction and precariousness. In Japan and elsewhere in Asia, for example, the potential for the current crisis to spread is overwhelming. The parasitic and destructive free flight of volatile capital is a clear expression of *the structural character of today's crisis.*

Latin America is 'integrating' with so-called globalisation while destroying itself at the level of society. The levels of social deprivation speak for themselves from Argentina to Mexico, through to Fujimori's Peru. Not to mention Brazil's Fernando Henrique Cardoso (FHC), the *prince* of *servitude to large capital*. Asia's sharp growth is built upon the brutal super-exploitation of labour, of which the workers' strike in South Korea in 1997 is a serious denunciation. Super-exploitation also profoundly affects women and children. And from

---

2. See, for instance, Tomaney 1996; Amin 1996; Antunes 1995a; Lima 1996; Gounet 1991 and 1992; and Bihr 1998.
3. Mészáros 1995; Chesnais 1996a.

Africa, capital now seeks hardly anything. It is only interested in its richest areas.

What can be said of a form of sociability that results in unemployment and precariousness for more than 1 billion people, *around a third of the global human work-force*? This is the result of capital's inability to self-valorise without the use of human labour. It can *reduce* living labour, but not *eliminate it*. It can make vast quantities of workers precarious and unemployed, but cannot get rid of them.

This has led to severe consequences in the world of work. I shall briefly outline some of the most important:

1) a reduction in manual, factory-, 'stable' labour, typical of Taylorism/ Fordism during the phase of expansion of vertical, concentrated industry;
2) a sharp increase in the *new proletariat*, of new forms of *sub-proletarianisation or precarisation of labour*, deriving from the growth of part-time, subcontracted, tertiarised work *which is increasing throughout the world, both in the Third World as well as in the central countries*;
3) a sharp increase in female labour within the working class, on a global scale, particularly in (but not exclusively) precarious, part-time, subcontracted, etc. work;
4) a huge expansion of moderate earners, especially in the 'service-sector', that initially grew very rapidly, but is now also generating increasing levels of unemployment;
5) an increase in young and 'old' workers (as capitalism defines them, over around 40 years of age), in the labour-markets of the central countries;
6) an intensification and super-exploitation of labour, with the brutal use of immigrant- and black labour, as well as the increase in child-labour, in criminal conditions, in numerous parts of the world, such as Asia and Latin America;
7) a sharp rise in the process of *structural unemployment*, which, if we add this to precarious, part-time, temporary, etc. labour, affects around a third of the human labour-force; and
8) an increase in what Marx called *combined-social labour*,[4] in which workers from different parts of the world participate in the process of production and service-provision. This, clearly, is not moving in the direction of the elimination of the working class, but towards greater complexity, a more diversified and precarious use of its labour, underlying the need for an

---

4. Marx 1967.

international structure of workers to confront capital. Thus, the working class has become more *fragmented, heterogeneous and complex*.[5]

These consequences in the world of work show that, under capitalism, there has not been an *end of labour* as a measure of value, but a *qualitative* change. *On the one hand*, there is the increasing weight of its skilled dimension – of multifunctional work, of the worker skilled at operating computerised machinery, of the *objectification of cerebral activity*[6] – and, on the other, the extreme *intensification* of forms of labour-exploitation, present and growing in the *new proletariat*, in the *industrial and service-sector sub-proletariat*, in the broad array of workers who are increasingly exploited by capital, not just in the subordinate countries, but at the very heart of the capitalist system. There is, therefore, an ever greater *capacity for socially-combined labour*, which becomes the *real agent* of the total labour-process, which, according to Marx, makes the proximity of workers to or their distance from manual labour absolutely *irrelevant*. Moreover, rather than the end of *labour-value*, we can observe the increasing occurrence of a more complex interrelation between *living labour and dead labour*, between *productive and unproductive labour*, between *material and immaterial labour*, further strengthening the forms of *relative and absolute* surplus-extraction.

These elements – cursorily outlined here – cannot, I repeat, support theses that defend the idea of the *end of labour* under the *capitalist mode of production*. This is all the more evident when we observe that two-thirds of the labour-force is constituted by the so-called Third World (euphemistically called 'developing' countries) where the trends outlined above are moving at a *particular and differentiated* pace. To restrict oneself to Germany or France and, from there, make *generalisations* about the *end of labour* or the *working class*, ignoring the realities of countries such as India, China, Brazil, Mexico, South Korea, Russia, Argentina, etc., not to mention Japan, is profoundly misleading. It is worth adding, also, that the thesis of the end of the working class, even when restricted to the central countries, is, in my view, without foundation – both empirically and analytically. A *broader* notion of the working class that brings to bear its multifaceted character demonstrates the inaccuracy of this argument.[7]

Not to mention the fact that the elimination of labour and the generalisation of this trend within contemporary capitalism – embracing the vast contingent of Third-World workers – presupposes the destruction of the *market-economy*

---

5. Antunes 1995a.
6. This expression is used in Lojkine 1995a.
7. See Bidet and Texier (eds.) 1995.

itself, as capital would be unable to integrate its process of accumulation with robots that cannot participate in the market as consumers. The simple survival of the capitalist economy would be compromised, not to mention the many other dramatic social and political consequences that would arise from this situation.[8] This all indicates that it is a mistake to think of the *disappearance* or *end* of labour *as long as the capitalist commodity-producing society persists* and – crucially – neither is it possible to foresee any possibility of the elimination of the *class-that-lives-from-labour*[9] *while the constitutive pillars of the system of social metabolism of capital are in place.*[10]

The necessary elimination of wage-labour, of fetishised and estranged (alienated) labour, and the creation of *freely associated individuals,* is thus indissolubly tied to the need to eliminate capital *wholly* and its *social-metabolic order* in all its forms. While the end of fetishised, waged labour is a definitive social need, this should not however prevent the careful study of the working class today and how it is changing.

Of great importance is the question of how these transformations are affecting the *social and political movements of workers* (amongst which are the trade-union and party-political movements), especially in the central capitalist countries. If these transformations are significant and have an impact on the working class and its *social, trade-union and political movements* in the advanced-capitalist countries, they will also be significant in the *intermediary and subordinated* countries – with a significant *industrial base* – such as Brazil.

In the next section we shall examine the *main challenges* for the *social movement of workers,* with an emphasis on so-called *new unionism.*

---

8. Mandel 1986.

9. The expression *class-that-lives-from-labour* is used here as synonymous with the working class, i.e. *the class of workers that live through the sale of their labour-power.* As mentioned earlier, albeit briefly, in contrast to authors who defend the thesis of the end of labour and the end of the working class, this expression seeks to *emphasise the contemporary meaning of the working class (and the resulting centrality of labour).* In this sense, the expression includes: 1) all those who sell their labour-power, including both *productive* and *unproductive labour* (in the sense that Marx gives these); 2) wage-earners in the service-sector and also in agriculture; 3) the *sub-proletariat,* the precarious proletariat, without rights, and also unemployed workers, that make up the reserve-army of labour and are at the increasing disposal of capital, in this period of *structural unemployment.* The expression excludes, clearly, the owners and high-level functionaries of capital, who receive high salaries or live from interest. It fully incorporates the Marxian idea of *combined-social labour,* as it is described in Chapter VI (unpublished). See Mandel 1986 and Chapter 6 of this book.

10. Mészáros 1995.

II

Brazilian capitalism, particularly the pattern of industrial accumulation developed since the 1950s that intensified after the coup of 1964, has a *dual* productive structure. On the one hand, it produces durable consumer-goods such as automobiles, electro-domestic goods, etc. for a *restricted and selective* internal market, made up of the dominant classes and a significant portion of the middle-classes, especially the upper-middle classes. On the other hand, there is production for export, not just of primary products but also of industrialised consumer-goods. The growing fall in wages permitted levels of accumulation that were very attractive to monopoly-capital. Thus, industrial-capitalist expansion was sustained (and is still sustained) by a process of *super-exploitation of labour, through low salaries, and a long and very intense working day (during the expansionary cycle) within an industrial base that was significant for a subordinated country.* This pattern of accumulation developed with strength from the 1950s to the 1970s.[11]

During the 1980s, this process began to experience its *first* transformations. Although the basic features of the pattern of accumulation and its 'economic model' remained the same, it was possible to observe some *organisational and technological* changes inside the productive and service-processes, *although clearly at a much slower rate than that experienced by the central countries.* This is because until then the country was still relatively *distant* from the process of capital-restructuring and the neoliberal project that was unrolling in the central advanced countries.

From the 1990s, with the ascension of Fernando Collor and then FHC, this process increased exponentially, with the introduction of a number of elements that reproduced the essential features of the *neoliberal model.* The recent effects of the current stage of capital's productive restructuring in Brazil have been more significant. Downsizing, a sharp increase in forms of super-exploitation of the labour-force, and changes in the technological and informational processes have all taken place. Flexibilisation, deregulation and new forms of production-management are all evident, showing that Fordism, *albeit still dominant,* is also mixing with new productive forms, with forms of flexible accumulation and numerous elements taken from Toyotism that constitute the trends of contemporary capitalism.[12]

It is true that the absence of a 'qualified' or *multifunctional* workforce, in the sense given by capital (able to operate computerised machinery), could

---

11. Antunes 1998.
12. See Gorender 1997; Druck 1999; Colli 1997; Teixeira and Oliveira 1996; Ramalho and Martins 1994; and Antunes 1998.

constitute, *in some productive branches*, an element that could potentially prevent, in part, the advance of capitalism. But the *combination of the super-exploitation of the labour-force and its low remuneration, alongside some advanced productive and technological standards*, constitutes a key incentive for greater capital-investment in production. In fact, for productive capital, what is needed is *a 'qualified' labour-force able to operate microelectronic equipment, the existence of patterns of sub-remuneration and intense exploitation and the conditions of full flexibility and precariousness of the labour-force.* In sum, the existence of *labour super-exploitation*, combining the extraction of *relative surplus-value* with the expansion of forms of *absolute surplus-value* extraction, i.e. the combination of technological advance and increase and intensification of the rhythm of work and the working day.

This process of productive restructuring of capital that developed on a global scale from the 1970s led to the redefinition of Brazil inside the international division of labour. It also led to its (re)insertion into the global productive system of capital, during a period in which financial, unproductive capital has been increasing and profoundly impacting upon all capitalist countries. Clearly, the combination of these *universal* experiences with the *particular economic, social and political* conditions of Brazil has had important consequences for its social movements, especially among worker- and trade-union movements.

During the 1980s, prior to the full development of these general trends, *the trade-union movement (new unionism)* experienced a particularly positive and strong period. Amongst the key features of this period we note:

1) a powerful strike-movement, led by the most diverse set of workers, including industrial workers (particularly the metalworkers), rural wage-earners, public-sector workers and different groups of moderate-wage earners, in a vast movement characterised by: *general strikes by category* (such as the bank-workers in 1995), *strikes with factory-occupations* (such as General Motors in São José dos Campos in 1985 and the National Steel Company in Volta Redonda in 1989), innumerable *company*-strikes as well as *general national strikes* such as the one in March 1989 by 35 million workers which represented the largest and most far-reaching general strike the country had ever experienced. In 1987, for example, there were 2,259 strikes with 63.5 million lost working days;[13]

---

13. Antunes 1995b. For the CSN (National Steel Company) strike, see Graccioli 1997.

2) a significant increase in the number of moderate-wage earners and service-sector workers joining trade-unions, such as bank-workers, teachers, doctors, civil servants, etc., whose numbers grew throughout this period and who organised themselves into important trade-unions. By the end of the 1980s there were 9,833 trade-unions in Brazil, a figure that reached 15,972 in the mid-1990s, including urban and rural, professional and workers' unions.[14] There was a sharp increase not only of industrial-sector unions but also of unions of middle-income workers, with an increase also in the levels of unionisation across the country. In 1996, there were 1,335 public-sector unions, 461 unions of so-called 'professional' workers and 572 self-employed workers' unions;[15]

3) the continued advance of rural unions, evident since the 1970s, leading to a restructuring of the organisation of rural workers. In 1996, there were 5,193 rural unions, of which 3,098 were of rural workers. Rural unionism developed under the strong influence of the Catholic Left, and went on to influence the birth of the Landless Workers' Movement (Movimento sem Terra, MST);

4) the emergence of the trade-union confederations such as the CUT (Central Unica dos Trabalhadores), established in 1983 and originally inspired by a class-based unionism, autonomous and independent from the state. The heir of the social and worker-struggles of the previous decades, especially during the 1970s, the CUT resulted from the merger of *new unionism* that had emerged *within* the union-structure of that period (of which the Metalworkers' Union of São Bernardo is an example) and the movement of *'oposicoes sindicais'* – movements of workers acting *outside* the trade-union structure who fought against its statist, subordinated, old-fashioned and verticalised structures – such as the Movement of Opposition of the Metalworkers of São Paulo (MOMSP) and the Metalworkers' Opposition movement of Campinas;[16]

5) the attempt, although limited, to organise in the workplace (a chronic deficiency of our trade-union movement) with the creation of factory-commissions, among many other forms of workplace-organisation. Examples of these were the *trade-union* commissions of the ABC factories, such as Ford, that were linked to the São Bernardo Metalworkers' Union and the *autonomous* commissions of São Paulo, such as ASAMA, that was linked to MOMSP; and

14. Figures from the Ministry of Labour, in *O Estado de S. Paulo*, 8 September 1996, b3.
15. Nogueira 1996.
16. Possan 1997; and Nogueira 1998.

6) there was also significant progress in the struggle for trade-union autonomy and independence from the state, through the struggle against the
Trade-Union Tax and confederation-style, hierarchical trade-union structure, with strong corporatist traits that were used by the state to subordinate and control unions. Although much work still needs to be done
to eliminate these features of unionism in the country, there have been
significant victories along the way.

These elements, among many others that have not been mentioned here,
suggest that the 1980s presented a favourable context for the development of
new unionism (as a *social movement of workers* with a strong class-character), in
contrast to the trade-union crisis occurring in a number of advanced-capitalist
countries. Although, during the 1980s, Brazilian unionism moved in the *opposite direction* to the trends displayed in the advanced-capitalist countries, by
the end of the decade, it was possible to observe the economic, political and
ideological tendencies that led, in the 1990s, to its decline.

The transformations in the productive process and in the restructuring of
firms, often *during recession*, led to a process of de-proletarianisation of important groups of workers, as well precariousness and even greater intensification of the labour-force, especially in the automotive industry. In the ABC
area of São Paulo, there were around 200,000 metalworkers in 1987, whereas
by 1998 there were fewer than 40,000. The reduction in bank-workers was also
significant, as a result of the changes to the banking system and technological
advance: while in 1989 there were more than 800,000 bank-workers, by 1996
the number had fallen to 570,000 and it continues to fall.[17]

Proposals for deregulation, flexibilisation, accelerated privatisation and
de-industrialisation gained momentum initially under Collor's government
and subsequently under FHC's, as both embraced the essence of the neoliberal political model. At the same time as the industrial labour-force went into
decline, there was a growth in the *sub-proletariat, tertiarised and underemployed
workers* and different modalities of precarious worker. FHC's government
proceeded to dismantle the system of labour-rights that had been built over
decades of worker-struggle and -action.

Under this new reality, *new unionism was stifled and placed on the defensive*. It
was faced, on the one hand, with the emergence of a neoliberal unionism that
expressed a *new Right*, in line with a global conservative wave, of which Forca
Sindical (a trade-union confederation created in 1991) is the best example. And
on the other, it encountered the transition of the CUT, inspired by the Articu-

---

17. On the changes to the labour-process in the banking sector, see Segnini 1998;
and Jinkings 1995.

lacão Sindical, towards European social-democratic models of unionism. This has made it very difficult for the CUT to make qualitative progress, to make the transition from a period of resistance, such as the one in the early years of *new unionism*, towards a higher moment *of elaboration of alternative economic proposals to the pattern of capitalist development* that could improve the lives of the vast number of workers that represent the working class in Brazil.

In this respect, the greatest challenge for the CUT is to articulate its previous combative posture with a *critical and anticapitalist perspective*, with a *clear socialist design that is compatible with the new challenges faced at the end of the 1990s*. It could, in this way, provide *new unionism* with the elements necessary to resist external influences, the avalanche of capitalist and *neoliberal ideology*. At the same time, it needs to resist the trend towards *social-democratic acceptance* that is increasing its political and ideological influence within the Brazilian trade-union movement, despite its crisis in the West. Contractual, social-democratic unionism is attempting to present itself more and more as the *only possible alternative* to combat neoliberalism. Thus, the absence of an anticapitalist political and ideological stance is leading to its gradual approximation with the neoliberal agenda.[18]

For these reasons, the 1990s represent a particularly critical period in the development of Brazilian trade-unionism. Forca Sindical's trade-unionism, with a strong political and ideological stance, represents the unionism of the new Right, defending preservation of the order, in alliance with the objectives of global capital and Brazil's role as country of assembly, without its own technological and scientific capacity and entirely dependent on external resources.

The challenges for the CUT are formidable. A dominant wing of the CUT has abandoned socialist and anticapitalist conceptions, in the name of *accommodating the existing order*. The defence of a policy of 'partnership', of negotiations with employers, of tripartite sectoral chambers (*camaras setoriai*), of joint participation by labour and capital with a view to the 'growth of the country', are all in line with a social-democratic trade-union project and practice. The result is the *weakening of the political will to break with the persistent elements of a trade-union structure tied to the state and the concomitant acceptance of an institutionalised, bureaucratic structure that has been a feature of Brazilian trade-unionism since the 1930s*.

The results of this stance have not been encouraging: the more one acts *within the prevailing order*, the less the interests of the world of work can be preserved. The 'Camaras Setoriais', for example, that have been at the heart of the 'Articulação Sindical' programme and were conceived as a model for

---

18. See Bihr's critique of social-democratic unionism (Bihr 1991).

restructuring the productive base and increasing employment, have, after a number of trials, resulted in failure, bringing about huge job-losses – the 'Camara Setorial' of the automotive industry in the ABC of São Paulo is a case in point. Not to mention the political and ideological significance of this posture, which led the Metalworkers' Union of São Bernardo to agree with the proposal for lower taxes to capital tied to the automotive industry and in this way preserve jobs.[19]

The CUT's participation, led by its dominant wing, in the so-called welfare-reform (in fact, a process of dismantling the meagre pension-rights that exist in Brazil) during FHC's government, was another expression of this misguided trade-union and political stance. It had a demobilising effect on the workers' union-movement which had been organising actions of resistance and opposition to FHC and his welfare (counter-)reforms.[20]

Amongst the clearly socialist and anticapitalist segments that have grown within the CUT, the challenges and difficulties are formidable. But there have been some important experiences, such as, for example, the Metalworkers' Union of Campinas, which was always against participation in the 'Camaras Setoriais' and negotiations and pacts with the government. It is an important union based in a strong industrial centre of Brazil and is structured as a *grassroots-, class- and socialist union and social movement*. It has significant weight within the CUT, in contrast to the social-democratic position held by the dominant nucleus of the confederation, and pushes for more grassroots- and socialist actions by Brazilian union.[21] This challenge itself – to think of a critical alternative to the 'Camaras Setoriais' – has shaped the actions of the Metalworkers' Union of São José dos Campos, where the General Motors factory is located, as well as that of many other unions.

Similarly, there has been an important effort to bring together and more effectively articulate the numerous socialist and anticapitalist sections within the CUT, especially by the Alternativa Sindical Socialista (AAS) (Alternative Socialist Unionism) and by the Movimento por uma Tendencia Socialista (MTS) (Movement for a Socialist Tendency), among other strands active within the CUT. The Corrente Sindical Classista (CSC) (Movement for a Class-based Unionism), another important strand with a growing following within the CUT, has at times been more closely aligned with the Left, at others to the principles of the Articulação Sindical.

During the 1997 CUT Congress, there was an increase in left-wing groups within the CUT which had benefited partly from the emergence of new social

---

19. See Soares 1998; Alves 1998; and Galvao 1996.
20. See Marques 1997 on the limits to social welfare in Brazil.
21. See Possan 1997.

movements, especially the MST. The MST was responsible, in 1997 (the year that followed the barbaric massacre of landless workers in the state of Pará), *for the most important popular act of opposition to FHC's government.* Marches and actions took place throughout the entire country calling for land-rights and against FHC's policies, converging in Brasilia, where the government was forced to receive the protesters in the midst of a thriving social and political mass-protest.

This scenario has made it possible to envisage a return to social action in Brazil, perhaps in an even more vibrant form in the coming years. For this to occur though, it is also very important to have a clear understanding of recent Brazilian unionism. Will it pursue actions *within* the current order, opting for negotiation as the dominant strand of the CUT has proposed, through the 'Camaras Setoriais' or negotiated participation, in 'partnership' with capital, to achieve 'growth', 'development', 'increased productivity', 'incentives for FDI', etc., all goals that are clearly in line with and subordinated ideologically to capital?

Or, instead, will the left-wing strands manage to elaborate, *in collaboration with social movements and socialist political parties,* an alternative that is *against the order,* with a clear anticapitalist agenda? In fact, the greatest challenge for the left-wing sections of the CUT that are closest to the MST and workers' social and grassroots struggles will be the elaboration of an alternative pro-gramme that is based on the viewpoint of workers, able to respond to the immediate demands of the world of work, *but aiming at the creation of a social organisation founded on socialist, emancipatory values* with no illusions as to the destructive character of the logic of capital.

The major challenge lies initially in the development of a society premised on the elimination of the *super-exploitation of labour,* which, as we saw above, is also particular to Brazilian capitalism where the minimum-wage is set at a degrading level despite the power and importance of our productive base. This project, in broad terms, should begin with the *dismantling* of the pattern of capitalist accumulation in place, through a set of measures that reject *glo-balisation* and *integration* imposed by the logic of capital, with the *destructive, fragmentary consequences this has for workers.* It must implement a *broad and radical agrarian reform* that reflects upon *solidarity and the collective* interests of workers and those *dispossessed from the land.* It must drive forward Brazil's technology, developing cutting-edge science and technology in co-operation with countries that have similar realities to Brazil and where the aim of tech-nological and scientific progress is *primarily* that of addressing the most fun-damental needs of our *working class.*

Moreover, it must monitor and curb the power of various monopolistic sec-tors, counteract the hegemony of financial capital, limit the forms of expansion and speculation of money-capital and, instead, provide incentives to forms of production aimed at meeting the social needs of the working population, *for the production of socially-useful things.* The collective farms and settlements organised by the MST are an example that allows us to think of the potential of Brazil's agrarian base and the brutal reality of its deficiencies – deficiencies that arise from a structure of concentrated ownership of and speculation on land, the produce of which is primarily for export.

A project of this kind, which we outline here only indicatively, *will be the result of a combination of grassroots-experiments and collective reflections.* It could provide the necessary, preliminary conditions for further elaboration, *with a greater universalising and socialist significance* relevant beyond national borders. Experiments in 'socialism in one country' have been, in fact, entirely unsuccessful. The challenge, therefore, is to look towards a society that goes *beyond capital*, but that also provides immediate solutions to the barbarism that plagues the daily lives of working social beings. In other words, it must make the necessary link between immediate interests and anticapitalist strategic action, with a view to a societal organisation based on socialist, emancipatory values. This, again, reaffirms the decisive importance of the creation of new forms of international worker-organisation.

As well as active participation in a project of this kind, in collaboration with left-wing parties and grassroots-social movements (with a view to a *society beyond capital*), left-wing Brazilian unions are also confronted with a set of *organisational challenges* affecting the very survival of unions as workers' social movements. These challenges confront the union-movement of both subordinated countries with significant economic, social and political bases – such as Mexico, Argentina, India and South Korea – as well as the union-movements of central countries that have undergone even more critical experiences.

The first challenge, fundamental to the very survival of unions, will be to *break the vast social barrier* that separates 'stable' workers – whose numbers are clearly falling – from part-time, precarious, sub-proletarianised workers, whose numbers, in contrast, are rising. Unions need to organise and help the self-organisation of the unemployed rather than exclude those who without a job can no longer afford to pay their dues. It is unacceptable that a worker is excluded from a union because she has been rejected by capital from the labour-market. *There needs to be a concerted effort to broaden the reach of trade-unions to unorganised workers.* Either unions organise the *working class as a whole*, or they will be increasingly limited and restricted to a small minority of workers.

Unions need to also *recognise the right of female workers to self-organise*, since they make up a decisive portion of the world of work and have traditionally been excluded within male-dominated unions. They must articulate *class*-issues together with issues concerning *gender*. In the same way, unions need to appeal to younger workers, who have also not found their aspirations echoed within the unions. They need to reach out to black workers, for whom capital has always reserved the most precarious, low-paid jobs. They need to incorporate the *new categories of workers* who have not had a tradition of union-organisation, or else remain limited to an increasingly restricted pool of 'stable workers'. Unions need also to include those large groups of workers who belong to the *new proletariat* who sell their labour-power in fast-food joints, etc., and many other areas in which wage-earners are growing in number.

Unions must make a sharp break from all forms of *neo-corporatism* that privilege the professional categories and *dismiss or abandon more deliberately class-based principles*. I am not merely referring to state-corporatism, of the kind that is widespread in Brazil, Mexico and Argentina, but also of *social neocorporatism*, on the rise in contemporary unionism, that excludes, is partial, and preserves and accentuates the fragmentary character of the working class, in line with capital's quest to promote individualism against solidarity-, collective and social interests. Similarly, all traces of xenophobic, racist or ultranationalist tendencies have to be eliminated.

Left-wing unionism must also break with the growing trend towards *institutionalisation and bureaucratisation*, which has made such a strong mark on the global union-movement and created a growing barrier from their social bases, widening the gap between the unions and autonomous social movements. The experiences of the Comitati di Base (COBAS) that emerged during the 1980s in Italy in response to the moderation of the dominant trade-union confederations – as well as many other grassroots worker-movements, such as the pressure exerted during the public-sector workers' strike in France in November–December 1995 in contrast to the cautious stance of some trade-union confederations – are important examples of the pressing need to reclaim the social bases of left-wing unions and dismantle their bureaucracy and institutionalism.

It is also essential to reverse the trend of reducing the remit of unions to the factory-space, to so-called enterprise-unions that are more vulnerable to employer-control. This trend has its origins in Toyotism and has been growing on a global scale. The response of left-wing unions should be of a different kind: The Fordist company had a vertical structure and generated vertical trade-unions. The Toyotist firm, following the Japanese model, has a horizontal structure. A union structured vertically cannot address the class-challenges of contemporary capitalism. Therefore, unionism needs to be established horizontally, which means it needs to be class-based, incorporating the vast array of workers who make up the working class today, from 'stable' workers to those more precariously employed in the 'informal sector' and the unemployed. Reclaiming the meaning of *class-belonging* is one of unionism's greatest challenges today.

There is another key challenge that I would like to mention here, without which the working class remains organically disarmed in its struggle against capital: *it must break the barriers imposed by capital between trade-union and parliamentary struggle, between economic and political struggle, and unify social, extra-parliamentary, autonomous struggles to enable class-actions. Since capital's power is extra-parliamentary, it is a grave mistake to seek to derail it with action exclusively restricted to the institutional sphere.*[22] Unions and workers' social movements should seek to expand and unify union- and political struggles, extending the reach of actions against capital and avoiding at all costs the disjunction, created by capital – and *also maintained by the social-democratic approach to trade-unionism and the labour-movement* – between economic struggle (led by the unions) and politico-parliamentary action (the responsibility of parties). *This mechanical segmentation is completely unable to derail the totalising system of capital-domination.*

It is imperative therefore for workers' social movements to move in the direction of a *social design based on a perspective of labour that is emancipated from and contrary to capital and its nefarious social and hierarchical division of labour.* Actions should be premised on the *concrete dimensions of everyday life* and on values that can bring about an *authentic, meaningful life.* The logic of social production needs to be significantly altered: it must be directed, primarily, at *use-values* and not *exchange-values.* We know that humanity would have the conditions to reproduce itself socially, on a global scale, if destructive production (including military production) were eliminated and if the results of *social labour* were not directed toward the logic of the market *but toward the production of socially useful things. Working just a few hours a day, under a form of self-determined labour, the world could reproduce itself while meeting basic social needs in a way that is no longer destructive. Free time, meanwhile, could acquire a truly free and self-determined significance.*

The production of socially-useful things must have *disposable time* and not *surplus-time* – which governs contemporary capitalist society – as its benchmark. In this way, labour, endowed with a greater human and social dimension, would lose its fetishistic and alienated (estranged) character, and besides acquiring the features of self-activity, it would open up a real possibility for

---

22. Mészáros 1995.

free, meaningful time beyond the sphere of work, which is impossible in a society ruled by the logic of capital. Genuinely free time cannot be built upon commodified labour. Currently, 'free time' is led by the consumption of commodities, whether material or immaterial. Time outside of work is also strongly contaminated by commodity-fetishism.[23]

For this *apparently* abstract formulation to obtain concrete and real significance, it is important to begin from *everyday life* and build on the manifestations of revolt and disenchantment of social beings who live from the sale of their labour-power or who are (temporarily) excluded by the destructive logic that structures our society. But it is essential for these actions to have deeper meaning and be directed against the logic of capital and the market. To illustrate with an example: the struggle for agrarian reform, led by the most important social movement in Brazil – the MST – allows us, through its land-settlements and occupations, to envisage collective forms of production. Or even the global struggle by workers for the reduction of the working day or working time, without a reduction in salary or loss of social rights, encourages us to place the following questions at the heart of the debate: *What kind of society do we wish to build? What and for whom should we produce?* This enables us to design a project of social organisation that is radically opposed to capital.

The social struggles in Brazil, and in particular its left-wing union-movement, have been both a part and a result of the class-actions that have been launched against capital. The public-sector workers' strike in France showed, for example, that it is possible to *resist* – and not *adhere to* – neoliberalism and its destructive goals. Recently, there have been many forms of resistance and strikes against capital. Let us recall the protests of 2 million metalworkers in South Korea in 1997, or the United Parcel Workers' strike in August 1997 or the General Motors metalworkers' strike in 1998, both in the US, or even the Liverpool dockers' strike, which lasted for more than two years – all of which were against attempts to introduce precarious working conditions or remove rights won by the workers. Or again, the riots in Los Angeles in 1992, the Chiapas Rebellion on 1 January 1994, which were manifestations by black workers or indigenous farmers, urban and rural workers, *against the brutal ethnic, colour- and class-discriminations* that characterise contemporary (de-)socialisation, against the growing degradation of living and working conditions of men and women.

---

23. Padilha 1995.

The example of the MST allows me to conclude with an observation that embodies the discussion above. It has emerged as the most important *social and political movement* of contemporary Brazil and is responsible for the *rebirth and resurgence* of the struggle of rural workers, placing this at the heart of political and class-struggle in Brazil. In so doing, it has become the most significant example of the need to re-establish *the centrality of social struggle* in Brazil. It has become the catalyst for recent social struggles and, *as a result of the strong ties it has with urban social sectors*, it has made it possible to envisage a return to mass-social action in Brazil, *perhaps on an even greater scale than we have witnessed in recent years.* The MST's importance and weight derive from the fact that:

1) Its activities are geared towards the *social movement* of rural workers and not towards *institutional or parliamentary activity*. The latter is a corollary of the former and not vice versa;

2) although it is a movement of rural workers, it has incorporated excluded workers in the cities who return to the countryside (in an inversion of the migratory flow that takes place in Brazil), expelled by the 'productive modernisation' of industries, resulting in a *synthesis that binds and articulates experiences and forms of sociability that derive from the world of rural and urban labour*;

3) it is the result of an amalgamation of the experience of the Catholic Left, linked to liberation-theology and grassroots church-communities and militant groups influenced by Marxist ideals and practice, reclaiming the two most important strands of recent social struggles in Brazil; and

4) it has a *national structure*, with a strong social base that gives it *dynamism, vitality and movement*. The MST's struggle for concrete goals, such as the ownership of land through collective actions and resistance, enables workers to gain a glimpse of a *meaningful everyday life*. This endows the movement with a great deal of strength and vigour. In the brutal social exclusion present in Brazil, there is a wealth of social power to be channelled by the MST. The greater its importance, and *the deeper its ties with urban workers*, the more it can encourage a resurgence of union-struggles in Brazil. And the fact that the objective of its action has been *concrete social struggles* has been a source of inspiration for left-wing unionism, an alternative to partnerships and ideological subordination to capital. It has encouraged direct action and a *social, political and union-movement* capable of participating in the construction of a society *beyond capital*.

It is, therefore, necessary to redesign an alternative socialist project that can reclaim the most essential values of humanity. A good starting point for such action could be to develop a deep, contemporary critique of the (de-)socialisation of humanity under capital, with the *social actions of rural and urban workers* and their social, union- and political movements against the destructive logic of capital at its core.

References

Ackers, Peter, Chris Smith and Paul Smith 1996, 'Against All Odds? British Trade Unions in the New Workplace', in Ackers et al. (eds.) 1996.

—— (eds.) 1996, *The New Workplace and Trade Unionism: Critical Perspectives on Work and Organization*, London: Routledge.

Alves, Giovanni 1998, 'Reestruturação Produtiva e Crise do Sindicalismo no Brasil', UNICAMP doctoral thesis, IFCH/, Campinas.

Amin, Ash 1996, 'Post-Fordism: Models, Fantasies and Phantoms of Transition', in Amin (ed.) 1996.

—— (ed.) 1996, *Post-Fordism: A Reader*, Oxford: Blackwell.

Amin, Samir et al. 1998, *Le Manifeste Communiste Aujourd'Hui*, Paris: Éditions de l'Atelier.

Antunes, Ricardo 1995a, *Adeus ao Trabalho? Ensaio sobre as Metamorfoses e a Centralidade do Mundo do Trabalho*, São Paulo: Cortez/UNICAMP.

—— 1995b, *O Novo Sindicalismo no Brasil*, Campinas: Pontes.

—— 2005, *O Caracol e sua Concha: Ensaios sobre a Nova Morfologia do Trabalho*, São Paulo: Boitempo.

—— (ed.) 1998, *Neoliberalismo, Trabalho e Sindicatos: Reestruturação Produtiva no Brasil e na Inglaterra*, 2nd edition, São Paulo: Boitempo.

Antunes, Ricardo and Ruy Braga 2009, *Infoproletários (Degradação Real do Trabalho Virtual)*, São Paulo: Boitempo.

Armingeon, Klaus et al. 1981, *Les Syndicats européens et la crise*, Grenoble: Presses Universitaires de Grenoble.

Berggren, Christian 1993, 'Lean Production: The End of History?', *Actes du GERPISA*, 'Des réalités du Toyotisme', 6, February.

Bernardo, João 1996, *Reestruturação Capitalista e os Desafios para os Sindicatos*, Lisbon: Mimeo.

—— 2004, *Democracia Totalitária*, São Paulo: Cortez.

—— 2009, *Economia dos Conflitos Sociais*, São Paulo: Expressão Popular.

Beynon, Huw 1995, 'The Changing Practices of Work', International Centre for Labour Studies, Manchester.

Bialakowsky, Alberto et al. 2003, 'Diluición y Mutación del Trabajo en la Dominación Social Local', *Revista Herramienta*, 23: 133–40.

Bidet, Jacques and Jacques Texier (eds.) 1995, *La Crise du travail*, Paris: Presses Universitaires de France.

Bihr, Alain 1991, *Du 'Grand Soir' à 'L'Alternative': le Mouvement ouvrier européen en crise*, Paris: Les Éditions Ouvrières.

Bremner, Brian and Chester Dawson 2003, *Business Week*, 18 November.

Brenner, Robert 1998a, 'The Looming Crisis of World Capitalism', available at: <http://www.solidarity-us.org/current/print/871>.

—— 1998b, *The Economics of Global Turbulence*, New Left Review, I, 229: 1–265.

Caffentzis, George 1997, 'Why Machines Cannot Create Value; or, Marx's Theory of Machines', in Davis et al. (eds.) 1997.

Callinicos, Alex and Chris Harman 1989, *The Changing Working Class*, London: Bookmarks.

Carchedi, Guglielmo 1997, 'High-Tech Hype: Promises and Realities of Technology in the Twenty-First Century', in Davis et al. (eds.) 1997.

Castel, Robert 1998, *As Metamorfoses da Questão Salarial*, Rio de Janeiro: Vozes.

Castillo, Juan J. 1996a, *Sociologia del Tra-bajo*, Madrid: CIS.

—— 1996b, 'A la Búsqueda del Trabajo Perdido', in *Complejidad y Teoría Social*, edited by A. Perez-Agote and I. Yucera, Madrid: CIS.

Castro, Nadya (ed.) 1995, *A Máquina e o Equilibrista: Inovações na Indústria Auto-mobilística Brasileira*, São Paulo: Paz and Terra.

Chesnais, François 1996a, 'Contribution au Débat sur le Cours du Capital-isme à la fin du XXᵉ Siècle', *Actualiser l'Économie de Marx*, Paris: Presses Uni-versitaires de France.

—— 1996b, *A Mundialização do Capital*, São Paulo: Xamã.

Colli, Juliana 1997, 'O Façonismo pelo Avesso', master's dissertation, IFCH/UNICAMP, Campinas.

Collingsworth, Terry, J. William Goold and Pharis J. Harvey 1994, 'Labor and Free Trade: Time for a Global New Deal', *Foreign Affairs*, 73, 1: 8–13.

Coriat, Benjamin 1992, *Pensar al Revés: Trabajo y Organización en la Empresa Japonesa*, Mexico City and Madrid: Siglo XXI.

Costa, Isabel and Annie Garanto 1993, 'Entreprises Japonaises et Syndicalisme en Europe', in Freyssinet (ed.) 1993.

Coutinho, Carlos Nelson 1996, 'Lukács, A Ontologia e a Política', in *Lukács: Um Galileu no Século XX*, edited by Ricardo Antunes and Walquíria Rego, São Paulo: Boitempo.

da Silva, Josué Pereira (ed.) 2007, *Por uma Sociologia do Século XX*, São Paulo: Annablume.

Davis, Jim, Thomas Hirschl and Michael Stack (eds.) 1997, *Cutting Edge: Technol-ogy, Information, Capitalism and Social Revolution*, London: Verso.

Dockers' Charter 1997, no. 21, November, published by the Liverpool Dockers Shop Stewards' Committee, Liverpool.

Druck, Maria da Graça 1999, *Terceiriza-ção: (Des)fordizando a Fábrica*, São Paulo: Boitempo.

Dussel, Enrique 1995, 'Sentido Ético de la Rebelión Maya de 1994 en Chiapas', in Noam Chomsky et al., *Chiapas Insur-gente*, Navarra: Txalaparta.

Elger, Tony 1997, 'Manufacturing Myths and Miracles: Work Reorganization in British Manufacturing since 1979', Cen-tre for Comparative Labour Studies, University of Warwick.

Elias, Norbert 1993, *Time: An Essay*, Oxford: Blackwell.

Foster, John Bellamy 1999, 'Is Overcom-petition the Problem?', *Monthly Review*, 51, 2: 28–37.

Freyssinet, Jacques (ed.) 1993, 'Syndicats d'Éurope', *Le Mouvement Social*, 162, January–March.

Fumagalli, Andrea 1996, 'Composizione di Classe and Modificazioni del Lav-oro nell'Italia degli Anni Novanta', in *Il Sapere delle Lotte: Saggi sulla Compo-sizione di Classe*, edited by Pino Tripoli, Milan: Spray.

Galvão, Andrea 1996, 'Participação e Fragmentação: A Prática Sindical dos Metalúrgicos do ABC', mas-ter's dissertation, IFCH/UNICAMP, Campinas.

Garraghan, Philip and Paul Stewart 1992, *The Nissan Enigma: Flexibility at Work in a Local Economy*, London: Mansell.

Gibson, Dot 1996, 'International Confer-ence of Dockworkers Called by the Liverpool Dockers Shop Stewards' Committee', 25 February, Liverpool.

—— 1997, 'The Sacked Liverpool Dock-ers Fight for Reinstatement', 26 Novem-ber, Liverpool.

Giddens, Anthony 1998, *The Third Way: The Renewal of Social Democracy*, Lon-don: Polity Press.

—— 1999, 'A Terceira Via em Cinco Dimensões', *Folha de S. Paulo–Mais!*, 21 February, São Paulo.

Gorender, Jacob 1997, 'Globalização, Tec-nologia e Relações de Trabalho', *Estu-dos Avançados*, São Paulo: IEA-USP.

Gorz, André 1982, *Adeus ao proletariado*, Rio de Janeiro: Forense Universitária.

—— 1990a, 'The New Agenda', *New Left Review*, I, 184: 37–46.

—— 1990b, 'Pourquoi la société salariale a besoin de nouveaux valets', *Le Monde Diplomatique*, 22 June, Paris.

—— 2003, *Metamorfoses do Trabalho*, São Paulo: Annablume.

—— 2005a, *Imaterial*, São Paulo: Anna-blume.

—— 2005b, IHU on-line, year 5, special edition, January.

Gounet, Thomas 1991, 'Luttes Concurrentielles et stratégies d'accumulation dans l'industrie automobile', *Études Marxistes*, 10, 35–51.

—— 1992, 'Penser à l'Envers… Le Capitalisme', Dossier Toyotisme, *Études Marxistes*, 14: 63–84.

—— 1997, 'La Stratégie "japonaise" de Jorissen', *Études Marxistes*, 37, 67–83.

Graciolli, Edilson 1997, *Um Caldeirão Chamado CSN*, Uberlândia: Edufu.

Gramsci, Antonio 1971, 'Americanism and Fordism', *Prison Notebooks*, International Publishers.

Gray, Anne 1998, 'New Labour – New Labour Discipline', *Capital & Class*, 65: 1–12.

Habermas, Jürgen 1975, 'Técnica e Ciência como "Ideologia" ', in *Os Pensadores*, vol. 48, São Paulo: Abril Cultural.

—— 1989, 'The New Obscurity', in *The New Conservatism: Cultural Criticism and the Historians' Debate*, Cambridge: Polity Press.

—— 1991, *The Theory of Communicative Action vol. 1: Reason and the Rationalization of Society*, London: Polity Press.

—— 1992, *The Theory of Communicative Action vol. 2: The Critique of Functionalist Reason*, London: Polity Press.

Harvey, David 1989, *The Condition of Postmodernity*, Oxford: Blackwell.

—— 1996, 'Flexible Accumulation through Urbanization', in Amin (ed.) 1996.

Harvie, David 1997, 'Review of *The Death of Class*', *Capital & Class*, 62: 192–3.

Hegel, Georg W.F. 1966, *Fenomenologia del Espiritu*, Mexico City: Fondo de Cultura Económica.

Heller, Agnes 1978, *Teoria de las necesidades en Marx*, Barcelona: Editorial Península.

Hesiod 1990, *Works and Days: The Works of Hesiod*, translated from the Greek by Cooke (London, 1728).

Hirata, Helena 1993, 'Paradigmes du Travail: "Un point de vue transversal"', *Futur Antérieur*, 16: 5–10.

—— 1995, 'Rapports sociaux de sexe et division du travail', in Bidet and Texier (eds.) 1995.

Hirsch, Joachim 1997, *Globalizacion: Transformacion del Estado y Democracia*,

Córdoba: Universidade Nacional de Córdoba.

Holloway, John 1987, 'The Red Rose of Nissan', *Capital & Class*, 32: 142–64.

—— 1997, 'A Note on Alienation', *Historical Materialism*, 1: 146–9.

Huws, Ursula 2003, *The Making of a Cybertariat (Virtual Work in a Real World)*, New York/London: Monthly Review Press/The Merlin Press.

Ianni, Octávio 1996, *A Era do Globalismo*, Rio de Janeiro: Civilização Brasileira.

Ichiyo, Muto 1995, *Toyotismo: Lucha de Classes e Innovacion Tecnologica en Japon*, Buenos Aires: Antídoto.

Japan Press Weekly 1998, 14 February, Tokyo.

—— 2004, 21 February, Tokyo.

Jinkings, Nise 1996, *O Mister de Fazer Dinheiro*, São Paulo: Boitempo.

Kamata, Satoshi 1982, *Japan in the Passing Lane: An Insider's Account of Life in a Japanese Auto Factory*, New York: Pantheon Books.

Kelly, John 1996, 'Union Militancy and Social Partnership', in Ackers et al. (eds.) 1996.

Kenney, Martin 1997, 'Value Creation in the Late Twentieth Century: The Rise of the Knowledge Worker', in Davis et al. (eds.) 1997.

Kurz, Robert 1992, *O Colapso da Modernização*, São Paulo: Paz and Terra.

—— 1997, *Os Últimos Combates*, Rio de Janeiro: Vozes.

Lavinas, Lena 1996, 'Aumentando a competitividade das mulheres no mercado de trabalho', *Estudos Feministas*, 4, 1: 171–82.

Lazzarato, Maurizio 1992, 'Le Concept de travail immatériel: la grande entreprise', *Futur Antérieur*, 10: 54–61.

—— 1993, 'Le "Cycle" de la production immatérielle', *Futur Antérieur*, 16: 111–20.

Lessa, Sergio 1997, *Trabalho e Ser Social*, Maceió: Edufal/UFC.

Lima, Eurenice 1996, 'A Construção da Obediência', master's dissertation, IFCH/UNICAMP, Campinas.

Lojkine, Jean 1995a, 'De la révolution industrielle à la révolution informationnelle', in Bidet and Texier (eds.) 1995.

—— 1995b, *A Revolução Informacional*, São Paulo: Cortez.

London Hazard Centre 1994, *Hard Labour: Stress, Ill-Health and Hazardous Employment Practices*, London.

Löwy, Michael 1998, 'Habermas et Weber', Dossier: 'Habermas, une politique délibérative', *Actuel Marx*, 24: 105–14.

—— 1999, 'Marx e Weber, Críticos do Capitalismo', *Cultura Vozes*, 2: 63–75.

Lukács, Georg 1975, *History and Class Consciousness*.

—— 1980, *The Ontology of Social Being: Labour*, London: Merlin Press.

—— 1981, *Ontologia Dell'Essere Sociale*, vols. 1 and 2, Rome: Riuniti

—— 1987, 'Prefácio', in Agnes Heller, *Sociologia de la Vida Cotidiana*, Barcelona: Península.

Maar, Wolfgang Leo 1996, 'A Reificação como Realidade Social', in *Lukács: Um Galileu no Século XX*, edited by R. Antunes and W. Rego, São Paulo: Boitempo.

Magri, Lucio 1991, 'The European Left Between Crisis and Refoundation', *New Left Review*, I, 189: 5–18.

Mandel, Ernest 1986, 'Marx, la crise actuelle et l'avenir du travail humain', *Quatrième Internationale*, 2: 9–29.

Manpower Brasil, Disponível, available at: <http://www.manpower.com.br>.

Marques, Rosa M. 1997, *A Proteção Social e o Mundo do Trabalho*, São Paulo: Bienal.

Marx, Karl 1967, *Capital: A Critique of Political Economy*, 3 vols, New York: International Publishers.

—— 1974, *Grundrisse: Foundations of the Critique of Political Economy*, Harmondsworth: Penguin.

—— 1975 (1844), *The Economic and Philosophical Manuscripts of 1844*, in *Collected Works*, vol. 3, New York: International Publishers.

—— 1994 (1861–4), Chapter VI (unpublished), in Karl Marx and Friedrich Engels, *Collected Works*, vol. 34, London: Lawrence & Wishart.

Mazzetti, Giovanni 1997, *Quel Pane da Spartire: Teoria Generale della Necessità di Redistribuire il Lavoro*, Turin: Bollati Boringhieri.

McIlroy, John 1995, *Trade Unions in Britain Today*, Manchester: Manchester University Press.

—— 1996, 'Trade Unions in Retreat: Britain since 1979', International Centre for Labour Studies, Manchester.

—— 1997, 'The Enduring Alliance? Trade Unions and the Making of New Labour, 1994–1997', International Centre for Labour Studies, Manchester.

McNally, David 1999, 'Turbulence in the World Economy', *Monthly Review*, 51, 2: 38–52.

Méda, Dominique 1997, *Società Senza Lavoro: Per Una Nuova Filosofia Dell'Occupazione*, Milan: Feltrinelli.

Mészáros, István 1986, *Philosophy, Ideology and Social Science*, Sussex: Wheatsheaf Books.

—— 1989, *The Power of Ideology*, London: Harvester Wheatsheaf.

—— 1995, *Beyond Capital: Towards a Theory of Transition*, London: Merlin Press.

Mouriaux, René et al. 1991, *Les Syndicats européens à l'épreuve*, Paris: Presses de la Fondation Nationale.

Muckenberger, Ulrich 1997, 'Trabalho, Modernização e Integração Social', in *A Sociologia no Horizonte do Século XXI*, edited by Leila da Costa Ferreira, São Paulo: Boitempo.

Murray, Fergus 1983, 'The Decentralisation of Production – The Decline of the Mass Collective Worker?', *Capital & Class*, 19: 74–99.

Neffa, Julio C. 2003, *El Trabajo Humano*, Buenos Aires: Conicet.

Negri, Toni and Michael Hardt 1998/99, 'Mutación de Actividades, Nuevas Organizaciones', *El Rodoballo*, 5, 9, 1198–9.

Netto, José Paulo 1998, 'Prólogo' do Manifesto do Partido Comunista, São Paulo: Cortez.

Nogueira, Arnaldo 1996, 'Trabalho e Sindicalismo no Estado Brasileiro', doctoral thesis, IFCH/UNICAMP, Campinas.

—— 1998, *A Modernização Conservadora do Sindicalismo Brasileiro*, São Paulo: Educ/Fapesp.

Offe, Claus 1989, 'Trabalho como Categoria Sociológica Fundamental?', *Tra-*

balho & Sociedade, vol. 1, Rio de Janeiro: Tempo Brasilieiro, 13–41.

Offe, Claus and Johannes Berger 1991, 'A Dinâmica do Desenvolvimento do Setor de Serviços', *Trabalho & Sociedade*, vol. 2, Rio de Janeiro: Tempo Brasileiro, 11–53.

Oldrini, Guido 1993, 'Lukács e la Via Marxista al Concetto di "Persona"', *Marxismo Oggi*, 6, 1 (new series): 131–50.

Oliveira, Francisco 1997, *Os Direitos do Antivalor*, Rio de Janeiro: Vozes.

Outhwaite, William 1994, *Habermas: A Critical Introduction*, London: Polity Press.

Padilha, Valquíria 1995, 'Tempo Livre e Racionalidade Econômica: Um Par Imperfeito', master's dissertation, IFCH/UNICAMP, Campinas.

Pakulski, Jan and Malcolm Waters 1996, *The Death of Class*, London: Sage Publications.

Paoletti, Grazia (ed.) 1998, 'Riduzione dell'orario e disoccupazione', *Marxismo Oggi*, 11, 2 (new series): 33–4.

Pelling, Henry 1987, *A History of British Trade Unionism*, Harmondsworth: Penguin.

Petras, James 1997, 'Latin America: The Resurgence of the Left', *New Left Review*, I, 223: 17–47.

Pilger, John and Bill Morris 1998, exchange of letters in *The Guardian*, 2 February 1998, available at: <http://www .hartford-hwp.com/archives/61/079. html>.

Pollert, Anna 1996, ' "Team Work" on the Assembly Line: Contradiction and the Dynamics of Union Resilience', in Ackers et al. (eds.) 1996.

Possan, Magali 1997, *A Malha Entrecruzada das Ações*, Campinas: Centro de Memória/UNICAMP.

Ramalho, José R. and Heloisa Martins (eds.) 1994, *Terceirização: Diversidade e Negociação no Mundo do Trabalho*, São Paulo: Hucitec.

Ramtin, Ramin 1997, 'A Note on Automation and Alienation', in Davis et al. (eds.) 1997.

Ranieri, Jesus 1995, 'Alienação e Estranhamento nos Manuscritos Econômicos-filosóficos de Marx', master's dissertation, IFCH/UNICAMP, Campinas.

Rifkin, Jeremy 1995, *O Fim dos Empregos*, São Paulo: Makron Books.

—— 2004, 'Return of a Conundrum', *The Guardian*, 2 March 2004.

Rosanvallon, Pierre 1988, *La Question syndicale*, Paris: Calmann-Lévy.

Sabel, Charles F. and Michael J. Piore 1984, *The Second Industrial Divide*, New York: Basic Books.

Sader, Emir 1997, 'Para um Novo Internacionalismo', in *O poder, cadê o poder?*, São Paulo: Boitempo.

Saffioti, Heleieth 1997, 'Violência de gênero – lugar da práxis na construção da Subjetividade', *Lutas sociais*, 2: 59–79.

Sayer, Andrew 1986, 'New Developments in Manufacturing: The Just-in-Time System', *Capital & Class*, 30: 43–72.

Scarponi, Alberto 1976, 'Prefazione', in Georg Lukács, *Ontologia Dell'Essere Sociale* [I], Rome: Riuniti.

Segnini, Liliana 1998, *Mulheres no Trabalho Bancário*, São Paulo: Edusp/Fapesp.

Shimizu, Koichi 1994, 'Kaizen et gestion du travail chez Toyota Motor et Toyota Motor Kyushu: Un problème dans la trajectoire de Toyota', GERPISA Réseau Internationale, June, Paris.

Singer, Daniel 1997, 'The French "Winter of Discontent"', *Monthly Review*, 49, 3: 130–9.

Soares, José de Lima 1998, *Sindicalismo no ABC Paulista: Reestruturação Produtiva e Parceria*, Brasília: Centro de Educação Popular.

Soon, Hochul 1997, 'The "Late Blooming" of the South Korean Labor Movement', *Monthly Review*, 49, 3: 117–30.

Stephenson, Carol 1996, 'The Different Experience of Trade Unionism in Two Japanese Transplants', in Ackers et al. (eds.) 1996.

Stewart, Paul 1997, 'Striking Smarter and Harder at Vauxhall: The New Industrial Relations of Lean Production', *Capital & Class*, 61: 1–12.

Strange, Gerald 1997, 'The British Labour Movement and Economic and Monetary Union in Europe', *Capital & Class*, 63: 13–24.

Takaichi, Tsugio 1992, 'Rapport sur le movement ouvrier au Japon', Dossier Toyotisme, *Études Marxistes*, 14: 53–9.

Taylor, Andrew 1989, *Trade Unions and Politics*, London: Macmillan.

Teague, Paul 1997, 'New Institutionalism and the Japanese Employment System', *Review of International Political Economy*, 4, 3: 587–607.

Teixeira, Francisco and Manfredo Oliveira (eds.) 1996, *Neoliberalismo e Reestruturação Produtiva*, São Paulo/Fortaleza: Cortez/Uece.

Tertulian, Nicolas 1990, 'Introduzione', in G. Lukács, *Prolegomeni all'Ontologia dell'Essere Sociale: Questioni di Principio di Un'Ontologia Oggi Divenuta Possibile*, Rome: Guerini e Associati.

—— 1993, 'Le Concept d'aliénation chez Heidegger et Lukács', *Archives de Philosophie: Recherches et Documentation*, 56: 441–3.

Tomaney, John 1996, 'A New Paradigm of Work Organization and Technology?', in Amin (ed.) 1996.

Tosel, André 1995, 'Centralité et non-centralité du travail ou la passion des hommes superflus', in Bidet and Texier (eds.) 1995.

Vasapollo, Luciano 2005, *O Trabalho Atípico e a Precariedade*, São Paulo: Expressão Popular.

Vega Cantor, Renán 1999, *El Caos Planetario*, Buenos Aires: Editorial Antídoto (Coleção Herramienta).

Vincent, Jean-Marie 1993, 'Les Automatismes sociaux et le "General Intellect"', *Paradigmes du Travail, Futur Antérieur*, 16: 121–30.

—— 1995, 'Flexibilité du travail et plasticité humaine', in Bidet and Texier (eds.) 1995.

Visser, Jelle 1993, 'Syndicalisme et Désyndicalisation', in Freyssinet (ed.) 1993.

Wood, Ellen 1997a, 'Modernity, Posmodernity or Capitalism?', *Review of International Political Economy*, 4, 3: 539–60.

—— 1997b, 'Labor, the State, and Class Struggle', *Monthly Review*, 49, 3: 1–17.

Wood, Stephen (ed.) 1989, *The Transformation of Work?: Skill, Flexibility and the Labour Process*, London: Unwin Hyman.

Subject Index

new configuration of the   xix, xxiii,
   81, 86, 90, 93, 155, 179, 188, 189, 193,
   196, 220, 221n60
relation between state and   47, 50, 75,
   185
See also working class today
working class today   80–95, 178, 192,
   193, 194, 195–6, 201, 220, 230
working time   xv, 19, 40, 67, 154, 162,
   176, 232
free time and   146–151
reduction of   40, 73, 147, 148, 147n3,
   150
See also reduction of labour-time

work-society   149, 207, 214
crisis in   207
See also society of labour
world of work   2, 21, 21n, 22, 26n13, 28,
   30, 56, 58, 69, 71, 86, 87, 89, 91, 98, 161,
   170, 185, 186, 188, 191, 194, 202, 206,
   208, 214, 226, 228, 229
changes within   1, 37, 44, 49, 52, 54,
   79, 82, 84, 161, 185, 187, 188, 189, 202,
   204, 216, 219
crisis of the   21n, 184, 188, 190
today   xxiii, 90, 166, 168, 170, 189, 193,
   196

Author Index